NAVAL WIVES AND MISTRESSES

1750 – 1815

NAVAL WIVES
& MISTRESSES

MARGARETTE LINCOLN

M NATIONAL
ARITIME
MUSEUM

First published in 2007 by National Maritime Museum Publishing, London, SE10 9NF

www.nmm.ac.uk/publishing

© National Maritime Museum, London, 2007

A CIP catalogue record for this book is available from the British Library.

1st edition
Printed and bound in the UK by Cromwell Press Ltd.

ISBN: 978 0 948065 92 7

Editor: Stephanie Egerton
Design: Poise Design
Photography: Josh Akin, Ben Gilbert, Ken Hickey, Andrew Holt and Tina Warner
Picture credits: National Maritime Museum unless otherwise stated
Picture research: Sara Ayad
Project Management: Sarah Thorowgood
Production Management: Geoff Barlow

For Andrew

CONTENTS

LIST OF ILLUSTRATIONS

All illustrations are held in copyright by the National Maritime Museum, Greenwich, unless otherwise stated.

Jacket Illustration
Taken from Dispatch or Jack Preparing for Sea, by T. Rowlandson (artist and engraver). NMM Repro. ID PW3835.

Colour plates
Plate 1: *A Sailor's Marriage*, by George M. Woodward (artist), Thomas Rowlandson (engraver) and Rudolph Ackermann (publisher), 25 May 1805. NMM Repro. ID PW3853.

Plate 2: *The Neglected Tar* (press gang), n. d., NMM Repro. ID PU4772.

Plate 3: *Rear-Admiral Fremantle*, by Domenico Pellegrini (artist), Charles Picart (engraver). NMM Repro. ID PU3287.

Plate 4: *Admiral George Brydges Rodney, 1st Baron Rodney, 1719 – 92*, oil painting by Jean-Laurent Mosnier, 1791. NMM Repro. ID BHC2970.

Plate 5: *Alexander Hood, 1st Viscount Bridport (1726 – 1814)*, by Lemuel Francis Abbott (artist) and Samuel Freeman (engraver). Hope Collection. NMM Repro. ID PU3204.

Plate 6: *Captain Flinders R. N.*, published by Hargrove Saunders. NMM Repro. ID PW3511.

Plate 7: *Admiral Edward Boscawen (1711 – 1761)*, oil painting by Sir Joshua Reynolds. Greenwich Hospital Collection. NMM Repro. ID BHC2565.

Plate 8: *Captain the Honourable Augustus Keppel (1725 – 66)*, oil painting by Sir Joshua Reynolds, 1752 – 53. NMM Repro. ID BHC2823.

Plate 9: *Vice-Admiral Cuthbert Collingwood, 1st Baron Collingwood, 1748 – 1810*, oil painting by Henry Howard, Greenwich Hospital Collection. NMM Repro. ID BHC2625.

Plate 10: Fan commemorating the Battle of the Nile, 1798. NMM Repro. ID D5541-2.

Plate 11: *Frances Nelson, 1761 – 1831, Viscountess Nelson*, British School, *c*.1800. NMM Repro. ID BHC2883.

Plate 12: *A Mansion House Treat or Smoking Attitudes*, published by S.W. Fores, 18 November 1800. NMM Repro. ID PW3887.

Plate 13: *Captain Inglefield of His Majesty's Ship The Centaur Wrecked in 1782*, by George Engleheart (artist) Benjamin Smith (engraver) and Thompson (publisher), 14 September 1815. NMM Repro. ID PU4608.

Plate 14: A copper commemorative coin, the obverse engraved with a sailor and his wife, and the legend 'JOHN AND MARTHA CROUCH', late eighteenth-century. NMM Repro. ID E3908-1.

Plate 15: *ACCOMMODATION or Lodgings to let at Portsmouth!!*, by T. Rowlandson and/ or George M. Woodward (artist), Thomas Rowlandson (engraver) and Thomas Tegg (publisher), 30 June 1808. Macpherson Collection. NMM Repro. ID RM/66/340 or PX8580.

Plate 16: *Sweet Poll of Plymouth*, by H. W. Bunbury (artist), G. Shepheard (engraver) and T. Macklin (Publisher), 10 June 1790. NMM Repro. ID PU4734.

Plate 17: *Shiver my Timbers Poll your grown out of Compass. I can scarcely embrace you*, by S. Jenner (artist), *c.*1820. Macpherson Collection. NMM Repro. ID PX8640.

Plate 18: *Men of War, Bound for the Port of Pleasure*, by Carrington Bowles (publisher), 25 April 1791. NMM Repro. ID PW4036.

Plate 19: *Jack in a White Squall, Amongst Breakers – on the Lee Shore of St. Catherines*, published by Thomas Tegg, 16 August 1811. NMM Repro. ID PW3862.

Plate 20: *The Sailor's Return*, engraved by C. Mosley, *c.*1750. NMM Repro. ID PW3801.

Plate 21: *Poll and my Partner Joe*, published by Robert Laurie & James Whittle, 12 May 1794. NMM Repro. ID PW4034. [or RM/41/452?]

Plate 22: Large creamware jug, transfer-printed in black and hand-coloured, Liverpool, Merseyside, England, after 1789. NMM Repro. ID E5680.

Plate 23: *Jack's Fidelity*, published by G. Thompson and I. Evans, 14 January 1796. NMM Repro. ID PW4042.

Plate 24: *The Token, or Jack safe Return'd to his True Love Nancy*, published by John Fairburn. NMM Repro. ID PW3798.

Plate 25: *Yo Heave Ho*, published by Laurie & Whittle, 24 April 1799. NMM Repro ID PW4013.

Plate 26: An earthenware jug showing a sailor departing from his family, Sunderland, England, 1810. NMM Repro. ID E6064.

Plate 27: *Exporting Cattle Not Insurable*, by W. Elmes (artist), Thomas Tegg (publisher). NMM Repro. ID PW4163.

Plate 28: *Loading a Smuggler*, by 'Giles Grinagain' (designer and engraver), S. W. Forres (publisher). 2 January 1804. NMM Repro. ID PU4736.

Plate 29: *A Seaman's Wife's Reckoning*, by George M. Woodward (artist), Thomas Rowlandson (engraver), and Thomas Tegg (publisher). NMM Repro. ID PW3844.

Plate 30: *Wrecks of the Britannia, & Admiral Gardner, East Indiamen, on the Goodwin Sands, 24 Jan. 1809*. NMM Repro. ID PU6386.

Plate 31: A large porcelain jug painted below the lip with an oval portrait of Admiral Edward Boscawen (1711 – 1761), *c.*1760. NMM Repro. ID E5623.

Plate 32: *A Sailor's Return in Peace*, oil painting by Thomas Stothard. NMM Repro. ID BHC1125.

Plate 33: A creamware mug, transfer-printed and hand-coloured with a portrait of an officer intended to represent Vice-Admiral Horatio Nelson, *c.*1800. NMM Repro. ID D5859.

Plate 34: A painted earthenware figure group depicting a sailor and his lass, early nineteenth century, (Fawssett Collection). NMM Repro. ID E6188.

Plate 35: *The interior of R. Ackermann's Repository of Arts, no. 101, Strand*, by Augustus Charles Pugin and Thomas Rowlandson, 1809. John Johnson Collection, © Bodleian Library.

Plate 36: *Wedgwood and Byerley in York Street, St. James's Square* in no. 2 of R. Ackermann's *Repository of Arts, Literature Fashions, Manufactures &c*, published from 1809 until 1828. John Johnson Collection, © Bodleian Library.

Plate 37: From 'Kettles to mend', by John Phillips (artist). John Johnson Collection, © Bodleian Library.

Plate 38: Oval patch box with a mirror inside the lid, from Bilston, West Midlands, England, commemorating the naval heroes of the French Revolutionary War, *c.*1800. NMM Repro. ID F4277.

NOTE ON THE TEXT

Original spelling, punctuation and capitalization have been retained throughout. At this period it was usual to abbreviate many words, including 'which' and 'would', 'the' and 'that'. Where such abbreviations are not clear, they are given in full in square brackets.

PREFACE

This book aims to fill a distinct gap in social and maritime history. It explores the lives and experiences of naval women who, for the most part, remained ashore when their husbands went to sea. While there has been keen interest in the minority of women who went to sea disguised as men, there has been virtually no research into the wives and mistresses of seamen who stayed at home, bringing up small children, earning their living as best they might, often enduring years of absence and uncertainty. This study examines the lives of naval women during the years 1750 – 1815, a time of heightened naval activity unparalleled in Britain until then, when men served at sea for extended periods. It also aims to advance the current renaissance of naval history, illustrating the importance of maritime sources for inter-disciplinary research and drawing attention to little-used materials (many housed in the National Maritime Museum, Greenwich). It considers a variety of visual and textual sources, from newspapers, pamphlets, prints and letters, to love tokens, jewellery and tableware. Each item reflects a range of vested interests and ideologies, and offers a window to a different world in time and space. Given the nature of surviving records, the work cannot claim to offer a comprehensive account. Instead, it seeks to combine an overview of the varied experiences of sailors' women at this period with a more detailed examination of certain women from different social levels so that shared ideas and topics emerge for investigation.

The book is structured into fairly long chapters. The introductory chapter contextualizes the work, explaining contemporary issues such as the status of women in marriage and outlining everyday practicalities that impinged on regular communication, including aspects of the transport network and the postal service. In the central portion of the book, individual chapters examine the lives of naval women from different social ranks. Within this framework, each chapter offers a broadly thematic approach to allow comparison between the different elements of society. The structure aims to facilitate an appreciation of the interconnections between the different social groupings as well as offer specific insights restricted to individual social orders. It also aims to challenge perceptions of gender roles: the image of women waiting on the shore after the departure of their men folk has a long history, but during these years the familiar image was both reproduced and subverted. Evidently, at the higher end of the social scale, women maintained widespread networks of power and communication, while at the lower end they had active resource to complex networks of support and interdependence. There is much to be uncovered about the lives of naval wives and mistresses of this period.

ACKNOWLEDGEMENTS

I should like to thank the past Director of the National Maritime Museum, Roy Clare, for granting me an initial sabbatical to commence work on this book, and I gratefully acknowledge my debt to many others for advice and assistance. I am particularly indebted to Roger Knight, formerly Deputy Director of the National Maritime Museum and now Professor of Naval History at the University of Greenwich, for his extremely helpful comments on the manuscript and for the additional leads and information he generously gave me. For specific help with eighteenth-century ceramics, I should like to thank Tony Tibbles, Keeper of the Merseyside Maritime Museum; Robin Emmerson, Head of Decorative Arts at the Walker Art Gallery, Liverpool; Maurice Hillis of the Northern Ceramic Circle, and Hilary Young, Senior Curator, Ceramics and Glass Collection, Victoria and Albert Museum.

The book has benefited much from the advice and suggestions of expert colleagues at the National Maritime Museum, particularly from Rina Prentice, former Curator of Antiquities and now a Curator Emeritus, who also offered valuable advice on ceramics. The Museum's Centre for Imperial and Maritime Studies has provided stimulating discussions, as has the Museum's programme of maritime history seminars, run with the Institute of Historical Research. Thanks are due to the Museum's library and manuscripts staff for their unfailing assistance with inter-library loans and enquiries; to the Museum's Photographic Studio; to Pieter van der Merwe, the Museum's General Editor, to Rachel Giles, the Museum's Head of Publications and to Abigail Ratcliffe and Sara Ayed from the publishing team. I also owe a great deal to Sarah Thorowgood for her expert project management and wise advice on the text. My final thanks, as ever, go to my family.

Margarette Lincoln

ABBREVIATIONS

Add. MSS	Additional Manuscripts
Adm.	Admiral
BL	British Library
GM	*Gentleman's Magazine*
CWPR	Cobbett's Weekly Political Register
OBP	*Old Bailey Proceedings*: consulted at www.oldbaileyonline.org prior to 18 January 2007
NMM	National Maritime Museum
TNA	The National Archives

Chapter One
NAVAL WOMEN AND SOCIETY

Jenny, who married Captain George Brydges Rodney in 1753, could never reconcile herself to his long absences at sea or summon the fortitude to say goodbye to him without breaking down. Rodney (see Plate 4) was related to the aristocracy but came from an impoverished younger branch of the family. He improved his situation significantly by his marriage to Jenny, who was a daughter of the Earl of Northampton, but the couple were also very much in love. In 1755 she wrote to him, 'without you life is not worth my care, nor would millions make me happy', and she urged him to give up his naval career, 'I hope you will then, as soon as you possibly can, give up that vile ship that causes us so much pain'.[1]

Jenny's situation affected thousands of women, and the suffering they endured and sacrifices they made in the cause of British sea power have yet to be fully acknowledged. This study of British naval wives and mistresses reveals how imperial ambition and the politics of warfare impacted on domestic arrangements at all social levels. During the period 1750 – 1815, a time of unprecedented naval activity for Britain (by the early 1800s one in five adult males was engaged in some form of military activity), most sailors' wives stayed at home, enduring years of separation and anxiety, bringing up small children, managing domestic affairs and making ends meet as best they could while their men were at sea. In the process they took on far more responsibility than other women whose husbands lived with them at home, often crossing the boundaries of what was understood to be conventional female activity. The impact of this remarkable naval effort on seamen's wives or women has until now been largely unexplored. This book sets out to illustrate the domestic role of these women and their social position within the context of Britain's growing imperial power. It looks at the fascinating interaction between the military and the domestic, and at the increasing power of women as consumers. It helps to throw light on the education of women and on the nature of contemporary marital relationships, and it reveals that the absence of men folk who were at sea for long, emotionally distressing, periods led to a range of practical consequences. These complicated family life but also had a broader impact on society while women's work, both inside and outside the home, helped the Admiralty to keep men at sea for long periods.

A study of naval wives in this period offers a snapshot of contemporary class structure since the Navy contained people from all social ranks and many of the sources explored are domestic and personal. In eighteenth-century Britain the traditional authority of monarchy, church and family seemed to be weakening. Steady economic growth meant that consumer expectation rose, and those who could afford to improve their lifestyle developed marked behavioural changes. In this period many of the middling and upper ranks felt an underlying sense of insecurity and there was periodic social unrest, particularly in London where rapid population growth exacerbated crime and civil disorder. Some elements of society reacted by trying to strengthen the established means of combating crime, such as increasing the number of offences that carried the death penalty. Others supported reforming methods, for example, setting up philanthropic institutions like London's Magdalen Hospital for penitent prostitutes. Britain was almost continually at war from 1750 – 1815, which had an enormous impact on family life. This was not an easy time for women, and most certainly not for those whose husbands were absent for long periods at sea. As a rule, the position of naval wives worsened the lower they were down the social scale and single naval women, whether unmarried mothers, deserted wives, or widows, had to earn a livelihood largely by their own exertions – though some benefited from charities.

Although seafaring is a predominantly male profession, naval wives had a degree of influence: they helped to provision ships by sending food parcels and lifted morale by sending letters and gifts. Most British sailors were born within sight of the sea and followed their father's profession and many sailors' wives would therefore also be the mothers of sailors. In port thousands of women were linked in some way to seafarers, through employment or kinship, helping to produce maritime subcultures in different locations. With the developments in printing, transport and the postal service, Britons were becoming more aware of foreign affairs and home news. The letters men serving overseas sent home helped form opinion there, particularly as the growth in newspaper production and rising literacy levels allowed people to compare different opinions. The sight of so many naval families on the move – whether in post-chaise, stage coach or trudging on foot – helped to bring home to people the impact of Britain's foreign policy on domestic life.

Emerging class structure

In the eighteenth century, notions of class became increasingly distinct – although where individuals placed themselves in the social hierarchy was not always clear. For example, the 'middling sort' of people became increasingly aware of themselves as a separate class but at the upper end there was always an overlap with the elite: because England was a trading nation gentlemen often set up their younger sons in trade while many rich merchants married their daughters into the aristocracy.[2] Because of their common interests, the landed gentry and the upper elements of the merchant class were often aligned on issues of the day. Below them the rest of the middling folk comprised a range of people of finely graded status, with an obvious line between those who engaged in commerce and those who were involved in the retail trade. The more powerful merchants asserted themselves in both economic and political arenas, yet as a rule they self-consciously aimed to be 'polite' and 'genteel' rather than lavish or fashionable. Above them were the gentry, old landed families who were often proud holders of local office and, at the very pinnacle of society, the landed elite comprising only two or three hundred families. Social commentators, anxious to maintain what appeared to be a fragile social stability, often criticized the aristocracy as debauched, profligate and dissolute, urging nobles to accept more responsibility and to bring their private lives into line with their public role. Reformers, eager to curb the power of the nobility and even to bring them down, were equally critical. Accurate or not, negative representations of the upper classes helped both the lesser gentry and the 'middling sort' to define their own status and consciously to align themselves with respectable codes of behaviour. Below were the labouring classes who constituted approximately 80 per cent of England's population, which by the mid-eighteenth century numbered about six million. Already, at this time, the phrase 'lower class' was quite frequently used. By the 1770s the term 'upper class' was also common, but the term 'middle class' took much longer to enter into common use. (Today, social historians generally prefer to call these people the 'middling sort'.) Only when they had developed for themselves a set of positive values and manners did people in this category become willing to accept a term that seemed to preclude aspiration to higher status.

Eighteenth-century society did not permit a great deal of movement between social levels: women were reluctant to marry beneath their station and those without riches had little hope of marrying above it. Despite this limited social mobility women still played a key role since, while aristocratic women had little freedom in their choice of partner, their male relatives were often encouraged to marry for money. The daughters of naval officers who made a fortune through promotion and prize money in wartime certainly benefited from this. Admiral Cuthbert Collingwood (see Plate 9) was denigrated in his own day as tediously strait-laced and provincial by those who had little personal knowledge of either his capabilities or his humanity. On his death in 1810 he left each of his two daughters £40,000 (over £2 million in today's money), which enabled them to marry well, though his repeated applications to parliament that they inherit the title he had earned were unsuccessful. His younger daughter, Mary Patience, was for a time betrothed to W. R. Cosway, her father's capable secretary, but the engagement was broken off and she married another – largely because her uncle considered that Cosway, a baker's son, was no fit match for a girl who was now the daughter of a peer of the realm. On the other hand, the daughters of less fortunate naval officers, though raised in upper-class gentility, might lack the wealth that would enable them to make a good match (unlike the daughters of rich merchants). Unable to marry beneath them, many were doomed to spinsterhood.

Women's role in the process of class formation has to some extent been ignored by historians, who have tended to focus more on the masculine role. This study aims to help redress the balance, showing how frequently naval women shouldered domestic responsibilities while their husbands were away and how women in general, despite legal constraints and notions of propriety, were far more active than many have supposed. Women never competed on equal terms with men but the degree of social inequality they experienced often depended on their own characters and on local circumstances. Many enjoyed a capacity for influence and actively contributed to urban economy and society, where they usually outnumbered men partly because so many sought work in urban areas. Admittedly this process became more circumscribed in the course of the century but it seems that even then it was fitful and ill-defined.

Women's social role

Women's actions in this period would have been framed by their awareness of the social expectations of their sex and status. Contemporary publications indicate that in the 1760s and 1770s there was a particularly keen and widespread interest in the position of women in society and in relations between the sexes. Much popular writing was dedicated to examining women's behaviour and social development, possibly because there was a growing realization of women's influence in society and a desire to channel this influence into approved courses. Women might have a range of responsibilities and labours, according to their status, but all were expected to exhibit female decorum unless they were at the very bottom of society. Yet although many contemporary works set out an ideal code of female behaviour, it is not sensible to think that eighteenth-century women entirely agreed with or adhered to such expectations.

Women from the labouring classes had always worked to supplement the family income, and now the growth of industrialization offered women new possibilities for employment in potteries and factories. In maritime communities, sailors' lengthy absences generally made it imperative for their women to develop independent sources of income.[3] It is true that as Britain became richer, the more prosperous tradesmen and artisans no longer needed their wives to labour alongside them and may also have employed domestic servants. But it is simplistic to think that women with more leisure became increasingly passive in this period or that they had no economic purpose. Women helped drive consumer markets by their strong presence as retailers and shoppers. The language of burgeoning consumerism – advertising and shopping, not to mention the design of products themselves – point to a feminization of consumption. A recognition of women's increasing consumer power is evident in the many advertisements in contemporary newspapers that were addressed to women: they were lured by 'female pills', violet soap, remedies for sore nipples after childbirth or for their children's illnesses, furs, muffs and trimmings. They were tempted by an increasing range of domestic goods – the more expensive items usually endorsed as already popular with the nobility and gentry. These British-made products helped the middling sorts to assert their status and cemented ideas of national identity. They also indicate rising expectations of material comfort and point to the kinds of artefacts that people who aspired to higher social status would need to acquire. Consumer products were particularly important to naval wives who accompanied their husbands when they were posted overseas. Mrs Susanna Maria Middleton, wife of Captain Robert Gambier Middleton, the commissioner in the dockyard in Gibraltar, wrote in 1805 to her sister in Harley Street, London, begging her to send out her usual tooth powder, some Nankeen bonnets, an almanac and a lady's pocket book. Such conspicuous consumption helped, in a small way, to promote British manufactures overseas while providing the Middletons with comforting reminders that they belonged to a dominant English culture as they were trapped in a strange environment. Susanna reported, for example, that English gingerbread was regarded as a dainty in Gibraltar and asked her sister to send out more of that, too. Her obsession with small luxuries, when in Gibraltar even everyday items such as butter and mattresses were difficult to obtain, shows how essential these trappings of 'politeness' had become to the self-image of the respectable middle ranks of society.

Women's letters were a medium for social gossip at all levels. At the lower end of the social spectrum, women's capacity for gossip and their use of topical material in songs and ballads was a force to be recognized. Ballads helped to inflame public opinion against Admiral Byng after he failed to relieve Minorca in 1756, contributing to a political crisis resulting in his execution for failing to do his duty. At a higher social level, men would also use letters home for their own political ends, knowing that their wives would circulate the information at social gatherings even though women's influence in the public arena was limited. Certainly genteel women were active in a world that extended beyond the household and family.[4] Provincial gentry had both considerable affluence and power. They purchased goods in London, where they lived for part of the year, as well as in the regional areas where their roots were, helping to spread the latest fashions and patterns of consumption, which would otherwise have been limited to existing trade links between particular regions and the metropolis.[5] The nobility were able to afford expensive purchases from both London and abroad. For example, Lady Anson, the daughter of Lord Hardwicke, the Lord Chancellor, who married the circumnavigator Captain George Anson in 1748 had expensive tastes. Anson had been made a peer after his victories at sea and had accumulated of a huge amount of prize money; he was also to serve twice as First Lord of the Admiralty. He bought Dresden china from Holland, and he and his wife ordered Chinese furniture and expensive fabrics from London for Shugborough, their Staffordshire estate.[6] Similar spending patterns can be found in the account books of Lady Mary Duncan (1731 – 1804), aunt of Admiral Lord Viscount Duncan. She had a house in Hampton Court Green and a town house in Queen Anne Street, London, and kept meticulous account books for both household and personal expenditure. She continued to order goods from London suppliers even when not resident in the capital. She also spent considerable sums to celebrate her connection with the famous admiral. For example, on 22 December 1797, after Duncan's great victory against the Dutch at Camperdown, she noted in her accounts, 'Paid the server tradesmen per bills and receipts for the entertainment of Admiral Lord Viscount Duncan consisting of illuminations, painting, transparencys [sic], fireworks which altogether comes to … 101 – 10 – 6.' In 1801 she recorded, 'Paid to Mr Copley, painter, for print and frame of Lord Duncan's victory 11 – 17 – 6.'[7] At this period genteel women, 'turned to personal and household artefacts to create a world of meanings' and arguably at every social level when women acquired everyday items with naval connotations they helped to fashion a sense of national as well as personal belonging.[8]

To some extent the middling sort aped the minor gentry, helping to spread metropolitan culture to provincial towns. Yet many had distinctive, even trend-setting, patterns of consumption either because they lived in urban or port areas where the latest manufactured goods and imports were more evident or because they traded in these goods themselves. Sailors' wives in particular might obtain novel items from abroad as their husbands travelled or had means to trade privately.

Women and marriage

To understand the social position of naval wives it is important to consider how marriage was viewed by contemporary society. Among people of social standing, marriage was a highly public institution; a couple's relationship was considered and judged within a larger context that included conceptions of female virtue, honour, reputation and social stability. Among the upper and middling ranks of society marriage was used for economic and political advantage. The 1753 Marriage Act, pushed through Parliament by Lord Chancellor Hardwicke and not reformed until 1822, set out to prevent clandestine marriage and bigamy so that heirs and heiresses would not be tricked into unsuitable marriages. The Act appealed primarily to ideals of patriarchy and family interest among the elite. It enforced public marriage and promoted parental (preferably paternal) consent because the aim was really to ensure the safe transmission of family property from one generation to the next. This suggests that the propertied elite, at least, did not greatly support marriage for love, or freedom of choice in marriage. Their children, and their daughters in particular, continued to be regarded as objects of commerce in the race to accumulate property. At the other end of the social scale, the Act did nothing to support the common law rights of poor or jilted women because in forbidding private marriage contracts it withdrew the protection such women had enjoyed under ecclesiastical law. (Formerly, the ecclesiastical courts had invariably supported court actions brought by young women who were seduced and impregnated on promise of marriage.) Yet even the middling sort, eager to progress socially, limited freedom of choice in marriage. Captain Matthew Flinders (see Plate 6) who, partly from ambition and partly to secure financial independence, accepted a commission to survey the coasts of Australia was abroad when his sister married. He was not pleased with her, writing that, 'the idea that young girls are at liberty to marry whom they please, without consulting any of their friends, may do much harm in society, and should be opposed'.[9]

The 1753 Marriage Act made Fleet marriages illegal. These were cheap marriages, needing no banns or licence, which had been carried out since 1710 by parsons operating within the 'Rules' or precincts of the Fleet prison, London – a sanctuary area just outside the prison where clergymen imprisoned for debt could obtain licence to live. As they were already in prison for debt, they could not be forced to pay the £100 fine imposed for performing such marriages nor could they be suspended from their parish as they had none or had already been suspended. Virtually immune from punishment, they married customers freely and cheaply at any time of day, any day of the week. Records of the marriages were kept, however, and these were recognised for legal and administrative purposes. While such clandestine marriages may have been the undoing of many young heiresses, they also seem to have been popular not just because they were cheap but because people wanted to marry privately, without banns, since many Londoners could have married at a comparable cost in their local parish church. By 1753 one in five marriages was clandestine, and Fleet marriages were exceptionally popular among sailors since they could be contracted almost on the spur of the moment (see Plate 1). They were also important for sailors' women because they gave them a legal claim to their husbands' wages.

In a regular marriage contract there were two main elements: the portion brought by the woman and the settlement to provide for her maintenance if the husband should die before her. Landed classes usually took care of the settlement by means of a jointure whereby lands to a certain value would be set aside to provide an annual income in widowhood. (Middling ranks might undertake to bequeath a widow a certain sum.) The marriage contract for the better off might also stipulate that the wife should receive an annual amount as 'pin money' for her personal expenditure. Any money a woman saved from this allowance was her own, though if her husband got into debt it could be used to pay his creditors. There was unease about even the limited independence this assured, since it seemed to threaten the 'natural' subordination of a woman to her husband.

A married woman's legal and financial identity was subsumed into that of her husband. Husband and wife were one person in law, the legal existence of the woman being suspended during the marriage, or consolidated into that of the husband under whose protection and *cover* she performed every thing. Her condition was termed her 'coverture' and, as a 'feme covert' rather than 'feme sole', strict limitations were placed on her economic activity so that, for example, she was unable to make contracts in her own right. But outside the common law of coverture other equity operated and an affluent bride's family might draw up settlements to secure her property. A woman with property of her own might have it put under the management of trustees prior to her marriage, although often such arrangements were made with the aim of protecting family interests from a possibly improvident husband, rather than providing financial independence for the woman. As a woman with a separate estate, she could then make contracts and incur debts in her own right. At all levels of society, different prenuptial settlements could be drawn up to preserve the wife's property interests. Some wives lost all legal rights to their wealth after marriage and might even be ruined by spendthrift husbands but others were able to protect their ownership of property and, in most cases, dispose of it as they wished.

Married women were certainly oppressed under common law, but on a day-to-day level, there were means of getting round the restrictions. For example, in law a wife could not purchase goods on credit since she owned no property in her own right under common law but under the law of necessaries, she could legally supply herself with *necessaries* for her own use while she remained chaste and continued to live with her husband. It was assumed that the husband, having taken all his wife's possessions, would not deny his wife the necessaries suitable to his own station in life and therefore would be willingly liable for any such purchases she made in his name. This applied especially to household goods and drapery and helps to explain why the didactic literature of the time condemned women's increasing levels of consumption just at the time when their formal economic rights under the law seemed to be diminishing after the 1753 Marriage Act tightened procedures.

The law of necessaries allowed women of more privileged status considerable power in matrimonial conflicts. Under the law of coverture, married women could not be imprisoned for debt since they were not allowed to contract debts at all. Estranged wives could run up large bills, which their husbands were bound to settle, and in this way they could force husbands to accept a compromise or face financial ruin. Women who were thrown out of their homes because they had committed adultery lost the right to their husband's credit but those forced to leave on account of their husband's cruelty kept it, as did adulterous women who remained in the marital home. The painter John Thomas Serres (1759 – 1825) was ruined by the extravagances of his unstable wife, Olivia. As marine artist to George III, Serres spent months at sea with the fleet. At home, his wife indulged in numerous adulteries and frauds, signing banks drafts in his name until he was declared bankrupt. They separated by mutual agreement in 1802. Serres afterwards started a new life in Edinburgh but Olivia pursued him there and he was imprisoned for debt. He never recovered his fortunes and died under the rules of the King's Bench, an area outside the gates of the King's Bench debtors' prison in London, where inmates of some means could wander or reside. However, the law of necessaries was of no help to very poor women, who could hardly form a case that their husbands needed to give them the means to support a lifestyle suitable to their rank.

Marriage was considered the most important choice a woman would make in life, and conduct manuals for women emphasized traditional gender roles in an effort to counterbalance an apparent trend towards greater female independence. Religious works similarly directed that, in a divinely-ordered world, wives should defer to their husband's better understanding. Some took issue with this. A Methodist tract of 1809 offered the conventional view that 'judgement in men is more solid, their minds more firm, and their knowledge more extensive than what is generally found in the other sex' but the owner's annotation in the margin reads, 'This in my opinion is far from being an universal truth, and is liable to many exceptions'.[10] It was accepted that good husbands would trust their wives with their property, or at least a sufficient proportion of it for housekeeping, unless wives forfeited that trust through extravagance. In contemporary literature, women were frequently linked to luxury and debt. They might be criticized for leading the family into debt by encouraging uxorious husbands to spend too much on needless fripperies, or they might be accused of wantonly accumulating gambling debts that they had no means of paying off. At the same time, it was recognized that women were having an expansive effect on western consumer markets and thereby helping to develop the economy, as well as being actively involved, as far as their circumstances would permit, in trading and business.

Writers of the day firmly insisted that the wife should be subservient to her husband but they also stressed the need for a loving, companionate relationship in marriage. While we cannot judge the extent to which conduct books actually influenced women's behaviour, they sometimes found it convenient to use the language of these books for their own ends. Many self-consciously displayed themselves in their letters as loving, obedient wives to assert an element of moral authority over their husband. They could also make fun of themselves and their subservient role in a self-deprecatory and ultimately subversive way. This tongue-in-cheek tactic might actually affirm their devotion and virtue; or they might be subtly undermining their husbands. Much depends on the rhetoric they used, and therein lies much of the drama of their letters.

Men and women were not expected to conform to the same moral standard. In 1775 one writer commenting on seduction, adultery and divorce explained that, 'carnal commerce of a married man with a woman whom he does not know, or had not reason to believe, is married; is not adultery in the man'.[11] On the other hand, a woman was guilty of adultery if she slept with any man but her husband – principally because there was a danger that she might bring another man's children into the family – and if she did this she should be turned out. In 1805 Randle Lewis, a lawyer producing a guide for 'the middle class of society' on how to end unhappy marriages, made a similar point: the injury caused by a husband's adultery was 'but skin deep' but an unchaste wife 'cast an indelible stain on her own offspring' and deserved to be shunned by society. If a husband was unfaithful or abusive, it was considered no reason to challenge his authority. His wife should instead examine her own conduct to see if she had given offence, and continue to be submissive in the hope that her husband would regret his infidelity. Conduct book writers presented this situation as a true test of womanhood, arguing that a wife could only question her husband's authority if he proved so abusive that she feared that her life or her children were in danger. Then she was advised to turn to a trusted relative who might confront her husband rather than confront him herself – even in these situations it was essential to maintain an appearance of submissiveness and reluctance to withhold her obedience. Jane Prescott, the daughter of the Chaplain at Plymouth Dockyard, suffered savage cruelty at the hands of her husband, a captain in the Navy. Her father, relying on the captain's honour and generosity, had given him a portion of £2000 when he married his daughter without insisting on any settlement, but Captain Prescott often beat his wife with a stick and threatened her with a poker hot from the fire. She concealed his ill treatment but finally in 1785 obtained a legal separation and an allowance of £90 per annum on grounds of cruelty.

Nevertheless, eighteenth-century writers continued to portray marriage as the only state that could provide true happiness for women, and conjugal love was supposed to stop a husband's authority from becoming tyrannical. Matthew Flinders, who sailed for Australia only weeks after his marriage to Ann Chappelle, was perhaps still speaking theoretically when he wrote to assure her that their's would be a marriage in which each had the confidence of the other: 'there is a medium between petticoat government and tyranny on the part of the husband, that, with thee, I think to be very attainable; and which I consider to be the summit of happiness in the marriage state.'[12] Admiral Sir William Young, writing to his old friend Admiral Sir Charles Morice Pole on his marriage to the daughter of a wealthy merchant, wrote:

> I am confident that an affection once raised may be easily kept up, remember this, my dear Pole! A little kindness, a little attention may preserve the heart of her we love, if she has ever loved us. Never forget that an inattentive husband has no case of complaint against a negligent wife.[13]

Even within aristocratic marriage, love was expected to flourish – but it was to be a controlled emotion, tempered by a mutual respect. In the reasoning of the time, a woman's total submission to her husband was therefore not meant to be a kind of abject slavery but a means of demonstrating her virtue and moral authority. Whatever the difficulties of the married state, commentators advised young girls to choose it in preference to spinsterhood, a condition that was heavily stereotyped and often held in disrespect. Dr John Gregory wrote of, 'the forlorn and unprotected situation of an old maid, the chagrin and peevishness which are apt to infect their tempers'.[14]

Divorce

In the mid-eighteenth century it has been estimated that only about 4 per cent of all marriages ended in break-up, a low percentage that may be partly explained by the high adult mortality rate.[15] However, one commentator revealingly argued that divorce was far preferable to the husband poisoning or murdering his wife if they were incompatible. Couples of any social level who could no longer live together might obtain separation by private deed. The husband agreed to pay his wife an annual allowance for life – usually about one third of his net income. In return she indemnified him against any suit by creditors for debts she might run up in future. The deed was not enforceable in common law but kept the domestic situation out of the courts and the public eye. For the woman it entailed loss of status, loss of social life and restrictions on her ability to see her children – although by the end of the century it had become common to award custody of children under the age of seven to the mother. Women were therefore under some pressure to remain in an unhappy marriage.

After 1750 most divorces came from the middle rather than the upper ranks, and the divorce rate rose considerably between the 1770s and 1790s. Lewis's 1805 guide to ending unhappy marriages sets out the options open to the middling ranks. He condemned the practice of those who rushed into print and published details of elopement or adultery in the newspapers. Where there was evidence of a wife's adultery or if the husband's cruelty was life-threatening, 'separation from bed and board' with no permission to re-marry could be obtained in the ecclesiastical courts. If there was no proof of a wife's adultery, or if the parties lacked funds to pursue a legal case, it was better to come to a private arrangement in a deed of separation.

If it could be shown that both parties were guilty of adultery, divorce could not be granted in the ecclesiastical court but only by act of parliament. Reliable witnesses would be needed to avoid any accusation of collusion. When Mr Esten, a purser in the Navy, brought an action of 'criminal conversation' 'or crim. con.' against the Duke of Hamilton who had lived with Esten's wife for six years, the House of Lords threw the case out because they suspected collusion. Since a man's wife was in a sense his property, if she was seduced he could bring a common-law action against his wife's lover for damages. The adulterous third party bore the cost of divorce, which brought it within the reach of the less affluent. The injured husband stood to gain from the proceedings, which may have encouraged more to punish their wives for adultery. But in this case, before Esten returned to sea, he and his wife had signed a deed of separation so no divorce was possible and no damages liable to be paid since the husband had not been injured. However, if evidence of adultery were incontrovertible, witnesses would not be needed. Lewis's guide gave as an example the case of a naval officer whose wife had a child during his absence abroad, and who upon his return was several months pregnant with a second, although he could not discover who the father was. In a pointed aside, Lewis remarked that generally only the lower orders settled their family quarrels before a magistrate because, he said, they were ill-bred enough to throw knives and domestic utensils at each other so that often a dangerous fracas ensued.

Because the wife could continue to accumulate debts for which her husband would be liable, many husbands advertised the separation, or at least informed the tradesmen whom they used regularly – an important consideration in a society that increasingly relied on credit and which punished debtors with indefinite imprisonment. Unless it could be proved that the tradesman had actually seen a notice advertising the separation, the husband was still responsible for his wife's debts. For this reason, it was more prudent to come to an arrangement and allow the wife an annual income, as Nelson did when he separated from his wife. If a man wilfully turned his wife out without making any provision for her he implicitly gave her a claim to credit for necessary food, clothing and lodging, according to his circumstances. On the other hand, if a wife left her husband, it was unlikely that an action would be brought against him for her debts because, if upheld, it would constitute a means whereby one man could financially ruin another simply by enticing away his wife.

By the 1760s it was usual to sue for crim. con. in order to prepare the way for parliamentary divorce in the House of Lords, the obligatory route by 1798, extremely expensive and at first confined to the landed elite so that they would have another opportunity to beget heirs. Contested crim. con. suits could also be expensive and were generally pursued only by the upper middling sort and landed elite. Recorded cases rose steeply in the period 1780 – 1800, though afterwards declined. Crim. con. cases became notorious as, with the increase in marital litigation, adulteries were featured in the popular press. The large number of military officers and West India merchants who appeared in the pages of the *The Bon Ton Magazine* (1791 – 96), a monthly which offered predominantly sexual gossip about the rich and famous combined with sensationalized news and fantastic everyday-life stories, reveals how war and imperial expansion generated marital breakdown. It also contributed to the prevalent anxiety about the perceived breakdown of social and sexual hierarchies. The issue for January 1795 explains, 'when the wife is gay and handsome, and the husband, poor soul, far away at sea, we but too often find the good old proverb verified: "Out of sight, out of mind." A man, in such cases, may be considered as dead for the time being.'[16]

Newspapers also carried notices of more prominent divorces. The front page of *The London Chronicle*, 24 – 26 May 1785, reported the marital break-up of John Inglis, late captain of the *Pandora*, who married in 1770. He was ordered abroad in 1780 and he left his wife and son in a house at Gosport, 'where she entered into an unlawful familiarity with Joseph Lancaster, late a midshipman in his Majesty's navy, and with whom she lived in open adultery'. The paper reported that when Inglis returned, his wife exclaimed that she thought he was dead – but she may only have wished him so. Inglis sued for crim. con., and won damages of £500 in the Court of King's Bench. His wife could put up no further defence and Inglis was granted his divorce.

Poor people and moderately paid artisans could not afford legal divorce or separation so records tell us little about marital breakdown at the lower levels of society. Husbands just deserted their wives, often joining the forces, but this may have been under pressure of poverty rather than estrangement. Recorded wife sales increased from 1750 due to the rigours of the Marriage Act, then evened out in the repressive 1790s and afterwards peaked around 1830, although when these separations were tested in courts they were declared invalid. When an ordinary seaman did obtain a formal divorce it was something of a novelty. In 1791 a seaman's wife was successfully tried for adultery during the absence of her husband at sea and it was reported as such in a compendium of divorce trials:

> This trial presents us with a feature of novelty upon its very first face; viz. A Sailor's divorce; a thing as remarkable for its rarity, at least according to the forms of law, as Sailors' weddings, without these forms, are for the frequency of their occurrence.[17]

Letter writing

In this period letter writing was the chief means of communicating at a distance and the ability to write good letters was highly regarded. It was considered bad manners not to reply to a letter, in the same way that it would have been bad manners not to return visits or reciprocate gifts, and the cost of carrying a letter meant that writers were often compelled to use a neat hand and cram as many lines on the page as possible.

Since marriage was so important to women and their social status and personal happiness depended so crucially on choosing the right partner, it is not surprising to find women commenting on their marriage, and those of friends and acquaintances, in their personal correspondence. It has been argued that one of the functions of letters between husband and wife was for both parties to assert and reinforce their understanding of the proper relations that should exist between them. Far from taking such letters at face value, since all letter writing is in a sense a performance, it is interesting to see how each partner reflects an awareness of the other's expectations. In many letters, the woman seems to be constructing her wifely identity, and perhaps testing the limits of that role. In her husband's absence, she could present a more positive side to her character by demonstrating responsibility, the ability to make choices and a degree of autonomy. Letters were an acceptable method of conducting business outside the family – and in some cases correspondence could be used to extend the limits of power.

Male commentators of the time noted that letters seemed particularly suited to the female voice.[18] Young women were recommended to maintain a correspondence because it encouraged habits of reflection, reduced the temptation to dissipate their time and enabled them to be more rational and pleasing companions to men of sense when they married. Letter-writing manuals had always described letters as 'conversation between absent friends'.[19] Such 'conversation' disclosed one's breeding and status. In 1801 Jane Austen could write to her sister, 'I have now attained the true art of letter-writing, which we are always told, is to express on paper exactly what one would say to the same person by word of mouth.'[20] Collingwood urged his eldest daughter, Sarah, to write her letters with great care, so that nothing would give offence or betray vulgarity:

> Remember, my dear, that your letter is the picture of your brains; and those whose brains are a compound of folly, nonsense and impertinence, are to blame to exhibit them to the contempt of the world, or the pity of their friends. To write a letter with negligence, without proper stops, with crooked lines and great flourishing dashes, is inelegant: it argues either great ignorance of what is proper, or great indifference towards the person to whom it is addressed, and is consequently disrespectful. It makes no amends to add an apology, for having scrawled a sheet of paper; of bad pens, for you should mend them; or want of time, for nothing is more important to you, or to which your time can be more properly devoted.[21]

However, even in this age when people had to communicate by letter, extended personal correspondence was rare and was only required when families were separated for long periods, which naval families were. It also helped to ease anxiety about illness, accident or travel.

Letters received or written by naval wives give an insight into their lives but cannot be taken at face value. It can be difficult to judge how honest and 'authentic' the views expressed are since the writer is always aware of the established etiquette of what the recipient expects or wants to read, and how far polite conventions can be manipulated. Personal correspondence is also clearly a means of self-expression: the letter form allows the writer to construct a particular image of themselves for the reader. It is also the case that relatively few letters from naval wives of the period survive: often seamen destroyed their wives' letters before a battle in case personal or perhaps even political exchanges fell into the wrong hands. We know that Nelson, for example, sorted through his wife's letters and burnt them before the action at Tenerife where he lost his arm. Wives, on the other hand, tended to preserve their husbands' letters more carefully, partly for sentimental reasons and partly because they often related to important events. The whole picture can be difficult to obtain when only one half of the correspondence survives.

While those at home could track a person's career in the *London Gazette* or, after 1799, the monthly *Naval Chronicle*, published until 1819, receiving a letter was a prestigious event. Some letters from naval officers were clearly intended to be read aloud and passed among friends and family, especially if they brought news of encounters with the enemy. Since letter-reading could be a social affair, writers often marked those passages which were not to be shared. In wartime, letters brought sought-after news – and an account from a trusted correspondent might be considered more reliable than a newspaper report. Such letters often had political importance. When Collingwood wrote home to his wife after the victory at Cape St Vincent in 1797, he first assured her that he was well and then began, 'Now for history'. The account he gave of the battle was clearly intended for a wider audience.

Yet inevitably there were times when those at sea had no news at all. Frequently husbands, since they were so cut off, wanted their wives to send details of national affairs as well as news of their family. On one occasion, when Collingwood had received no letter for three months, he complained that he knew no more of the world his wife was living in than if he were an inhabitant of the moon.[22] Most correspondents were aware of the need to avoid writing about trivia, or at least understood that they should try to make such details interesting and the letters of wives and children to men at sea were especially useful in keeping up their morale. Collingwood, almost continually afloat during the French wars from 1793 until his death in 1810, asked his wife to tell him everything she could think of about their family and about the countryside around Newcastle that he loved so much, 'the oaks, the woodlands, and the verdant meads'.[23] When no letters arrived, husbands naturally worried and feared the worse. Letters could be a lifeline.

Though literacy levels were higher than has previously been thought in the eighteenth century, not all wives of seamen were literate and communication by letter would not have been an option for many of the lower classes. Some figures suggest that literacy was as low as 30 per cent but others indicate that between 1700 and 1790 literacy remained fairly steady at 60 per cent for men, rising in women from 40 to 50 per cent. The papers of the Charity for the Relief of Officers' Widows indicates that even in the early nineteenth century, some wives of warrant officers could not sign their name. They had to take regular oaths that they remained widows in order to continue to receive the pension and many simply made their mark in the presence of witnesses. Despite the fact that printed materials were in wider circulation than ever before, there were many, such as labourers and farmers who did not need to read regularly and also a number of people who could not write but who were able to read a variety of cheap, popular materials such as ballads, tracts, familiar tales and pamphlets.[24]

There is little correspondence written by ordinary seamen, whether at sea or from a foreign port, to be found in regional archives. However, letters that survive offer insights into the management of mariners' domestic affairs and the relationship between them and their families. For example, fathers unable to watch their children growing up treasured specimens of their early handwriting. James Whitworth, an impressed man separated from his family for over two years in the early nineteenth century, wrote that he longed to see an example of his daughter's handwriting. Jean Grant explained in a letter to her father Samuel, a purser, that her younger sister had not yet mastered 'small hand' but that she would sign her name at the foot of the letter and, as a postscript, there duly appears a short, carefully written message in a different hand: 'Margaret Grant Gives her duty to her father'. Samuel Grant was also sent a lock of the child's hair which he kept carefully folded in a paper marked 'Little Peggy's 27 June 1801'.[25]

Although as a historical resource letters offer illuminating insights into aspects of social and cultural history, the gender and power structures within society, codes of behaviour, and language, yet they can be difficult to interpret. Contemporary conventions mean that much in the correspondence can seem now to be encoded, and what is left unsaid is often significant. Moreover letters offer the seductive possibility of identifying too closely with the recipient or reader. Like diaries, they can be personal and immediate – yet though not fiction, sometimes they need to be read carefully, as has been remarked upon in connection with politicians' correspondence:

> 'private letters', in the politician's world is a misnomer. A letter is a
> political action. It is not private, even if marked 'Private'. A political
> letter is an act of persuasion or deception taking place on a smaller
> stage. Its contents are conventional, not natural outpourings. It is not
> a message, but a form of art and craft. We can no more be naïve about
> private letters than about public speeches.[26]

Such warnings are also relevant to the reading of naval letters from this period, partly because the writers knew they would be read aloud to others and partly because politics often loomed large in their content.

The postal service

It is clear from contemporary letters that official timetables for postal collection and the actual operation of letter delivery were always at the back of correspondents' minds. Depending on where seamen were stationed, communication could be very irregular and many women kept a letter to their husband 'on the go' so that it could be hurriedly finished if a chance occurred to send it or if they received a letter that needed a prompt reply.

Highway construction in the mid-eighteenth century permitted a more rapid, extended postal service between major towns. 'Flying coaches' could now provide faster communication than the former post boys on horseback. But to avoid breaking the rules of the postal monopoly any letters sent by coach had to be made up into parcels. Everybody understood that when coach owners discreetly advertised their parcel service, it was a polite fiction and they were actually offering to carry letters. Eventually, market pressure prevailed and in 1784 a coach service was established to carry both mail and passengers. The standard service was a coach drawn by four horses and, since the team was changed at regular intervals along the road, the vehicle kept up a cracking pace of about eight miles an hour. The mail coach service proved so reliable that people would set their watch by it. Coaches made a colourful spectacle when they arrived at their destination and in wartime they would be decorated with flowers and ribbons when they carried news of a British victory. Inevitably, the early intelligence they brought was sometimes imperfect: when the mail arrived in Newcastle bringing news of Trafalgar, the coachman, who was wearing a black hatband, announced that Nelson and all the admirals had been killed. Admiral Collingwood's wife, Sarah, out shopping in the town, promptly fainted. The news that her husband was alive after all was only confirmed later in official reports.

The cost of postage was high as it was based on a single sheet of paper and regulated according to distance, measured by the routes of the mail. Most letters were paid for on receipt but any government official or Member of Parliament could send letters free of charge simply by signing or 'franking' the cover of the letter. This privilege was naturally exploited, with officials signing scores of letters for family and friends. In 1784 Pitt ordered a substantial increase on postage in place of a tax on coals. Postage rates were increased again in 1797, 1801, 1805 and 1812 in order to help pay for the war against France. As an example, after the 1801 increase it cost three pence to send a single sheet to a destination not exceeding 15 miles away, and four pence to one not exceeding 30 miles away. All double, treble and other letters were taxed in proportion to a single postage. Influential people could generally find someone with franking privileges to ease the cost of postage but regular correspondence was generally beyond the means of the lower classes: 1d was equivalent to a day's pay for many agricultural labourers and account books show that in 1808 two quires of paper (48 or 50 sheets) could cost 3s 2d. There were, however, devious ways of sending messages free of charge: if individuals just wanted to reassure their family that they were well, they could send a blank sheet with the family's name and address on it. The recipient could then refuse to pay the postage but would still know their relative was safe. (If the letter did contain important news and needed to be accepted by the recipient, the writer could signal that the letter had to be paid for by some pre-arranged variation, perhaps in the way the family name was written.) Brief notes could be written in the margins of newspapers, which were carried free of charge, or certain words in a newspaper could be marked to convey simple messages. Underlining the name of a Whig politician commonly meant 'I am well', while doing the same thing with a Tory meant the opposite.

Overseas communication in this period was inevitably a much more hazardous business, especially in wartime. The Post Office contracted packet boats to take letters to Ireland, the West Indies, North America, Spain, Portugal, the Mediterranean, the Channel Islands, France and Holland. The packet service was often slow, though it aimed to provide a regular monthly service to the West Indies from 1744, and to North America from 1755.[27] It could also be dangerous: in wartime, the captains of these packet boats had orders to jettison the mail rather than allow it to be captured. For some, shipowners offered an alternative method of sending letters overseas. They had long offered their business contacts a free service, via bags hung up in London coffee houses labelled with the name of the ship, date of sailing and ports of call so that merchants could deposit letters for overseas destinations. Mail to India had always been carried free of charge by the East India Company: its ships called en route at the Cape of Good Hope and at Mauritius, so naval officers could always leave letters at either place to be taken home to Britain by a passing East Indiaman. These ships were designed for freight, not speed, so mail could take between 170 and 230 days – sometimes longer.

By 1798 the problems of getting overseas mail through in wartime had become so great that the Post Office set up the Ship Letter Office to try to regularise the free merchant system. The bags of letters were to be collected by the Post Office, stamped and charged, and sent by mail coach to the port from which the ship was sailing. There they would be handed over to the master of the ship, who received 2d for every letter he took (as an incentive to deliver them safely). This service was popular, as the rates were half those for normal packets. Even so, the Post Office could not enforce the system and many letters slipped through and were sent free of charge. Foreign letters that came in by ship other than packet boat were known as 'ship letters'. They were not taken to London but delivered to the postmaster at the port where the ship anchored, and from there the Post Office could levy the appropriate charge to cover inland delivery.

Only London had a penny postal service, until 1765, when a change in regulations allowed other cities to follow suit, and until 1773 only in London was mail delivered to houses. This service slowly extended to other large cities but mostly people had to take their own letters to the post office and collect them from there. No one could be certain that letters once posted remained confidential. People were aware that some letters were opened but were never sure where or how. In fact, successive governments tried to control the exchange of both national and overseas mail. The Post Office in London had sophisticated equipment for steaming open wafers and reproducing seals with bread impressions, and officials routinely opened suspect letters, especially in times of crisis, although they were not supposed to do this without a warrant. When Nelson, having anchored at Spithead in August 1805, wrote to Emma Hamilton to say that he was coming home, he asked her to imagine what was in his mind and what he wanted to say since he supposed his letter would be 'cut open, smoaked and perhaps read'.[28]

In wartime, the routes set up by government to maintain contact with officers at sea was also used for private correspondence. In 1795 an Act was passed 'further regulating the sending and receiving letters free from the duty of postage'. This allowed non-commissioned officers, seamen and private men, in the navy and army, to send and receive single sheet letters at a low rate of postage (one penny, prepaid), while on active service. Letters were countersigned by commanding officers saying that the writer was employed on his Majesty's service. Many objected to this concession on the grounds that allowing men to write in this manner was treating them like citizens rather than subjects and that it would inflame radical tendencies. Admiral Collingwood, for example, wrote in 1801, 'The intention was kind and considerate, but the allowing seamen's letters to pass free of postage has done infinite harm. Of a hundred letters not more than five are from wives or relations, but either scrawls from the nannies, or plans of resistance from other ships.'[29] His point was that cheap correspondence increased the risk of men plotting mutiny within the fleet rather than improving general morale.

Practicalities of travel

Naval wives had to be prepared to travel at short notice to see their husbands if their ship anchored at a home port, although sometimes seamen were able to make a visit home. Travel costs could be high. The development of a turnpike road network in England (when travellers were charged a fee for the use of a stretch of road which could then be maintained by the money they paid), encouraged the use of wheeled traffic. Some important towns in England, including Bath, Bristol and Cambridge, had enjoyed coach services from 1660, but most of the others had to wait until after 1750 to gain a waggon or stage coach service. Even then these unwieldy vehicles, drawn by four or six horses, lurched along badly made roads at an average speed of only four miles an hour. Northern manufacturing towns did not gain a coach service at all until the roads were turnpiked; Leeds and Sheffield, for example, only got a London coach in 1760. Even in 1800, travelling post on horseback was common in the West Country and in the Pennines. But by end of century turnpike roads had made a huge difference – there were still complaints about the quality of the roads but conditions were much better for wheeled traffic.

Improvements to coach design also made travelling easier. Steel springs were generally fitted in stage coaches from about 1760, which enabled them not only to travel more safely at speed but also allowed more people to be carried as the earlier coach carrying 4 to 6 people inside was replaced by the 'flying coach' with up to 4 additional passengers on the roof. In the second half of the eighteenth century better coach design and faster, better bred horses, enabling longer journeys without breaks, and, crucially, improved roads all contributed to faster journey times; but the increase in speed was also accomplished by tighter schedules. Costs could be substantially reduced too, as journey times were cut by travelling through the night rather than breaking the journey at an inn, thus sparing passengers the price of food and accommodation, though coachmen and guards still expected tips. For example, in 1763 the Bath coach left London at 11pm and arrived in Bath the following evening. The increase in wheeled traffic made the upkeep of turnpiked roads more difficult but roads had to be well maintained if coaches were to travel by night in darkness.

These shorter journey times made a great difference to naval families. In 1750 a stage coach from London took more than a day to get to Portsmouth, a day to get to Ipswich and over two days to get to Plymouth. There were marked improvements on these journey times after 1784 when the stage coach began to be replaced by the mail coach. By 1811 a mail coach leaving London at 8p.m. could get to Portsmouth by 6.15a.m. the next day, to Ipswich by 5.30a.m. and to Plymouth by 8a.m., although the journey was extremely tiring as passengers had to endure long hours of non-stop travel over relatively poor roads. Seasonal schedules gradually became more flexible. In the first half of the eighteenth century many stage coaches, like the flying service, did not run in the winter months, and from 1750 many routes kept to a less exacting schedule in winter. By the 1770s summer times operated throughout the year on some routes and, from the 1780s, mail coaches ran on non-seasonal schedules. By the early nineteenth century their arrival could be timed within minutes and after 1820 horseback travel declined because by then it was no faster than the stage coach. Increasingly, travellers had a choice of quality, speed and expense as types of service and competition increased. Even within the limits of a single service, passengers often had the choice of 'inside' or 'outside' travel – the latter at half the price. The middling ranks of people chiefly used mail and stage coaches. In 1752 – 3, passenger fares were 2.2d per mile; in 1782 – 3, 3d per mile, and in 1808, 4.5d per mile, so travellers still had to be reasonably well or and engaged in important business.[30] (Stage coaches were often used by business men as they sought to widen their market or take control of deals formerly left to agents.) Obviously, the mail coach was much too expensive for labouring people: if the poor needed to travel they walked or paid a small sum to travel on a carrier's cart or waggon.

At the upper end of the market, travellers could take advantage of several options: they could hire horses to ride or to draw their own carriage, or if they could afford it they could pay a considerable premium to travel by post-chaise. These, with just two passengers and four horses with two postilions, combined both speed and exclusivity. Post-chaise charges were generally between 7d and 9d per mile on turnpike roads and 9d to 1s, or up to a third more, on the unturnpiked crossroads (because post-chaises were also used to link places off the main roads with coach services). When Lady Mary Duncan travelled she took her own carriage or travelled by post-chaise but her servants were put in a stage coach. Private transport was a mark of nobility – only the lesser classes tolerated the chance companions that might be found in a stage coach. Nelson wrote to his wife Frances (see Plate 11) from his ship *Agamemnon* in October 1794, 'All I beg is that you will not travel in a stage coach, this I insist upon' but by 1798 she was pointedly complaining that 'postchaise hire comes to too much money'.[31] Yet Betsy Fremantle, the wife of one of Nelson's captains, frequently travelled in a chaise to see her husband (see Plate 3) when his ship anchored. She recorded in her diary for 7 August 1801 that Fremantle had written to summon her to Portsmouth since he had been unable to get leave of absence. She travelled from Reading with her sister and son Tom, 'It was an excessive hot day and very uncomfortable travelling being four in the chaise.'[32] On another occasion she learnt by letter at 1p.m. that Fremantle's ship was detained at Portsmouth. She set out as soon as she had packed, at 3p.m., and got to Portsmouth just before gates shut at 12.15a.m. All the town seemed asleep but fortunately Fremantle from his bed heard her carriage as it pulled up opposite Fountain's Inn and was able to meet her.

With the increase in wheeled traffic, roads had to be well maintained, especially if coaches were to travel safely at night. But despite this, travelling could still be a dangerous business. Stage coach accidents made the news regularly as drivers went through low arches forgetting passengers on the top, or overturned their coaches through negligence or in bad conditions. In 1796 the Bath stage coach overturned when the horses set off before the coachman had scrambled onto the box. It fell onto John Baker, a gunner, who had been travelling as an outside passenger on his way home to his wife in London whom he had not seen for ten years.[33]

Naval life and seamen's wives

Admiralty regulations of 1731 stipulated that '[a captain] is not to carry any women to sea ... without orders from the Admiralty'. However, officers' wives might be given official permission to accompany their husbands, and the wives of warrant officers (including the boatswain, carpenter, gunner and master) went with them to sea as a matter of course. When Fanny Martin, a boatswain's wife, provided details of the bloody mutiny that took place on the *Hermione* in 1797, nothing was made of the fact she was on board, or that she remained on board after the mutineers had thrown the bodies of the murdered officers, including that of her husband, over the side.[34] If officers did carry their wives to sea with them it was often to save money, if their main source of income was their pay and they had married a woman without fortune. Admiral Sir William Young, who never married, wrote with shocked disapproval to his friend Admiral Pole about some officers who sailed with their wives during the 1797 fleet mutinies, 'A fine school to teach delicacy to one's wife!' In 1799 he passed censure on another captain who had his wife and family on board with him, averring that he would have been disposed to suspend him and send him home.[35] Young was a member of the Board of Admiralty so his view may have had some influence. In 1801, when Captain Flinders tried to take his wife with him on his voyage to Australia against the wishes of his superiors he received orders before he reached open sea to put her ashore. Most naval wives therefore had to resign themselves to extended periods of separation. In addition to worrying about their husbands' health, they probably worried about their fidelity because the temptations that assailed seamen in port were well known. One mother, writing to her son in 1801 as he returned from his first voyage, bluntly warned him not to spend his hard-earned money on prostitutes.[36] Popular songs and prints either depicted seamen as having a choice of sexual partner in every port or as steadfastly faithful to their chosen loved one at home: the deciding factor on which version was used probably depended on the intended audience. For example, Charles Dibdin's popular song 'Jack in his Element', in which the sailor boasts of sampling a range of beauties, 'In every mess I find a friend, | In every port a wife', may well have been used to help make the navy seem more attractive to young men in wartime. But another of Dibdin's songs, 'Jack's Fidelity' (see Plate 23), in which the young sailor withstands all temptations and remains constant to his loving 'Poll', may have been more suited to mixed audiences. Such affective tales served as a foil to the salacious anecdotes about life at sea and were often used as a poetic device to help raise funds for widows and orphans.[37] Inevitably, many seamen did succumb to temptation, particularly given the double standards adopted towards adultery: Nelson, for example, had a mistress in Leghorn during 1794 – 6 when he was stationed in the Mediterranean, long before his more public affair with Emma Hamilton.

The conditions under which men served, and the pay they received, impacted in various ways on the lives of their women. Only a small proportion of common seamen joined the navy from choice. Men were divided into three categories: able seamen who were well trained and highly prized, ordinary seamen who were useful on board but not yet skilled, and landmen who came from a variety of trades and backgrounds but had no experience of the sea. In wartime many ordinary seamen and landmen were pressed, or forced to join the service. Particular ships might land recruiting parties ashore. On a larger scale, an organization that came to be known as the Impress Service sent out gangs of men, each under a 'regulating captain', to round up recruits across the country. If these press gangs were composed of sailors they were sometimes able to persuade men to join the navy by talking up the daring and exciting aspects of naval life. But press gangs often resorted to violence to obtain the quota of men they needed. Impressment was generally regarded as a necessary evil and was legal because it was recognized that national safety depended on manning the navy (see Plate 2). In the mid-eighteenth century Admiral Vernon, arguing against impressments in a speech to the House of Commons, gave a clear idea of why many objected to the practice:

> When our ships are to be fitted, an impress is sent into the streets, to bring those who shall fall in the way, by force into the vessels; from that time they are, in effect, condemned to death; since they are never allowed to set foot again on shore, but turned over from ship to ship, and when they have finished one expedition, hurried into another, without any regard to the hardships they have undergone, or the length of the voyage; so that they must live upon salt provisions, without their pay, till they shall be consumed by the scurvy, or die of some other distemper, which they have contracted by the hardships they have suffered and the provisions on which they have been obliged to subsist: a practice so horrid and barbarous, that it is sufficient to deter anyone from entering into the service at all, and to oblige those who are so unfortunate as to be engaged in it, to desert to the enemy or fall upon the most desperate means to set themselves free from such dreadful servitude.[38]

Yet no better system could be found to man the navy and the practice persisted. Women often gathered together to prevent the press gang taking away their men. At the quarter sessions held at Durham in November 1803, Elizabeth Johnson and Ann Richards pleaded guilty to making a riot and to obstructing the impress service in South Shields. They were given a severe warning but released on condition of good behaviour. Wives of pressed men also did what they could to improve conditions for their husbands while ships were in port, for example, by smuggling liquor aboard.[39]

But though press gangs were at the heart of naval recruitment, other means had to be found during the long wars against France from 1793 – 1815 to raise the numbers of seamen needed for an extended fleet. Some landmen were attracted by the bounty offered to join the service. Others were caught up in the Quota Acts, passed in 1795, which required each county to provide a certain number of able-bodied men to serve in the navy. Each area was expected to provide the men from the poor of the district or to raise the bounty to encourage volunteers. In order to prevent desertion, the crew of a ship coming into port for a refit might be 'turned over', as Vernon described, to one that was ready to sail. This was a major grievance since the men were denied any opportunity to see their families. Also, if they missed pay day on their old ship they were issued instead with tickets redeemable at the Navy Pay Office in London, so they might not be paid for years. In wartime those who joined the navy would have no idea when their service would finish: the only release they could envisage before war ended would be through death, desertion, or illness and incapacity. During these wars more men were court-martialled for desertion than for any other offence, and punishment was severe. A list of deserters, with their descriptions, was published regularly in *The Hue and Cry, and Police Gazette*, which was issued once every three weeks and cost 2d per issue.

Women might be able to glean some news of their menfolk from the regular newspapers. By 1758, provincial newspapers were available in twenty-eight towns from Newcastle to Exeter, usually (as already mentioned) taking their cue on national events from the London press. They reported fleet movements but the details were not always reliable, nor was the construction put upon those details necessarily reassuring. *Schofield's Middlewich Journal or General Advertiser* for 31 August to 7 September 1756 reported:

> The Government have certain Intelligence, of the Toulon Fleet being put to Sea, so that the News of an Action is every Hour expected. We are assured that if all Sir Edward Hawke's Strength be together, he will only have a Majority of one Ship, and the Weight of Mettal [*sic*] will be on the French Side.

Newspapers, feeding on catastrophe, kept the dangers of the sea at the front of people's minds, carrying reports of storms around the coast, shipwrecks in all parts of the world, and the numbers of seamen lost.

Their women had another fear when men went to sea, and that was disease. The wife of the purser Samuel Grant (known as Jeanie to distinguish her from their daughter Jean), was already worried about her husband having to endure the rigours of service in the Channel Fleet during winter, but when she heard that his ship was to be sent instead to the West Indies, notorious for disease, she was distraught. Grant's daughter Elizabeth wrote, 'my mother is very much troubled about you going to Jamaica for she says she never shal [*sic*] see you again'[40] At the beginning of this period, the Admiralty found the logistics of supplying ships with the fresh produce very difficult, though the link between fresh food and good health was obvious. *The Evening Advertiser* for 24 – 26 August 1756 noted indignantly that earlier reports of ill-health in Admiral Boscawen's fleet, returning after a six-month turn of duty were all true: 'the men are sickly, and numbers die. All this proceeds from the length of the cruise, and the want of fresh provisions and garden stuff.' The officers, who had better food, were still in good health, and the paper complained: 'Why are not these necessaries sent duly, and charged to the ships stores? It would cost the public little or no more than at present.'

Pay was a major cause of discontent in the navy and low pay had a direct effect on naval families. Before the 1797 fleet mutinies, common seamen had not seen a pay rise since 1653. Pay was calculated on the basis of a 28-day, lunar month; each month 6d was deducted for Greenwich Hospital and 1s deducted for the Chatham Chest, a fund for distressed seamen (of which 6d actually went to the Chest, 4d to the chaplain and 2p to the surgeon). After deductions, an able seaman had 22s 6d a month, an ordinary seaman 17s 6d and a landman 16s 6d. These wages were less than merchant crews earned – a great deal less in wartime when merchant crews could demand higher wages because manpower was so scarce. By comparison, common labourers in London were earning 1s 6d a day in 1775, and skilled craftsmen 2s 6d. After the 1797 mutinies, naval pay was increased by 5s 6d a month for an able seaman and by 4s 6d for the lower rates. There was a further increase in 1806 which brought the monthly pay after deductions to 35s for an able seaman, 23s 6d for an ordinary seaman and 20s 6d for a landman. Wages were generally kept six months in arrears to prevent men from deserting, except when the ship was finally paid off. In home waters, a ship's crew should have been paid once a year, after a year in commission, but this did not always happen. In foreign waters, the men might go for years without being paid. They did have the right to have some of their pay deducted at source and sent to dependents at home. They could also receive prize money, from the sale of captured enemy ships. Their share of prize money was tiny compared to that of the officers but could occasionally yield substantial sums. Those serving on frigates had more opportunity to search for prizes and on a typical cruise could perhaps earn enough to double their wages if they were fortunate. The hope of prize money was a considerable incentive although it was rare for seamen to earn a large amount. Officers understood that this incentive was important: Nelson proposed that every man who had served five years in the navy should get an annual bounty of two guineas after that time. In a telling remark he pointed out that though the bounty might seem generous, since the average seaman only lived to be 45 years, it would not have to be paid for long and would actually save the government money since fewer men would desert.[41]

Seamen sometimes asked trusted officers to help them send money home to their wives. Edward Boscawen (see Plate 7) was one such officer, and once his men had been paid he was prepared to transfer money to their wives using his own private agent or banker. At intervals, the Government took steps to make it easier for seamen to remit part of their wages for the support of their families. The 1758 Navy Act allowed men serving in ships abroad to send money home on the same terms as those in home waters were paid, that is, on a yearly basis six months in arrears. This was a free service using government channels but fewer than 5 per cent of seamen at this date used it.[42] The 1795 Navy Act allowed petty officers, seamen and landmen to allot a portion of their wages for the provision of their wives and children, or mother, and stipulated that this money should be paid every 28 days even if the ship had not been paid. If the wife or mother lived in London, they were paid by the Treasurer of the Navy; if at Portsmouth, Plymouth, or Chatham, or within five miles of those places, by the accounting officer of the dockyard; and if they lived anywhere else, payment was made by the nearest Receiver General of the Land Tax, or Collector of the Customs or Excise. For some women, collecting this payment could mean a considerable journey. The wife had to apply in person for the money unless she was disabled or infirm – and the infirmity needed to be certified by a minister, churchwarden or elder, or by the physician, surgeon or apothecary attending her. The payments continued for as long as the husband or son served in the navy, payment ceasing if no person came to demand the money for a period of six months. If the wife died leaving young children, the Commissioners of the Navy had to be informed, naming the person in the parish who would receive the father's money for the upkeep of his children until they reached the age of 14. The allotment of wages could be increased if the sailor was promoted. If he died or was discharged, his family received payment only up to that date. If the wife deserted her children and any under 14 had to be supported by parish for one month or more, the parish could inform the Commissioners of the Navy and could appoint another person to receive the husband's allowance. It was a felony punishable by death to impersonate the wife or mother entitled to receive the monthly payments, or to procure anyone else to do the same. In spite of these stringent regulations, the navy seemingly understood that in order to encourage men to enlist and keep them at sea it was important to consider the material needs of seamen's women.[43]

Officers' wives also suffered from financial worry. Increasingly, the navy appealed to men of good family and to the younger sons of the landed classes, yet the basic pay for naval officers was not good, and they also had to find money for their uniform, some equipment and to keep a good table on board ship when in command. Between 1747 and 1807, the pay of a captain of a first rate rose from

£28 to £32 4s a lunar month, and a captain's pay depended on the size of ship he commanded. In 1808, for example, the captain of a sixth rate earned £16 16s a month. During most of the period, though, as Britain was at war, men could hope for prize money. When peace arrived, officers were put on half pay and paid half yearly, not monthly, as in wartime. Yet they got no money until two instalments were due at the end of the first year, and in the meantime many found themselves in financial difficulties, especially as there was no prospect of prize money in peacetime, so there were frequent calls for their half pay to be increased.

At the end of a war the size of the navy was reduced as soon as possible and officers and common seamen were paid off to lessen the expense on the public purse, although mutinies caused by the slowness in paying off ships were common at the end of every eighteenth-century war. Some men joined merchant ships; others had difficulty in finding employment and for months the papers would be full of the crime and civil disorder caused by so many unemployed seamen. Naval towns were generally described as places of drunkenness, profane swearing and riot – so much so that when travellers found that seafaring people could conduct themselves respectably they were amazed – but when war ended, lawlessness in other major towns increased.[44] Before Britain lost the American colonies, the possibility was voiced that indigent seamen, accustomed to a life of dissipation and riot, and quite likely to die at the hands of the common executioner, should be sent to cultivate land in North America. Newspaper reports of the time suggest that seamen were a cause of many brawls, and that women were particularly vulnerable and liable to be robbed by them. Fighting the Irish chairmen in Covent Garden, as they waited with their sedan chairs to be hired by the wealthy, seems to have been a popular amusement for many London-based seamen. In an age without a police force, the sheer numbers of unemployed seamen could be frightening, especially if they gathered as a crowd with a common purpose. At the end of the Seven Years War, *The St. James's Chronicle; or the British Evening-Post* for 19 – 22 March 1763, reported that peace officers had searched the bawdy houses around Tower Hill in London on Sunday night, arrested women of ill repute with some sailors and taken them to the round house (the lock-up where arrested persons were detained). On Monday morning a crowd of sailors demanded their release and when the authorities called up a file of musketeers, the enraged sailors mustered more support until allegedly they numbered 1000. A passing naval officer persuaded most to disperse, but that evening as the prostitutes were being taken to Clerkenwell Bridewell, a gang of sailors managed to overpower the accompanying guard and released them.

Pensions

For the wives of those seamen who did not return, various arrangements were made. A lump sum of one year's wages known as the Royal Bounty was payable to widows, dependent children or indigent mothers aged over 50 of officers, ratings and marines killed in action. In addition, philanthropic societies such as Lloyds Patriotic Fund or the Society of Shipowners provided irregular relief for the families of seamen killed in wartime. The Navy Society, a club founded by naval captains in 1765, decided in 1792 to use its surplus funds for the relief of members' widows and 'legitimate orphans' and a sum of £1,300 was invested in 3 per cent Consols for the purpose.[45] This scheme had a remarkable effect in inducing members to pay up their arrears and the first recorded donation out of the fund was one of £20 to the widow of a post captain who had been a member of the club. Churches were another source of relief: they often opened subscriptions for the benefit of bereaved naval families, and the contributions of parishioners would be listed to encourage charitable giving. Naval institutions also provided pensions of various kinds to widows and orphans.[46] Widows of commissioned officers killed in service received an Admiralty pension. From 1809 the Admiralty also administered the Compassionate Fund (later the Compassionate List) voted by Parliament, which paid grants and pensions to the dependants of officers killed in battle. An Act of Parliament of that year allowed those on the list to be paid their pension at or near the place of their residence as opposed to at the Navy Office in London. The wives of warrant officers and ratings received a pension from the Chatham Chest. This naval charitable foundation was transferred to the management of Greenwich Hospital in 1803 and its pensions were combined with those of the Hospital from 1814. Greenwich Hospital, which was supported by 6d. a month deducted from the wages of both naval and merchant seamen, employed seamen's widows as nurses in its infirmary and ran a school for the children of officers and men, giving orphans priority of admission. Finally, relief might be had from the Charity for the payment of Pensions to the Widows of Sea Officers. This charity derived from Parliamentary grants and a compulsory deduction of 3d in the pound from officers' wages. It paid pensions to the poor widows of all sea officers regardless of how or when they had died, as long as they were in service at the time.

When applying to this charity, widows had to produce a marriage certificate and take an oath that they were left with only a modest annual income. Thereafter they would have to make an affidavit each year to the effect that their circumstances remained unchanged. A captain's widow had to take an oath that her annual income was less than £45; a lieutenant's or master's that it was less than £30; a purser's, or other warrant officer's that it was less than £20. For a widow to receive benefits, her husband would have had to have paid the regular contributions into the Charity and be in service when he died. The applicant also had to prove that she had been married more than a year, and apply within a year of his death. This last clause was sometimes waived if the widow only learnt of the event years afterwards. The pension was paid quarterly from the date of the man's death and had to be collected from the London pay office between the hours of 10 a.m. and 12 noon. At one point the widows complained that Mr Jackson, clerk to the paymaster, demanded a shilling from each widow for payment of her pension, and that if the clock struck twelve before he had paid them all, he told those who were still waiting that they must call again or pay 6d more. The charge was investigated, and proved, and Mr Jackson was ordered to stop his practice immediately, though he explained that he was legitimately charging for working longer hours. Since Jackson earned only £80 a year, less than that of a junior clerk in any public department, the temptation to supplement his salary is understandable. When he retired in 1813, being too old and infirm to continue, the Paymaster sought permission to increase the salary in order to recruit a replacement. This is just one of many instances of women from seafaring communities acting collectively to get what they wanted from the naval authorities.

The Court of Assistants who ran the charity were impressively efficient and they tried to apply the rules strictly but fairly. In May 1815 they decided not to pay a pension to the widow of Lieutenant John Sandys, because although they had lived for years as man and wife, they were not legally married. They allowed that the widow of Joseph Malpas, a gunner, should be paid a pension because although he was not in service when he died, having been confined for madness, he could not be said to have quit the service of his own volition. Another widow whose husband had lost his post on account of his drunkenness and mutiny but who was then shipwrecked before his replacement arrived on board was also paid a pension, but the widow of a boatswain actually deprived of his rank by court martial for drunkenness and neglect of duty, and turned before the mast, was refused. The administration of the Charity had also to be alert to the possibility of fraud. For example, when the papers of two widows were laid before the court on the grounds that there was a variation in the signing of their names at different periods, the court decided that the variation proceeded from ignorance, and want of ability to write better rather than from any design to defraud. But frauds were certainly attempted: informers were encouraged to write to the Charity if widows had remarried and these whistleblowers received a reward. This in itself became a scam, and accusations were made that proved false when investigated.

Whereas some officers were improvident, many petitioned the Charity to be able to contribute to the fund in special circumstances so that their wives would be able to benefit if widowed. On 23 September 1812 Lieutenant Charles Turner, Tide Surveyor of the Customs at Belfast, made such a request. In his current post he could not receive half pay and so without making special arrangements he would not otherwise be contributing. His request was allowed. Such requests are a testimony to the efficiency and fairness with which the charity operated.

The pension fund gives an insight into class differences. In October 1812 the widows of gunners, boatswains and carpenters residing at Plymouth applied to the Charity for an increase to their pension. On 19 November those at Deptford, Greenwich and Woolwich followed suit. Their petition read:

> Your Lordships most humble petitioners are in general in very indigent circumstances, and many of them have large familys and much increas'd in years, and have not any other Dependance either on the Compassionate Fund or on any other Institution for themselves or their Children but their small pensions.[47]

The Charity's administrator made a note that the petition would be discussed at the next meeting of trustees but wrote that there was little chance of increase since the widows of warrant officers could not reasonably expect to be paid a pension approaching that of senior naval officers' widows, 'who are from connections, & habits of Life in the station of "Gentlewomen"'. He thought that an increase to all classes of widows' pensions, might be thought very reasonable in those difficult times, but it would add greatly to the expenditure of the Charity and also burden the country because the pensions of widows of army officers would also have to be raised. All the same, the pensions were increased in 1814.

There are some indications that contemporaries considered the impact of wartime trauma on women. For example, a correspondent to the *Gentleman's Magazine* in 1788 wrote a letter explaining that females suffered more from bereavement than men, not simply because of the limited range of employment open to them but also because of the social prejudice against single women:

> The female mind is usually affected most deeply with despair. The employments of the man give him some relief; the retired occupations of the woman require little or no attention, and therefore, as they leave her at liberty to continue her reflections on the subject ever present, they prove no remedy to her misery. In widowhood woman is the greater sufferer. She is doomed not only to mourn in solitude,

but to contend also with the malevolence of the world, unless her condition makes its frowns or its favours indifferent. Indeed sometimes even wealth and dignity are ineffectual towards securing widows from insult, offered, if not to their persons, then to their understandings, by the undue advantage which artful knaves will meanly take of their forlorn state and inexperience in business.[48]

This correspondent suggested that widows from the lower ranks were worse off as the poorly educated treated them with even less generosity.

An examination of surviving records and possessions reveals aspects of naval women's lives that we can immediately relate to today, but also many circumstances that are now totally alien to us. N. A. M. Rodger, Britain's leading naval historian, makes the point that our knowledge of the social history of the navy will never be complete until more research is undertaken into 'what one might call the female half of the naval community as a whole; not the minority of women who went to sea, but the wives and mothers who stayed at home'.[49] This book aims to reveal key aspects of this neglected subject and to highlight areas of future study.

1. David Spinney, *Rodney* (London, 1969), p. 113.

2. James Nelson, *An Essay on the Government of Children, Under Three Heads: viz, Health, Manners and Education*, 2nd edn (London, 1756), p. 317.

3. See Margaret Hunt, 'Women and the Fiscal-Imperial State in the Late Seventeenth and Early Eighteenth Centuries' in *A New Imperial History: Culture, Identity and Modernity in Britain and the Empire, 1660 – 1840*, Kathleen Wilson ed. (Cambridge, 2004), p. 31.

4. See Amanda Vickery, *The Gentleman's Daughter: Women's Lives in Georgian England* (New Haven and London, 1998).

5. Helen Berry, 'Prudent Luxury' in *Women and Urban Life in Eighteenth-Century England*, Rosemary Sweet and Penelope Lane eds (Aldershot, 2003), p. 134.

6. Staffordshire Record Office, D615/P(S)/1/3/G, Lady Anson to Mr Thomas Anson, 16 Aug. [?1749], 1 Dec. 1750.

7. NMM MSS/86/080 0, Accounts kept by Lady Mary Duncan (1731 – 1804).

8. Vickery, *The Gentleman's Daughter*, p. 194.

9. www.nmm.ac.uk/flinders accessed 18 Jan. 2007, 2 Feb. 1808, Captain Matthew Flinders to his wife Ann Flinders.

10. Valentine Ward, *A Short Essay on the Duties of Husbands and Wives* (Liverpool, 1809), p. 16.

11. A Civilian, *Free Thoughts on Seduction, Adultery, and Divorce* (London, 1775), p. 98.

12. www.nmm.ac.uk/flinders accessed 18 Jan. 2007, 2 Feb. 1808, Flinders to his wife Ann Flinders.

13. NMM WYN/104, 11 June 1792, William Young to Admiral Sir Charles Pole.

14. John Gregory, *A Father's Legacy to His Daughters* (Dublin, 1774), p. 61.

15. Lawrence Stone, *Broken Lives: Separation and Divorce in England 1669 – 1857* (Oxford, 1993), p. 12. The following discussion is indebted to Stone.

16. *The Bon Ton Magazine*, 47 (1795), 399.

17. *The Cuckold's Chronicle; being select trials for adultery, imbecility, incest, ravishment etc*, 2 vols (London, 1793), II, 3.

18. Elizabeth C. Goldsmith, ed., *Writing the Female Voice* (London, 1989), p. vii.

19. Rebecca Earle, ed., *Epistolary Selves: Letters and Letter Writers, 1660 – 1945* (Aldershot, 1999), p. 19.

20. Chapman, R.W., ed., *Jane Austen's Letters to her Sister Cassandra and Others*, 2nd edn (Oxford, 1952), p. 102.

21. Cuthbert Collingwood, *A Selection from the Public and Private Correspondence of Vice-Admiral Lord Collingwood, interspersed with memoirs of his life by G.L. Newnham Collingwood*, 2nd edn, 2 vols (London, 1828), II, 307-8, 5 Feb. 1809, Collingwood to his daughter Sarah.

22. Oliver Warner, *The Life and Letters of Vice-Admiral Lord Collingwood* (London, 1968), p. 102.

23. Newnham Collingwood, I, 149, 21 Aug. 1805, Collingwood to his wife.

24. Carey McIntosh, The Evolution of English Prose, 1700 – 1800: Style, Politeness, and Print Culture (Cambridge, 1998), pp. 36, 171

25. NMM X2002.047.1, 7 Nov. 1812, Edward Whitworth to his wife; NMM GRT/23, 5 Oct 1801, Jean Tyler Grant to her father.

26. J. Vincent, ed., *Disraeli, Derby and the Conservative Party: Journals and Memoirs of Edward Henry, Lord Stanley 1849 – 1869* (Hassocks, 1978), p. x.

27. Ian K. Steele, *The English Atlantic 1675 – 1740: An Exploration of Communication and Community* (Oxford, 1986), pp. 10, 273.

28. NMM SUT/1-2, 18 Aug. 1805, Nelson to Emma Hamilton.

29. Oliver Warner, *The Life and Letters of Vice-Admiral Lord Collingwood* (London, 1968), p. 102.

30. Eric Pawson, *Transport and Economy: The Turnpike Roads of Eighteenth Century Britain* (London, 1977), p. 291.

31. George P. B. Naish, ed., *Nelson's Letters to his Wife and Other Documents 1785 – 1831*, Navy Records Society, 100 (London and Colchester, 1958), p. 434, 11 June 1798, Fanny to Nelson.

32. Anne Fremantle, ed., *The Wynne Diaries*, 3 vols (London, 1940), III, 58.

33. *GM*, 66 (1796), 75.

34. *The New Annual Register For the Year 1798* (London, 1799), p. 32.

35. NMM WYN/104, 2 Sept. 1797 and 19 June 1799, Young to Pole. Cf. NMM WYN/104, 1 Dec. 1788, Young to Pole. I owe these references to Roger Knight.

36. [J. Davis], *Letters from a Mother to her son: written upon his return from his first voyage at sea* (Stockport, 1801), pp. 27, 29.

37. Timothy Jenks, *Naval Engagements: Patriotism, Cultural Politics and the Royal Navy, 1793 – 1815* (Oxford, 2006), p. 105.

38. A.F. Scott, *Everyone a Witness. The Georgian Age* (London, 1970), p. 402.

39. M. D. Hay, ed., *Landsman Hay: the Memoirs of Robert Hay 1789 – 1847* (London, 1958), pp. 42 – 8.

40. NMM GRT/23, 18 Nov. 1801, Elizabeth Grant to her father.

41. *GM* , 84 (1814), I, 432.

42. N. A. M. Rodger, *The Wooden World: An Anatomy of the Georgian Navy* (London, 1986), p. 78.

43. Margaret Hunt, 'Women and the Fiscal-Imperial State in the Late Seventeenth and Early Eighteenth Centuries', *A New Imperial History: Culture, Identity and Modernity in Britain and the Empire, 1660 – 1860*, ed. Kathleen Wilson (Cambridge, 2004), p. 34.

44. *GM* 73 (1803), 114.

45. *Historical Memoirs of the Royal Naval Club of 1765 and the Royal Navy Club of 1785 to the time of their Amalgamation as the Royal Navy Club of 1765 and 1785 United 1889* (London, 1925), p. 27. I am indebted to Roger Knight for this information.

46. N. A. M. Rodger, *Naval Records for Genealogists* (London, 1984), p. 34.

47. TNA ADM6 386.

48. *GM* 58 (1788), 861-3.

49. N. A. M. Rodger, *The Command of the Ocean. A Naval History of Britain, 1649 – 1815* (London, 2004), p. 407.

Chapter Two
THE ARISTOCRACY AND THE GENTRY

The aristocracy, with its power based primarily on landowning, counted for just a tiny percentage of the British population at this period, yet there was no serious challenge to its authority or its right to govern until the end of the eighteenth century.[1] True, radical groups in the 1760s and 70s launched sporadic attacks on this propertied elite, and these were to grow more concerted in the 1780s as radicalism in Britain gained force and criticism of the aristocracy became part of political debate. By the mid-1780s the British electorate expected the men they elected to parliament to show some moral consistency in their private life as an illustration of their fitness to govern. But only in the next turbulent decade did critical voices grow so clamorous that the elite could ignore them no longer. Although the British aristocracy did not enjoy the generous tax privileges and seigneurial dues that their counterparts on the continent did, and although many from the highest rank actually engaged in capitalistic enterprise, nevertheless a widespread, negative image of the feckless, degenerate aristocrat persisted – constituting an increasingly serious threat to aristocratic domination. In the 1790s, for example, *The Bon Ton Magazine* offered readers gossip about prominent people in society. Much was of a sexual nature, derived from topical crim. con. cases that excited prurient interest and highlighted the debauchery of the aristocracy, marking them out for moral judgement. Key stories would be illustrated with audacious images of couples caught in the act. 'The Instructing Captain and the Horn-Pipe Matron' (1792) relates how a naval captain seduces the wife of a squire while he takes his daily ride, under pretence of teaching her the hornpipe. The wife's maid betrays the couple but the squire ignores the captain's challenge to fight a duel, intending instead to sue him for crim. con. since he thinks him worth at least 40 or 50 thousand pounds.[2] This kind of erotica usually highlighted the debauchery of the aristocracy and marked them out for moral judgement.[3]

The stereotypical image of the decadent aristocrat given to whoring, gaming and duelling became politicised, with many calling for aristocratic moral reformation as an essential prerequisite to any claim that the elite had a right to rule. In the face of this challenge, members of the nobility in Britain consciously began to re-model themselves. King George III set the tone, his faithfulness and obvious pleasure in domesticity increasingly represented in popular media after 1786, so that his court provided a marked contrast to the anarchy of the French Revolution.[4] Members of his aristocracy started to demonstrate a greater willingness to take on official employment, although after 1801 the majority of those who were rewarded with a peerage were already active servants of their country. (Also, coincidently, power in the state was becoming more centralized so that in any case official posts now offered the nobility more attractive opportunities to exert power and influence.)

In the 1790s, revolution in France emphasized that in Britain aristocratic rule needed to be presented as somehow compatible with the people's sense of their individual liberties. The Establishment therefore claimed that the character of a 'gentleman' of the ruling class was distinctive. While differences in rank and the principle of subordination in British society were needed in order to preserve civil discipline, it was alleged that the true gentleman possessed a certain 'elevated sensibility of mind', which carried no threat of oppression or tyrannical rule. An article, typical of the period, in the *Gentleman's Magazine* for 1795 explained that Britain's hierarchical society was really the effect of a 'temperate and well ordered freedom', which enabled independent people voluntarily to see that their petty passions were better sacrificed to a greater duty of subordination, and that it was this voluntary acquiescence in a proper respect for birth and station that distinguished true British Liberty.[5]

Such explanations were more convincing at the time because of the role, in provincial communities at least, of the lesser gentry. The gentry amounted to well over ten thousand families, in contrast to the two or three hundred that comprised the nobility. As a comparison, extremely wealthy merchants might earn in excess of £10,000 a year, while annual incomes for the gentry ranged from between £200 – 300 at the lower end up to those who enjoyed incomes close to £5000. By 1790 there were about 800 gentry families with around £5000 a year and 3000 to 4000 with annual incomes of between £1000 and £3000.[6] At parish level, these old landed families were often bound through ties of kinship to the higher professional or wealthy mercantile families, all sharing the same values of politeness and gentility. At this local level, it was the gentry that constituted the elite. They were confident holders of local office, content with their respected status and they harboured no automatic desire to rival the higher nobility. While many of the lesser gentry may have been fascinated by the glitter of high society, since the antics of the rich and famous helped to sell magazines, then as now, others were just as likely to adopt a kind of superior indifference to the behaviour of the highest families in the land, though as a rule they remained deferential. The conspicuous consumption of the landed classes at all levels was recognised as a welcome spur to economic growth, although the national economy clearly also benefited from bourgeois patterns of consumption, as well as from the industry and ambition of the upper tier of the middling sort who often sought to rival their social superiors.

The rise of 'politeness' in this period, defined as a secular code of behaviour that prioritised easy and inclusive social intercourse, helped in due course to bring together the different levels of British society. Initially, it simply added to the behavioural demands placed on the elite at the very time that the group was under increasing scrutiny, showing how judgemental society was and how difficult it was to live down the past. For example, in 1807 Captain Edward Codrington often dined with Susannah Middleton and her husband Robert Gambier Middleton, then Commissioner of the Dockyard at Gibraltar. Susannah reported to her sister in London that Codrington was a sensible, clever man and a great poet but continued:

> He is rather high, but can make himself very pleasant sometimes, he made himself very famous I understand some years ago by I believe running away with another mans wife, or something of that sort, but, as I never heard the whole story, & have forgot what I did hear, I cannot let you much into the secret, except that he was made to pay £10,000 damages.[7]

Codrington came from an old Gloucestershire family and was the grandson of a baronet. He distinguished himself at the Battle of the First of June in 1794 and was to fight at Trafalgar. In 1802 he married Jane, the daughter of Jasper Hall of Kingston, Jamaica, but clearly his past errors could not be buried, though he was conscious of the need for good deportment and lectured Jane on the importance of an easy manner with social inferiors.

Against this background, and since many people questioned whether the nobility was actually fit to rule, high ranking women could not help but see that their virtuous conduct in marriage was important to help safeguard their social position. Even so, the admonition was often reiterated to them since an aristocratic wife's fidelity was the only guarantee of a title's legitimate succession. For instance, the author of *A New Collection of Trials for Adultery* warned in 1790, 'In vain shall we expect the laws will be obeyed by the middling orders of society, unless the example is set by those of higher rank.'[8] He went on to explain that the upper classes had the good fortune to be born with superior advantages: they possessed the means of cultivating their minds and their education would acquaint them with the duty they owed society. Having been placed in such an eminent situation, any immorality on their part would obviously set a bad example to the lower orders. Publications of this nature indicate that, as far as the upper classes were concerned, there could be no fixed boundary between private and public behaviour.

The task of avoiding social criticism was made harder for the fashionable elite because they lived in the public eye. They were the subject of gossip, newspaper columns, periodicals and, of course, each other's letters – all of which passed judgement on individual behaviour. For example, *The Bon Ton Magazine* for January 1795 relates the story of 'The Tender Nurse, and the Willing Substitute' in which the older brother of a captain in the navy, absent with the fleet, seduced the captain's wife left at home nursing her four-month-old baby. The older brother is portrayed as a stereotypical aristocrat, 'who preferring ease to the laborious duties of military service, spends his time in the usual dissipation of fashionable life'. Since he was unmarried, he often lived for periods at his brother's house and now the absence of the captain seemed to render it almost a duty to visit his sister-in-law, in order to protect and solace her during the absence of her husband. Their close relation silenced rumours for a time but having servants meant that there was almost a total absence of privacy in domestic life. When the servants finally circulated news of the affair, the couple eloped. The title of the piece is ambiguous in its allocation of blame for the affair. Presumably the wife is the 'Tender Nurse' and the brother 'the Willing Substitute' but both descriptions could apply to either party. The piece ends with the warning that the captain would take his revenge when he returned home.

In another even more high-profile adultery case between a naval wife and another man, the abused husband was Captain William Henry Ricketts, eldest nephew and heir to Earl St Vincent, and his adulterous wife was Lady Elizabeth Lambert, daughter of the Earl of Cavan. The break-up of their marriage was reported in The Times and in collections of adultery trials. The couple were at first devoted to one another, had two small daughters and were devastated when Ricketts was ordered to the West Indies at the end of 1795. His wife had hoped to go with him, but friends dissuaded her from venturing to a place so dangerous to health. Ricketts settled his family in cottage near Southampton under the protection of his wife's mother, and proceeded to send prize money at regular intervals. His wife lived with propriety for six months or so until she met the dashing Captain Hargreaves who began to visit her almost daily in her cottage and dined and stayed till late. As soon as news of their affair reached Ricketts, he obtained leave of absence. The defending counsel in the case tried to argue that young Hargreaves had been seduced by the lady but the court ordered him to pay damages of £1000. Next month Ricketts sued for divorce in the House of Lords and also sued for bastardising his children – he got the divorce but the bastardising clause was rejected. One commentator concluded with a warning to women that underlines the double standard of the day:

> Were ladies carefully to peruse these pages, not from motives of mirth and levity, but with a view of improvement, they would see how the odium of these cases generally falls upon them. Instead of their despoilers, the gallant captains, being called seducers, the seduction is artfully attributed to them! This surely should put them more upon their guard, and be a useful lesson – for, let learned counsel say what they will, the temptation generally belongs to the men. The lady was allowed to be a good virtuous wife till she saw – the captain![9]

In Britain in the 1790s, popular fear of a revolution like that in France led to a repressive backlash and growing pressure to regulate female sexuality within dutiful marriage. An early nineteenth-century ballad called *The Sea Captain* tells the story of a naval captain who married a young lady for her estate and then was called away to sea. A neighbouring squire propositioned her, 'The slice off & cut loaf can never be missed [sic]'. Though the wife was afraid that her husband would call her a whore, she and the squire went to bed nonetheless. In a night of debauchery, the squire's servants also bedded the captain's female staff. Nine months later the husband returned and that same night all the women of the house were delivered of boys. The captain was complaisant and forgave his wife as he himself had fathered a child while away in the West Indies. While there is a certain balance, in that each partner has been unfaithful, the open amorality of the tale is very unusual. In fact high-ranking women were increasingly expected to set a standard, and though Emma Hamilton climbed up the social ranks chiefly through her wit and beauty, it says much for the force of her personality that she was used to set a contrast to those who failed to meet the standard. In 1794 Admiral Howe's sister Caroline wrote to her friend Lady Georgiana Spencer:

> What a charming character Ly Hamilton's is, notwithstanding the great disadvantages of her early education, & how different from many who have had every advantage, & not allowed themselves to profit from such good fortune![10]

This was written before Emma's affair with Nelson and helps to explain why some elite women, anxious to maintain their status and possibly feeling duped, turned on Emma so completely after Nelson's death.

Upper class married women were often required to be circumspect about their intelligence as well as guarding their morality. If they happened to have any learning, they were warned to keep it a profound secret, especially from their husbands, who generally looked 'with a jealous and malignant eye' on a woman of great parts and a cultivated understanding. Commentators explained that men 'of real genius and candour' were far superior to this meanness – but were seldom found'.[11] Despite the elevated social status the elite enjoyed, aristocratic women lacked standing within their own families, being chiefly regarded as a means of consolidating or enhancing a family's position through carefully planned marriage. Since the consequences of a poor marriage could be disastrous to a noble family, this care is understandable. The Honourable Augustus Hervey, for example, admiral and later third Earl of Bristol, contracted a clandestine marriage in his youth. Though his wife had a son by him, she chose not to regard herself as legally married; the marriage had not been made public and she took a number of lovers while he was away at sea. Hervey was later unable to obtain a divorce and ultimately this ill-advised marriage prevented him begetting legal heirs to his title.

Patronage and influence

The informal networks maintained by high-ranking women were recognised as playing an important role, by contributing to the patronage and influence on which much of public life depended. Husbands were happy to tap into these informal networks as it suited them. Lady Elizabeth Anson, married to Admiral George Anson, was an intelligent woman who took a close interest in naval affairs and in her husband's political career. However, as the daughter of Lord Hardwicke, the Lord Chancellor from 1737 – 1756, she was arguably always her father's daughter first and Anson's wife second. In 1748 she wrote to Anson's elder brother, Thomas, explaining that her husband needed his brother's presence for the discussion of the Navy Bill in the House of Commons.[12] George Anson was of a reserved nature and he disliked paperwork. Until her death in 1760, Elizabeth often served as his secretary, especially when he served as First Lord of the Admiralty (1751 – 1756 and again from 1757 – 1762), during which time she had ready access to politicians and political news. Her favoured position meant that she received a steady stream of patronage requests. Naval officers' wives were often approached to help get sons and relatives started on a naval career, especially in peacetime when there were fewer warships in commission. In 1779, for example, Lady Robert Manners asked Admiral Rodney's wife if she could ask her husband to take a boy on board with him. Rodney was about to sail from Spithead to relieve Gibraltar and Minorca but replied that if the boy was not under 13 years old and had £30 p.a. (as boys received no wages), he would do it if he could, but that he had already received his sailing orders and would leave as soon as the wind set fair.[13] Middle-ranking naval wives were approached in the same way if their husbands attained positions of influence. Fanny Nelson was always being asked if she could recommend somebody or other to Nelson for preferment or office, and as his consequence grew she was sometimes able to place young boys at the start of their naval career with other captains who had served with her husband. Yet aristocratic wives usually had much greater influence and individuals often found it advantageous to oblige them because of their own personal status rather than that of their husbands. When in 1812 Caroline Smith, the wife of Sir Sidney Smith, wrote to Vice-Admiral Sir Richard Hussey Bickerton at Portsmouth to ask a favour for Captain Blyth of the sloop Boxer, she explained that Blyth was a 'very brave and good officer' who had distinguished himself under Sir Sidney and who now wished to serve again under her husband's flag. Sir Sidney thought so highly of him, he would be happy to have him under his command, so now she asked Bickerton to recommend Blyth to the second Lord Melville, whom she had learnt would soon be in Portsmouth, for service in the Mediterranean. She concluded her letter to Bickerton with some assurance, 'shou'd an opportunity offer & that you can comply with the request I have ventured to make you will infinitely oblige me'.[14]

Some political wives disliked having to mix with people from the lower ranks. Lavinia Lady Spencer famously kept such duties to a minimum. When her husband was at the Admiralty during the French Revolutionary Wars it was customary to invite all returning sea officers to dinner. She invited the men but refused to receive their wives in order to pre-empt any need to maintain their acquaintance later.[15] Yet naval captains would happily keep up a correspondence with aristocratic women with whom they had any social contact if they thought it could help them to preferment, and their wives would be expected to support them. Captain Charles Tyler's wife, for example, took great care to cultivate her husband's acquaintance with the elderly Lady Dacre (d. 1806), potentially an important influence on her husband's career, by sending her regular news of Tyler and New Year's gifts such as two woodcocks from the Pembrokeshire countryside.[16] In 1798, after Tyler was wrecked near Tunis, Lady Dacre wrote to his wife:

The Captain has desired me to get a recommendation of him to Lord
Spencer, and in consequence I have written to Lord Camden to have
the goodness to send me a letter to that purpose, for Charles to
present, as a means of getting him another ship, which I persuade
myself, from your good sense, you will have no objection to as
certainly in times like the present, every officer would wish to be
employed in the defence of his Country.[17]

In contrast, Emma Hamilton's invidious position as Nelson's mistress meant that
after his death she could only appeal to sentiment if she wished to secure favours.
In 1808, for example, she wrote to Tyler, now a rear-admiral, recommending
a certain Mr Jackson, then a lieutenant on board his ship. She wrote, 'Dear
Lamented Nelson allways promised me promotion for young Jackson', and added
that if ever Tyler were near Richmond he should call on her so that they could
speak of past times.[18]

Elite women with strong family links to the navy were often extremely
knowledgeable about the chain of command and the status of individual officers.
Caroline Howe, for example, was able to send Lady Georgiana Spencer a complete
list of the ships in Lord Howe's fleet and name the captain of each.[19] Much could
depend on the discretion of high-ranking naval wives, as they often had access
to sensitive information. The aristocratic Frances Boscawen, explained to her
husband that when she last went to Court she assured the King that he was well.
The King had asked if any of Boscawen's squadron had become separated from
the fleet but Frances had been diplomatic. She reported to Boscawen that she
had replied:

"Not that you mentioned to me." I thought that was best to say,
not only because 'twas true, but because I would not seem to have any
other information than that you was [*sic*] well and had had a fair, or a
contrary, wind.[20]

Later, when Boscawen (see Plate 7) sailed for America in 1755, Frances assured
her husband that he could depend upon her silence – whatever information he
chose to entrust to her about his orders, and that she would never, even by some
look or sign, convey that she had important knowledge. Frances was an extremely
intelligent woman, a superb letter writer and close friend of the bluestocking author
Elizabeth Montague. She valued her husband's confidence because she thought
that in having that she was sure to have his esteem. Though she understood that
in public life there might well be secrets that no man should impart to his wife,

she expected that there should be the kind of unreserved confidence between them that a friend might owe another, after many proofs of love and fidelity. Captain Codrington's wife Jane was also clearly a sensible, competent woman who had the full trust of her husband. In his letters home Codrington shared confidences with her, clearly noting when he did not wish them to fall into 'ungenerous hands'.

Elite wives could do much on their own initiative to further their husbands' careers. Frances Boscawen, for example, flattered herself that she took excellent care of her husband's public character. She understood that her behaviour could easily embarrass him in front of friends and colleagues, and unlike Lady Anson who, she reported, regularly gave naval officers unsolicited accounts of her 'friseurs', she made a point of entertaining her husband's friends and brother officers appropriately. She also thought to have a print of Boscawen framed and sent as a present to the Corporation of Truro, where he had many social networks to maintain. During the Seven Years War (1756 – 63) Britain acquired peoples and lands across the world, and one response to the scale of these new and intimidating responsibilities seems to have been the strengthening of regional and familial ties. Frances Boscawen's action was typical of this prevailing impulse to maintain local contacts but it also strengthened her husband's position: the wives of men in public life understood that it was part of their role to support their husbands by maintaining their professional networks. The difference for naval wives was that often they were doing this in their husband's absence. A letter from Charlotte Berkeley, the wife of Rear-Admiral Berkeley, to Lieutenant Charles Napier in 1801 is typical of this kind of networking: she wrote that she was glad to have been of service to the young man and that he must be sure to visit her when next in London.[21] For some naval wives whose husbands became famous, these networks could include the important figures of the day. In later life, when Codrington had become an admiral, Jane enjoyed the company of a range of interesting figures, including Charles Babbage, the mathematical inventor of calculating machines.[22] George Brydges Rodney (see Plate 4), as a rear-admiral, also came to rely on his wife. He married Henrietta (Henny), his second wife, in 1764 when she was 25 and he was 46. From 1774 he was forced to live in France because his gambling and electioneering debts were so great that he would be arrested if he set foot in England. She was left to run the home and bring up the children. By 1778 war was developing with France since the French King had signed an accord with America against Britain. Rodney was eager to be employed so that he could repair his fortunes and do more to support his family, but when the duc de Biron generously offered to lend him 1000 louis so that he could return to Britain, Rodney at first refused. He wrote to Henny explaining that in the current climate he thought he would be censured for accepting gifts from a high-ranking Frenchman and confidently expected that his refusal could only do his reputation good – he obviously expected that she would help to spread news of his honourable refusal in circles where it would have most effect. He also asked her to call on Lady Dunmore, wife of the ousted governor of Virginia, who was just leaving Paris and would soon be in England, again because he thought that this networking would help his cause. However, a month later he gladly accepted the duc de Biron's offer so that he could settle his debts before leaving Paris. Rodney would still be distressed for cash and risked arrest in England so he wrote again to Henny asking her to think of a safe place to stay if he did return, 'Think for me, for I can scarce think for myself'.[23] As a commander, Rodney was reputed to be arrogant, uncommunicative and reluctant to delegate. Given that he discouraged initiative in his subordinates and once famously observed that 'the painful task of thinking belongs to me', his sentiments to Henny are surprising and reveal another side to the man. Fortunately for him, the military crisis meant that he was soon appointed commander-in-chief in the Leeward Islands and, with family responsibilities and money worries to speed him on, began to win a series of actions. However, a decisive victory over the French in the West Indies, which would prevent a strong French threat to North America, eluded him for the next four years.

After a period in Bath in 1781 to recover his health, Rodney was made Vice-Admiral of Great Britain and returned to the West Indies, reaching St Lucia in February 1782. He was depressed at the situation he found there and wrote in detail to Henny on 17 March complaining about the inhabitants' collusion with the enemy. He asked her to convey this information to Richard Payne Knight, MP for Leominster in Herefordshire where his eldest son George had just married into the family of the Earl of Oxford and settled in Berrington Hall. At last, on 12 April 1782, Rodney won a decisive victory at the Battle of the Saints, thereby protecting British possessions in the West Indies. He wrote to Henny while still at sea the next day urging her to make the most of the effect that the battle would have on his reputation, 'I hope this joyful news will raise the spirits at home, and I do not doubt but that you will meet with a joyful reception at St. James's: do not forget to go.'[24] The emerging role of George III's court in celebrating national achievement in wartime and linking it with stable monarchy is evident here.

Codrington similarly relied on his wife to pass on sensitive information to influential people. In June 1810 he wrote to Jane from Cadiz saying that he believed that the Regency in Spain had invited the Duke of Orleans there and had deliberately spread the rumour that the invitation had come from the English. Codrington explained that without full details, which he had not had time to acquire, he did not feel that he could discuss this subject with others.

He told Jane, who might be pardoned a little ignorance, that she did not need to keep his theory and information a secret 'from those to whom you may wish to divulge them'.[25] He left it to her judgement how far to impress others with her husband's perspicacity and how far to evade further questions by pleading a limited knowledge of foreign affairs. Jane was also able to help her husband's career by ensuring the loyalty of valued members of his crew. On 28 November 1810, when his sailmaker was invalided home after falling into convulsions, Codrington asked Jane to do all she could to help because he would be sad to lose so valuable a man. She was also required to help Codrington discharge his obligations: he asked her to thank a certain Captain Jones if ever he were in Deal because he was indebted to him for a very good draft of men as well as for the three principal members of his band.[26]

Admiral Alexander Hood (1726 – 1814) (see Plate 5) relied heavily on the support of Mary, his first wife, when his reputation was damaged by the revelation that he had ordered the logbook of his ship to be altered after the engagement with the French off Ushant in 1778. This inconclusive battle resulted in the courts martial of both Admiral Augustus Keppel (see Plate 8), commander of the fleet, and Vice-Admiral Sir Hugh Palliser, who had led the rear division and been accused by Keppel of failing to support him quickly enough. It was at Keppel's court martial that evidence about Hood's logbook came to light, and although it is likely that the alterations were ordered for the sake of accuracy, Hood faced hostile reception at home because popular opinion sided with Keppel – a great favourite of the opposition party. His wife, who was well connected, worked hard to try to get Lord Sandwich at the Admiralty to promote Hood in order to demonstrate confidence in him. Even after he was appointed to a reasonably important command in the Channel Fleet in 1782, he was still urging his wife to petition the Admiralty for higher favours. He wrote from Gibraltar in 1783 to say that he missed her and was anxious about her (she was much older than him and now in her late 70s), ending his letter enigmatically with, 'Pray keep our Admiralty friend to our favorite point, as that is only thing [sic] that would give me most pleasure in obtaining, and he may do it with propriety, if he has our interest at heart.'[27] The key expression 'our interest' signals that Hood was confident that he and his wife were of one mind on this matter. By 1795, Hood's position was consolidated: the son of a country parson, he was promoted admiral and created Baron Bridport for his part in the Battle of 1 June 1794. He had by this time re-married and felt secure enough about his position to advise his second wife, Maria Sophia, that when he was at sea he did not want her to visit the Admiralty more than was necessary to keep up a 'friendly' interchange, as it might not suit him to become too embroiled in the 'Tittle Tattle of that House'.[28]

Lady Amelia, wife of Rear-Admiral Sir Robert Calder, knighted for his services as captain of the fleet at the Battle of Cape St Vincent in 1797, was also a great supporter of her husband. In October that year, Betsy, the wife of Captain Fremantle (see Plate 3) recorded in her diary:

> Dined at Southwick with Lady Calder, she is a clever pleasant woman but a bore for such a stupe as myself, she talks of nothing but ships and sea service and of the red ribbon that was given to Admiral Nelson, instead of very properly bestowing it on the great Sir Robert … The dear lady drank half a dozen glasses of wine after dinner, which made her still more talkative than usual.[29]

Lady Calder was not afraid to try her influence with the Admiralty on her husband's behalf. In May 1801 she wrote asking that Calder's ship, the Prince of Wales, might be allowed to refit at Portsmouth. This would clearly be in her husband's interest since he would be able to rest at home during the refit, yet she claimed it would also have a positive effect on his men's morale. Earl St Vincent, newly in post as First Lord of the Admiralty, had a low opinion of Calder, once describing him as, 'violent, impracticable, ignorant and illiterate, beyond description' and it seems that Lady Calder's letter did not elicit the response she hoped for.[30] In June she found it necessary to write to Sir Thomas Troubridge, as a Lord Commissioner of the Admiralty, berating the Admiralty for not sending a private letter to her husband at Portsmouth instead of the official letters sent to the Western Squadron, since it was clear that his ship was anchored at Spithead and that therefore that he would be at home with her. She explained that she had persuaded her husband to take a ride in the forest on her pony that morning because she knew it would do him good and anyway she wanted him out of the house when she wrote the letter. 'I think you are all a parcel of Savages', she wrote and professed herself very angry at their lack of consideration. Nevertheless, she concluded politely and added a teasing postscript, 'I do desire that you will not be such Savages tomorrow as you have been hitherto – and let us have proper letters by Tuesday's Post.'[31] Whether or not her husband was as ignorant of her activities as she made out, she was clearly in a position to use her influence on his behalf.

Aristocratic mothers also did all the networking they could to further the naval careers of their sons. Lady Cornwallis wrote to her son William in 1763:

> I'm told that Admiral Keppel is now upon his voyage home, which makes me very solicitous you should be inform'd that I have got you so well recommended to Sr Wm Barnaby who is to succeed Keppel in

that command that yr chance, if there is any beliefe in mankind, is not in ye least hurt by the change of admirals.[32]

Cornwallis's family and political friends were Whigs, and since Keppel was also a Whig, they could have expected his patronage if he had continued in that command, and in fact later Lady Cornwallis continued to discuss her son's career with Keppel. Now she solicited Admiral Barnaby to promote her son to post captain, and he promised to do so at the first vacancy. She also managed to obtain the Admiralty's consent to enclose the letter she had written to her son with the official mail that was being sent to the fleet in the West Indies. She continued with needless self-deprecation, 'I think I am a strong instance in many particulars that an insignificant person with great attention may be of some use, altho' far short of their wishes.' Lady Cornwallis also cultivated powerful female acquaintants that might help. She wrote again to her son on 17 September 1763, assuring him that she had reminded Barnaby of his promise, who would stand by it unless Lord Egmont asked him for a similar favour. Immediately, therefore, she had written to Lady Ferrers, a near relation and intimate friend of Egmont's family, asking for her help to ensure that Egmont did nothing of the kind. Lady Ferrers was happy to oblige and she in turn solicited Admiral Rodney's assistance. Consequently, Lady Cornwallis was now able to assure her son that all was set for his promotion – although she had always encouraged him also to deserve it through his own merit. Earlier she had cautioned him against 'bashfulness' and explained that he should make the acquaintance of superior officers who would help him to get on. After her husband died in 1762, she became particularly anxious about her son's naval career urging that he must be prepared to stand on his own feet and work hard to deserve promotion:

> You are my Dear Billy very young, but I hope you have sense and prudence enough to consider yr whole future happiness consists in getting an establish'd character of a good officer, and a sober man, you will then rise by yr own merit, which is ten thousand times more satisfactory than the doing it by ye assistance of friends, supposing you shou'd have them, wch is not always ye case.[33]

Cornwallis, who had entered the navy when he was just eleven years old, never achieved the social skills and polished manners of his elder brother Charles, who succeeded his father as Earl in 1762. He never married and remained shy and reserved. Yet family interest, and his own ability, enabled him to secure employment in the West Indies even in peacetime and though that station was unhealthy, the risk proved worth taking and he was promoted to captain in 1765. His influential mother played a large part in ensuring his steady promotion to this rank.

Lady Elizabeth Collier similarly badgered everyone with naval influence she could to secure promotion for her son Francis. One recipient of her fulsome letters was Nelson, who seems to have been helpful. When her son was finally promoted in 1803 he sent his commission from the West Indies to his mother to have it confirmed by the Admiralty without delay. Lady Collier then shamelessly wrote to Nelson again to fix a time to call upon him so that he could advise her exactly how to do this.[34] Other correspondents eventually lost patience with her. In 1805 Lord Barham, First Lord of the Admiralty, wrote:

> Madam, It would be very gratifying to me if I had the power
> to comply with the innumerable applications that are made to me
> for promotion, and particularly so with your Ladyships, but the
> number of officers on half pay is so great as to oblige the Admiralty
> to postpone promotion in every class where the service does not make
> it absolutely necessary.[35]

Nevertheless, Francis Collier eventually made it to Rear-Admiral and also secured a knighthood.

The correspondence of Rear-Admiral Philip Carteret's younger son, Samuel, is a further example of women's role in helping to advance naval careers. In 1795 Samuel went to sea and wrote to his mother in Southampton asking for her help in matters of etiquette. He explained that he had been given a number of letters of recommendation addressed to important people whose acquaintance might be of advantage to him but he had not the least idea of how to go about presenting these recommendations. He wrote, 'surely I am not to introduce myself to people with a letter in my hand telling 'em my name' and reminded her, 'Fail not to assist me in your next letter with your Advice about my Letters of Recommendation'.[36] With exchanges of letters, naval women could become more knowledgeable about distant places than their peers and equally, their menfolk often relied on them for the domestic political news of the day, of which they were supposed to have some understanding. Samuel wrote his mother long, informative letters from Gibraltar and the West Indies and, in April 1795, told her that political news in Gibraltar was so scarce that he would appreciate an insight into how things stood in Britain, partly so that he would be able to hold pleasanter conversation than the dull subjects he had already exhausted. Lady Cornwallis meanwhile gave her son the latest political information and forwarded London newspapers whenever possible. Captain Edward Riou's mother did not move in such elevated circles but, when he was shipwrecked at Cape Town and awaiting orders from the Admiralty, he also asked his mother repeatedly for newspapers so that he could keep up with current affairs, clearly stipulating that he did not want 'lady's magazines'.[37]

Yet although elite naval women had powerful networks and newspapers were becoming an increasingly important platform throughout this period, they seldom had a public voice and rarely contributed notices to the national press. When they did, they often used a pseudonym to protected their identity. Lady Anson, defending the Admiralty in the *Public Advertiser* after the loss of Minorca in 1756, used the pseudonym *Civicus*. As her husband had just taken up the post of First Lord of the Admiralty for the second time, she may have felt that her comments would have more effect if they seemed to come from an objective source.[38]

Anxiety and separation

The stress and anxiety suffered by women whose husbands were at sea were common to all naval wives. High-ranking women might exchange miniatures with their husbands and others less expensive love tokens or engraved coins but they all worried about storms at sea and their menfolk's health, and were sensitive to the weather conditions and wind direction. Caroline Howe, sister to Admiral Howe, maintained close contact with Lady Howe, his wife, and probably reflected their joint concerns when she wrote, 'I am still an observer of the wind, being anxious it should continue Easterly to carry my Brother clear of the Channel; he was out of sight of Portsmouth on Wednesday morning.'[39] The letters of Admiral Boscawen's wife, Frances, show how much women worried about bad weather at sea. When he was sent to take charge of the fleet off India in 1747, she complained, 'could I have persuaded myself that you had not sailed, I might have escaped a very bad night. But you know the situation of this chamber, and how a South West wind howls against our crazy bow-window.' In the same letter, she also revealed how constrained by social formality the lives of upper class women could be. The day before, acquaintances had called after dinner and prevented her from starting her letter: 'I attempted several times to escape and write to you, but a "Niece, where are you going?" gave me to understand 'twas expected I should entertain the company.'[40]

Husbands of this class hoped that their wives' upbringing and education would permit them to rationalize their fears but they also often advised wives to seek the support of friends and family during their absence. Admiral Alexander

Hood, for example, counselled Maria Sophia at the beginning of the French Wars in 1793 to make use of her 'reason and judgement' to support her spirits after their parting. Later, he wrote:

> I know my Love will keep up her Spirits, and I think it right that she should not be too much alone, but mix with such friends as will afford her comfort, from their amiable society.[41]

Hood (1726 – 1814) had married Maria Sophia in 1788 when he was 62 and she 42. As second in command of the Channel Fleet at this time, he was often at sea and surviving letters indicate that he was a regular correspondent. Hood used an odd construction when addressing his wife, never writing 'you will' but rather 'my Love will', which seems both formal but at the same time intimate. The couple had no children and Maria Sophia needed all her resourcefulness to find amusement, whether at their country house at Cricket St Thomas, near Chard in Somerset, or at their London house in Harley Street. Hood's father was the younger son of a country squire but his first wife Mary had possessed wealth and connections, which had helped him to advance his career so that he had the money to run two homes. This was made easier as transport improved and high-ranking seamen's wives, able to afford travel, became more mobile. Captain Tyler's wife, for example, did not stay in rural Pembrokeshire but spent periods socializing in Bath. Betsy Fremantle divided her time between Swanbourne in Buckinghamshire, where she doted on her children and worried about sick livestock, and London where she and her sisters enjoyed a varied social life, visiting panoramas, operas, concerts, plays and assemblies.

Many husbands understood that their wives needed reassurance. Captain John Child Purvis wrote to his wife from the West Indies, 'I am in the best of health and now perfectly seasoned to this infernal climate, tho' this is supposed to be the worst time of year, yet by living temperate and being careful, it is by no means dangerous.'[42] His reassurances may have been undermined somewhat by his revelation in the same letter that the troops who sailed with him had already lost 123 officers, and by a draft he enclosed for his wife's mother for the money raised by selling the effects of her son, who had recently died. Edward Codrington was similarly phlegmatic about danger when he took part in the ill-fated Walcheren expedition in 1809. During this period he wrote regularly from the Scheldt to his wife, Jane, in Berkeley Square who by this time had three young sons, and was pregnant with a daughter, Jane.[43] After a night of gales on 3 June 1809 he wrote to reassure her that all was well. His letters are written as if he were talking to her, and usually open informally, inserting Jane's name in the first conversational sentence. At times he adopts a humorous, slightly condescending tone, especially when making light of her fears, but of course husbands worried about their wives' health too, and all the more because they were in charge at home and so much depended on them. When Jane complained of a cough and pain in her side, Codrington at first dashed off a hurried reply and failed to mention it, later making up for the omission to the extent that Jane might well have regretted mentioning her indisposition in the first place:

> I do entreat, my dear Jane, that if your cough & pain are not both removed by the time you receive this, you will oblige me by taking decisive measures at once. I cannot help thinking that the ale you take by way of support would be well exchanged for a quick done beefsteak or mutton chop on your child's account and your own; well as you appear to have done hitherto.

Codrington was concerned in part for their unborn child. He reminded Jane that Lady Collier, a 'hectic beauty' with a family history of consuption, had also complained of pain in side, concluding in terms that Jane may or may not have considered flattering, 'though you may be as fat as she is lean, I cannot be quite at ease under such circumstances'.[44]

As letters often went astray or were delayed, both parties were sometimes writing in a vacuum and after months of absence could not predict how their more emotional outpourings would be received. Officers were frequently interrupted while writing letters home and might be pardoned for scrawls that were scarcely intelligible. On 28 November 1810 Codrington apologized to Jane in Plymouth that his 16th letter had reached her 'at so ill-timed a moment'. Clearly it had not been a cheerful letter and had added to her worries. By way of justification he suggested that she would just have to console herself that she was much in his thoughts whether he was sad or happy and that he rarely thought of her when he was merely in an indifferent mood. He continued more positively, 'I think a visit to Bath if your two friends should go also, will be a pleasant break to your sea-port weary eyes'. Instead of dwelling on sorrow in his absence, she would then be more likely to think of pleasure in the town where they first met. There is just a hint of manipulation in this exchange – possibly Jane reckoned she was more likely to get his approval for a trip to Bath if she made him feel guilty first.

Women's letters to their husbands at sea could be a great deal more intimate than the replies they received since it was less likely that they would be read aloud to company, although there was always the possibility of letters going astray. Frances Boscawen used this danger to heighten the intimacy of her correspondence, writing that she hoped her letters reached her husband safely since anyone else reading them would credit her with little sense as she filled her pages with dreams and fancies she could only properly share with her husband. At other times, she played with contemporary ideas about marriage to emphasize the quality of her love. When one of his letters was delayed she complained about the uneasiness it had given her, 'for 'tis not that I prefer you to solitude, but that I prefer you to all the world. A strange, old-fashioned sentiment this, to confess to a fine gentleman, but it escaped me, and you must not betray me'.[45] She had a happy knack of turning her anxieties into a positive force that strengthened the bond between them.

Often couples employed a code when writing sensitive information to each other. Edward Codrington sent his wife a code consisting of a simple substitution of letters in the alphabet. He gave it to her again on 10 December 1810 commenting, 'I dare say you have lost our alphabet' and asking her to 'copy it onto some other paper and erase it from this letter directly you have so done', although actually she did not trouble to do this. The Fremantles also used a cipher, which involved a transposition of letters so that to work out what had been written they also each needed a copy of the code.

Regularity of correspondence was an issue between couples, who needed to be careful not to set up expectations that could not be fulfilled. In 1805, Betsy was writing to Fremantle twice a week, sending letters post-paid to Plymouth Dock from where navy vessels could take them to the fleet. Codrington was clearly someone who paid strict attention to detail and Jane's failure to number her own letters consistently or to acknowledge when his letters reached her obviously irritated him. He complained that he was never sure whether or not he had received all of her letters, and since she failed to note receipt of each of his, he was in danger of repeating stories he had told her already.

In wartime upper class naval wives were acutely aware of popular pressure on their husbands to achieve success, and this must have compounded their anxiety as they waited at home. At the beginning of the French Revolutionary Wars, Admiral Howe was bitterly criticized for failing to engage the French fleet. The *Morning Chronicle*, an Opposition paper, printed satirical verses comparing Howe unfavourably to Admiral Hawke, a great hero of the Seven Years War:

WAPPING SENTIMENTS
May every British Tar fight like a hawke in
defence of his King and Country, and as howe
safe return into port.
May the eye of the British Tar never meet his

Glass [telescope] for the purpose of avoiding his country's
Enemy.
May the British Sailor never as now let his eye
daunt his heart.[46]

The insinuation that Howe was a coward who did all he could to avoid the enemy
must have wounded his family. As Howe attempted to bring the French fleet to
battle, the female members of his family shared his frustrations and were eager for
news. His sister Caroline explained to Lady Georgiana Spencer:

Yesterday we learnt by a frigate come into Plymouth from Ld Howe,
that he & all his Fleet were altogether coming into the Channel &
making for Torbay, (I went as soon as I had dined yesterday to Lady Howe
or shd have as I do sometimes before a post day begun this) alas all the
French fleet escaped flying into Brest as fast as they could, it is a vexating
business & we have no other comfort than his being well, which Lady
Howe sent me word he is & that she has had a letter from him off Scilly.[47]

Caroline later explained that the main French and English fleets had still not come
to blows, although there had been skirmishes between individual ships. No wonder
that when Howe finally achieved something like a victory at the Battle of the First
of June in 1794, King George III, who was fond of him since Howe was descended
on his mother's side from George I, wrote personally and sympathetically to Lady
Howe, congratulating her on her husband's victory and trusting that her mind
would soon be at ease now he was to return to Spithead.[48]

Whenever news of a fleet battle was received or expected, wives were
naturally in suspense until they knew the fate of their husbands. Frances Boscawen,
heavily pregnant, wrote to her husband after his victory at the Battle off Finisterre
in 1747, explaining that friends had attempted to conceal the fact that he had been
badly wounded in the shoulder and only decided to tell her once she had ordered
a newspaper. Later, other women showed her letters they had received from their
husbands saying that their captain was well, which was a comfort to her, and she
hoped to see Boscawen soon. 'I long for the pleasure beyond all expression. I do
not intend (and may Providence favour me!) to be brought to bed before you
come.' Betsy Fremantle suffered similarly after Trafalgar, having learnt that Nelson
and several other captains had been killed, but not their names. She explained:

I really felt the most undescribable [sic] misery until the arrival of the
Post, but was relieved from such a wretched state of anxious suspence by

a Letter from Lord Garlies, who congratulated me on Fremantle's safety & the conspicuous share he had in the Victory gained on the 21st off Cadiz. (III, 216)[49]

Contemporary concepts of masculinity required officers to make light of any injuries they received. When Captain Tyler wrote from Gibraltar after the Battle of Trafalgar to tell his wife Margaret that he was safe, he explained that the wound he had received in his right thigh had the 'best appearance' and the surgeons who had seen it pronounced that there was not the smallest danger and in the course of ten days he should be able to walk, though he was eventually awarded a pension of £250 for what had been a severe wound.[50] Friends would inevitably do all they could to relieve a wife's anxiety. Richard King, a fellow officer, wrote to Margaret Tyler as soon as he returned to Cawsand Bay, near Plymouth, on 1 December 1805 to say that her husband was doing well and would leave Gibraltar for home when his ship was ready.

By the mid-eighteenth century it was well-established practice that commanders would write promptly to their wives at home with news of a victory. In 1741, Admiral Vernon's letter to his wife carrying news of his victory against the Spanish at Cartagena was clearly intended for public consumption:

My dear,
After the glorious success it has pleased Almighty God so wonderfully to favour us with, Whose manifold mercies I hope I shall never be unmindful of, I cannot omit laying hold of the opportunity of an express I am sending him to acquaint you of the joyful news, though in my present hurries I have no leisure to enter into many particulars.

After properly ascribing his success to Providence, he gave a detailed account of the battle before concluding, 'I have only time to add, it has pleased Almighty God to preserve in good health, to go through all these glorious fatigues, and in a full disposition to push this beginning with all possible vigour, to humble the proud Spaniards, and bring them to repentance for all the injuries and long-practised depredations on us'. Finally, he sent his love to her and a 'blessing to his dear boys'.[51]

Though success in battle temporarily relieved the agony of suspense for naval wives, sudden fame brought its own pressures. After Howe's engagement in June 1794, for example, the government was anxious to turn the battle from a strategic stalemate into both a political victory for Pitt's government and an ideological victory for loyalists.[52] The great effort made to propagate a sense of victory proved effective. The 'Dress a la Howe' became the latest fashion as elite women strived to make their presence felt on the public stage, and Howe's wife and family were more than ever in the public eye.[53] Caroline Howe gives a vivid account of the attention naval families could receive:

> Half out of my senses, & wild with joy ever since ½ past nine last
> Friday, my dear Lady Spencer, you must not expect more than a few
> lines, & were I sober I could not send many, having hardly had a
> moment to my self since Wednesday morn all my friends &
> acquaintances, some even who have never visited me before, have
> come to give my joy, & except a quarter of an hour that I was obliged
> to shut my doors whilst I answered a Letter I had from the King, wrote
> before he left Windsor to come to his Levée on Wednesday, I have
> never been able to resist seeing every one who have chose to come in, I
> have millions of notes very few I have had time to answer.[54]

Lady Howe and her daughter hurriedly set out for Portsmouth to meet the admiral as he returned home. They had been assured that he was in perfect health, although a little thin and exhausted, he and his officers not having had time even to take their clothes off to sleep for four nights. Caroline Howe wrote simply to her brother that she was glad to have lived to see his success.

Children

Children were a key source of anxiety for couples when husbands were at sea. In 1747 Frances Boscawen was concerned to learn that her husband was sleeping badly and assured him that he need not worry on his family's account.

> Have no anxious thoughts for the children. Assure yourself they shall
> be my sole care and study and that my chief purpose and the business
> of my life shall be to take care of them and to procure for them a sound
> mind in a healthful body. God give me success! I do not ask you
> for any directions, as whether, if one has the Smallpox, I should put
> away the others, etc., for I reckon that in all these cases one's conduct
> must chiefly depend sur le conjecture, and therefore 'tis impossible to
> take any resolutions beforehand. Let it suffice that all my faculties
> and studies will have for aim the benefit of these dear children. And,
> generally speaking, where one applies one's whole strength, one brings
> the end to pass, and success crowns such hearty endeavours.[55]

In 1755, she ensured that her younger son was safely inoculated against the smallpox, and when her elder son went to Eton she reassured Boscawen that he had departed happily with his friends and joked that as the boy had shed all his tears on his father's departure he had none for her on this occasion.

When children were young, it was sufficient for absent husbands to show sympathy for their minor ailments. For example, on 4 August 1810 Codrington wrote to his wife about 'poor little Jane's teething' and hoped she would not have to endure a repeat of the torment her brother Henry had suffered. Yet as children grew older, there were more difficult decisions to make; with one eye on their future careers, Codrington had begun to worry about the characters or his boys. In June 1809 the schooner *Sea Lark* was lost at sea and only one member of the crew survived. Codrington deeply regretted the loss of life but stoicism seemed to him to be the proper response. He wrote to his wife:

> The more I investigate myself, the more I am assured that we ought to discourage in our children that excess of sensibility which must be offended by the many incidents which occur in the course of wartime, as well as what arise from service in any military or naval profession.[56]

There is an indirect warning here that he does not want his sons inculcated with excessive feminine sensibility in his absence, although boys under ten often spent more time in female company. By July 1810, Jane had written to Codrington asking what was to be done about the boys going to school. In reply he told her that at Harrow he had learnt more errors than good and that he considered all schools a bad idea. Between them he thought they had enough knowledge to teach their children the first rudiments – and beyond this stage he could teach the boys more – though admittedly not Latin and Greek. He did not want his son Edward to go to a boarding school because he believed the boy needed to learn the 'habit of attention' and did not think it could be achieved under the bad influence of a school. He considered that wherever Jane might live when he was at sea, it would be best to send the boys to a day school which would permit her to enquire into 'all their mental advances'. He did not hope to be away for long and concluded, 'I think we had better not to decide this matter until my return. Seven is not surely an age for hurrying any boy to school.' He recommended to her the two first volumes of Maria Edgeworth's book on educating the young (admitting he had not yet read volume three himself). But just four months later he was writing testily, 'I must say that I approve highly of your sending the boys to school, as it does not deprive me of their society.' But he and a brother officer in the same situation agreed that, 'had we been at home we should have marred the better determination of our wives'. Obviously Jane now found the boys hard to manage. Codrington reassured her, concurring with her view that she had 'done her truest duty' to them and that no woman could manage boys once they had passed a 'certain passiveness'; but during this critical stage in their upbringing his absence was clearly felt and his wife had to make the key decision.[57]

As children grew up, naval wives might have to oversee their engagement and marriage in their husband's absence. Admiral Sir Alexander Cochrane's daughter, Anna Maria, wrote to her father in 1809 when he was stationed in Halifax to reassure him that she was still unattached. She supposed that he might have heard that she was about to be married to Sir Edward Thomas Troubridge, just 20 years old, and continued, 'My Beloved Father, do you think that Mama or I would have kept you in the Dark if their had been any likelihood of such a thing taking place?' Yet just a year later, once Troubridge came of age, that is exactly what happened. Cochrane's wife had meanwhile written to her husband to reassure him and ensure that he approved of the match but their daughter was married in his absence while he was still in Halifax.[58] The supervision of older children of marriageable age was a heavy responsibility and the way in which mothers dealt with this task reflected their characters. The critical portrait of Lady Bertram in Jane Austen's *Mansfield Park*, who took to the sofa while her husband was in the West Indies and allowed her children and house guests to rehearse a play that included ardent love scenes, offers an insight into the moral and social consequences that might ensue from naval wives' complacency.

Running the home

Among the many additional responsibilities that might fall upon high-ranking wives while their husbands were away at sea was overseeing estate management. In this period, women generally made the decisions about daily household consumption (except among the peerage or the exceptionally rich), and the control and management of financial resources in the home is central to the understanding of female roles. Upper ranking households employed a housekeeper who supervised the maids and often took on a great deal more of the domestic management.[59] The position was usually filled by a woman, particularly after 1777 when a tax was imposed on male servants. Subsequently, employers tried to keep males, especially those of good carriage and physique, for the more visible positions of butler or footman. By this time, among the gentry too, it was no longer socially acceptable for the lady of the household to be seen as an active housekeeper herself and some among the middling ranks were anxious to avoid anything that might tarnish their gentility. It was more important that she be seen as a woman of fine taste and some knowledge. Nevertheless, it was still expected that her household would be well run, and so a woman might be torn between ensuring that she was clearly seen to be above the drudgery of household duties while demonstrating that she remained a capable wife who presided over a well-run and efficient household.

For affluent wives who took their household duties seriously, life was far from an untroubled expanse of self-indulgent leisure, for a genteel household could be larger than a small business and comprise a variety of activities. Among the gentry, a woman's role as housekeeper and consumer could involve the monitoring of possessions, the household accounts, the calculation of wages and other costs, domestic stock-taking and, for some, the recording of revenue derived from sales of home produce. Such women were exceptionally literate and their pocket books and diaries are an important source of accounting history, giving an insight into the kind of business that tied the genteel housekeeper to her desk every morning. These account books are almost exclusively concerned with expenditure but some indicate that women could also be well informed about livestock and crop yields, often through correspondence with other similarly placed women. Some women felt tied to a complex domestic role that they would rather not have had.[60] We know that some felt uneasy at the extent of their responsibilities when their husbands were at sea. When, on 10 July 1803, Captain Fremantle left home to take up his commission in the Ganges at Portsmouth, Betsy recorded in her diary how anxious she felt at being left alone with five young children and so much to manage.

Landowning aristocrats used property both to justify and advertise their claim to rule; large estates demonstrated their stake in the country's success and the careful management of these properties was one way in which the elite manifested and retained their power in society. The English country house was designed to display the taste of its owner and was intended to be a place of refined, polite sociability. The ideal country house displayed tasteful furnishings, had a well-stocked library and was ornamented with grounds that had been improved and shaped according to current fashions. Country estates were such powerful symbols that many aspired to own or improve them, and the importance of property management certainly impacted on naval wives of this class. Officers used the money they made in wartime to build up great estates, such as Hatchlands Park, near Guildford, bought with prize money by Admiral Boscawen. At first he and his wife Frances lived in the existing Tudor house there but later they built a redbrick mansion and commissioned Robert Adam to decorate the key rooms. When at sea, Boscawen amused himself by planning his estate but the running of it mostly fell to his wife, and he sent her detailed instructions to convey to the estate manager. She also had their town house to manage. She wrote to explain that the cost of repairing the sluices in the back house had cost £9, and that she was now having the street in front re-paved since the gutters where the rain settled were so worn the vaults underneath threatened to collapse. She supervised its decoration, ordering rooms to be papered, chintz hangings and carpets. In one letter she hinted broadly that if he could bring home with him carpets, matting and muslin, these articles would be very acceptable since all were very dear in London.[61]

Though she must have been extremely busy, Frances Boscawen seems to have been happy to supervise the estate in her husband's absence. In 1748, playing the role of the economical housewife, she boasted to her husband that she was 'a very house-wifely young woman' and that she kept her account book with such perfect exactness that she now knew her expenses to a shilling, alleging that the total sum frightened her (which she would never have dared confess if she had been truly extravagant).[62] In 1755 she explained proudly that the estate flourished under her administration: the hay was all got in and stacked before the end of July which brought heavy rain, her flowered walk looked charming, she had the best barley in the parish – ahead of neighbouring farms by a fortnight – and his horses all seemed in order. Her list of completed chores before leaving to meet him in Portsmouth one year gives a more detailed indication of the range of tasks she was expected to oversee. There was the farm, the garden and the house to look after. Dung heaps had to be distributed, apples and pears stored, thistles had to be rooted up from the park, the maids set to making shifts and tablecloths, wages and bills had to be paid, the land tax had to be settled, bricks for their new house were being delivered, and she also had to complete lists of work she wanted carried out in her absence. She contrasted this aspect of her role with that of 'the hero's wife' and during the early period of the Seven Years War, when major defeats caused many to debate the apparent 'effeminacy' of the British military, she played her part in boosting his image as a proud, honourable leader, the bravest and best officer available to the government in wartime. In similar vein, she was highly critical of Admiral Byng, court martialled for failing to relieve Minorca in 1756, sending in her letters a clear signal to Boscawen (if one were needed) of the kind of behaviour the country expected.

Rodney's first wife Jenny, pregnant with their third child, was also left to oversee the management of the wood on their estate at Alresford while he captained a ship on active service. In June 1756 Rodney wanted the beech cut down for firewood and the oak stacked in the field. If the faggots were brought home, she must remember not to let the horses go into the wood any more until after the leaf-fall as the animals would damage the underwood. She was also needed to oversee the purchase of an adjacent farm since investment in land would bring them more interest than the stock market would and help to secure their estate. In his absence he advised her that the purchase would have to be in her name.[63] Codrington sent even more detailed advice to his wife Jane, also kept busy running the house and bringing up their children. In September 1809 he told her to 'paint the garret floors and stairs after puttying well the seams' as it would keep out dirt and bugs and make the floors easier to wash. Now was the best time to do it, he wrote, as the surfaces would have to be dry before further decoration. When Jane was left to sell their filly, Codrington was clearly uncomfortable: horses and stables were deemed to be masculine affairs, and the buying and selling of horses part of male culture. He offered detailed guidance, telling her what he remembered about the horse's age and parentage; he also tried to explain just how to go about taking a horse's pulse. Yet this being a traditionally male province, he did not wholly trust her judgement. On 26 May 1810 he complained about her latest purchase, 'Your description of the horse does not make him quite of my taste.'[64] On the other hand, Codrington did sympathize when Jane complained about servants, who were often unreliable and likely to flit from one position to another. On 29 June 1809 he wrote, 'Your cook is like most of her predecessors, no great loss, but I think you must be badly off without somebody to supply her place.' The words 'your cook' suggests that this was an area of housekeeping deemed to fall squarely on his wife's shoulders.

When Admiral Alexander Hood's ship was in home waters there were periods when he wrote every day to his second wife, Maria Sophia. In 1793, anchored off Torbay, he reassured her that she need not reply to his letters individually because he knew she had so much business but at this time he was also sending her detailed instructions about what he wanted her to do on their country estate:

> With respect to the planting the chestnuts some of them, I should
> think might remain in the Hill, but planted at greater distances, some I
> think might be planted at the back of the North Lawn plantation [?]
> Building, by the same rule, that is they may be placed next to Chapple
> Field, but not in a strait line. Some may be planted as single trees, in
> different parts of the hill fields, and fenced in the same manner as
> other trees. This is all that I can suggest on this chestnut object. I
> know full well that the Hedge behind the building is a bad one, but
> you must take care not to take too much of it down to make an
> improper or irregular plantation in place of it. If you have taken it
> down to the gate, certainly you should go very near, if not quite so
> far, on the other side of the Building, and that must be well-fenced

against the sheep. All these improvements must be done by the Eye, and I can give no particular direction, only give the outline of the Plan.[65]

Hood trusted that his ideas agreed with his wife's, and one hopes that his rather imprecise instructions made perfect sense to her when she went to inspect the actual locations.

But not everything went according to plan and something catastrophic seems to have happened to their garden house. Shortly afterwards Hood wrote from the Royal George:

> The circumstance of the Garden House is a very serious one indeed. Though I do not quite understand whether it is the Roof, the Walls or the Floor that has fallen in. If the latter, the danger has been Great; but I scarcely know, how that can have happened, as I always understood that it was supported by an arch, and not by Timber. You must repair the damage without delay, the place being necessary for the convenience of Life. I will add no more upon this Edifice, but follow my Dear Woman's advice, upon the subject.[66]

He urged her to hurry up with her planting on the hill because if she left it too late it would be subject to frosts, more so than in the new flowered walk she planned to create at the foot of the hill. Hood wrote that he wished he could peep in on her while she was so happily employed – she obviously derived great enjoyment from gardening – but as this was impossible he could only wish that her ventures prospered. He valued her opinion about the landscaping and urged her to comment freely on every plan for the ornament or use of their estate. For the most part it seems that married women of the period were interested in flowers, shrubs and walks while landscaping was more of a male preserve.[67] But on the evidence of contemporary letters naval wives seem to have crossed this boundary and taken a personal interest in landscape planning, although often at the behest of their husbands. This was certainly also true of Collingwood's wife. Cuthbert Collingwood (see Plate 9) was promoted to Vice-Admiral and made a peer for his part in the Battle of Trafalgar, becoming Baron Collingwood of Caldburne and Hethpool – indebted properties close to the Scottish border that had he inherited through his wife's family. He took his duties as a landowner and a patriot seriously and, knowing that the navy suffered from a shortage of timber, wrote to wife on 21 March 1806 asking for the barer parts of his small estate to be planted with larch, oak and beech.

Money

Aristocratic naval wives enjoyed a comfortable standard of living yet the practicalities of managing domestic finances when their husbands were away from home still proved a source of anxiety because their liabilities would be on a scale commensurate with their income. Admiral Purvis told his wife that his agent, Cooke, should always send her an account of what he received from him, and that she should write to Cooke to make sure that he did. As an afterthought he sometimes jotted on the cover of his letters exactly what monies he had sent to Cooke to ensure that she was in a better position to check the account. Captain Codrington sent his wife money on a quarterly basis, almost certainly via his agent or his bank, and expected her to live within a budget, though he obviously had means. He gave Jane instructions, explained tax matters and asked her to pay his debts. On 10 September 1809 he wrote, 'Did you get my last quarterly bill? You have not acknowledged it – but if you had received it, it is surprising you should complain of being poor'. He then proceeded to give her a list of items that he wanted her to buy and send to his ship. By 15 November 1810, Codrington had read the radical William Cobbett's new publication criticizing government finances and been convinced that it was better to put the money into land than entrust investments to government funds. In his letter to Jane he wrote, 'employ your energies in finding some place which we can control ourselves for a home, or some land where we can lay out some of our [?] money to advantage'. He listed some suitable properties including one called High Down, assuring her that since buying land was the safest security for their children he would have no objection to her buying it without his first seeing it.

At the beginning of the war with France in 1793, Alexander Hood signalled in his letter to Sophia that they needed to agree some financial arrangements, but seems to have left the way open for her to suggest how she would prefer to handle such matters:

> I will now speak upon the subject of money and if my love finds no difficulty in drawing for a hundred pounds, she will do it, and I request that she will let me know by the return of post what plan she means to adopt.

Yet Hood on occasion had to make elaborate arrangements in order to send his wife money, resorting in one extreme instance to sending a trusted person ashore at Lyme who would then ride to their country house at Cricket:

I wish I could send the money to you, and I am sorry, I had any from my love when she kindly made me a visit in Torbay [*sic*]. Friday morning. We have a fine day here, and I am going to send Henderson on shore to get me some money for my draft, and I will send sixty pounds to my love to-morrow, by a trusty person, in the cutter to Lyme, perhaps Richardson who will take a horse ride to Cricket to see my love for a short moment, return again to Lyme, and be back the third Day, as I see no prospect of our moving from here before that time.[68]

Upper class naval wives regularly had to deal with the paying of taxes. In 1795 Hood wrote from Portsmouth:

I wish the Tax Gatherer had called for them, while I was in Town, as I always feel a pleasure in relieving my Love from these, or any other Payments of that sort. She will keep a separate account of them, that I may replay them, when we have the happiness to meet, which I sincerely hope may be soon.[69]

Some wives also had to keep an eye on their husband's debts even if they had not been given specific instructions to do so: when Betsy Fremantle received some of her husband's prize money, she immediately paid off his debts to an upholsterer. Even aristocratic naval wives could find themselves in serious financial difficulties. A letter of 1812 from the wife of Admiral William Bentinck to Alexander Davison, an army contractor and financier, illustrates the complications some had to cope with. The Honourable Frances Augusta Bentinck hesitantly explained to Davison that he was out of the office when she called in person, so that she was forced to write in spite of her embarrassment, 'It is my duty to overcome those feelings and to leave nothing untried to relieve my dear Husband from his present difficulties, of which I have not yet communicated to him the extent' (being anxious not to add to his burdens at sea).[70] She went on to explain that their property had descended to them hampered by mortgage, that the tenants were in arrears due to the failure of the previous year's wheat crop, and that the interest on the mortgage was due. This amounted to £450 and the creditor was pressing for payment although she had no means of settling the debt until after the harvest when she hoped that tenants would pay their arrears. Could Davison lend her the money for a short time? Davison must have offered to help because on 2 September she wrote to thank him but also to explain that her father had just offered to lend her the sum and had already written to his banker about the loan. In a later note to Davison, dated simply 'Wednesday morning', she wrote that she had just received a bill upon his House for acceptance, which she now enclosed, pleading:

> I really can do nothing about it in my husband's absence – I have no knowledge whatever of the transaction alluded to in the letter which accompanies the Bill, and certainly thought that in all my Husband's dealings on the continent he was creditor and not debtor'. I expect him home the end of October and shall immediately give him the letter and beg him to do what is proper about it.[71]

In the meantime she asked him to let his colleagues know her circumstances so that she would not receive more bills she was unable to pay.

Often elite naval wives were part of a network that financially supported seamen's wives lower down the social scale, most usually those women who were married to men on their husband's ship. Jane Codrington was a trusted mediator in financial affairs of this kind. On 14 May 1810 Codrington wrote to explain that she must accept on his behalf a draft drawn by a Dundee minister for £17 intended for a seaman's widow. She must also supply money as needed to a member of his crew named Dumnett, currently in hospital, because the loan could be set against the money the man still had on board. On 28 November 1810, he wrote explaining that if the wife of another of his crew were 'pressed for money by missing his bills, at any time', Jane must help her by making sure his agent gave the woman an advance. A captain's wife could also pass on to other wives regular news of the men serving with her husband. On 21 November 1810 Codrington confirmed that Jane's latest letter had arrived with parcels for his gunner and boatswain, adding, 'If you see their wives you may say their husbands are well'. Yet upper ranking wives did not usually consort with naval women of the lowest kind. Codrington gives an insight into the stratagems they employed for survival when he warned in December 1808 that she should be on her guard when she arrived at Chatham. He explained that it was likely that she would be approached by women begging for money, claiming that their husbands had gone to sea and left them behind. On no account was she to give them anything.

Supplying menfolk at sea

Officers often depended on wives and mothers to supply them with clothing and food while they were at sea. Jane Codrington sent her husband hampers of fresh produce when he was serving in the North Sea in 1809. In one letter he told her irritably not to send any more vegetables likely to perish as several 'stinking hampers' from her had turned up, but then rather inconsistently he asked her to send salads and mint for sauce.[72] In the summer of 1810 the Admiralty sent him to Cadiz to cooperate with Spanish forces and in August of that year Jane was sending him live sheep – though the heat was so intense there that Captains were expected to kill a sheep only when it was convenient for a sufficient number of officers to consume the meat quickly. She was also sending him English cherries, raspberries and currants. Notably, after Nelson had separated from his wife, Emma Hamilton took on the role of supplying his needs at sea. In 1803 she wrote to Nelson's secretary, John Scott, to explain that she had sent Nelson a box of clothes, a pot of butter and a view of Merton.[73]

When officers asked for clothing to be sent, wives could order items of uniform from established suppliers or tailors who would have their husband's measurements. In November 1808, Codrington was appointed to the Blake (74 guns). On 9 December he wrote to Jane explaining that he had only one pair of epaulettes fit for going on shore and asked her to buy another pair, stipulating that he did not like the ones with high cushions or stiff curling springs. Jane also had to send items of uniform for members of his crew. On 10 September 1809 he wrote that the hat she had sent for Clifton was too small and so had been given to someone else. Another man now wanted a hat of the same size and Clifton needed a larger one. Codrington himself needed leather to sole his boots and proper shoemaker's thread. And could she send him a brown and a white loaf as soon as soon as she could locate a speedy supply ship? Later in the year, on 8 November 1809, he wrote asking her to send a gross of 'small anchor buttons' for the jackets of the boys on his ship and also reeds for his band's instruments – particularly bass reeds. Off Cadiz, on 13 June 1810 he explained, 'I have only twelve pair of the short cotton stockings which are so much pleasanter for this climate that I should like to double or treble my number. Don't think me unreasonable. I will send by one of the ships a pair of long stockings which I can best spare as a pattern, which are quite easy in the feet; and perhaps you may have an opportunity of sending to Mr Radform 52 Cheapside.' One of the boys on the ship had no shirts or stockings and he asked Jane to buy some for him, with no other guide to size than, 'he is rather bigger than Hopkins'. Two weeks later he asked her to send sheet music – 'The Grenadiers March' – and a velvet cap to keep the flies off his bald head. She also supplied him with such necessities as toothbrushes. Simply keeping abreast of her husband's demands and replying to his letters must have kept Jane busy.

Since husbands often received sudden orders appointing them to a ship, they might have to leave home with insufficient linen and wives would be expected to forward additional items as soon as they could. If the ship actually sailed before the clothing arrived, the parcel would be held until the ship returned to port. Efficient wives would always be as prepared as possible. When Fremantle went to sea in 1810 as a Rear-Admiral, taking his son Charles with him, Betsy made an inventory of his wardrobe. She also arranged for her husband to be sent newspapers: the *Morning Post*, *Morning Chronicle*, and Cobbet's *Political Register*. Unmarried men often relied on their mothers to supply clothes as soon as their ship had been commissioned and family correspondence can reveal much about the kind of clothing that men preferred to wear at sea. In 1794 Samuel Carteret, waiting to sail from Spithead, wrote urgently to his mother in Southampton:

> I could wish you, as soon as possible to send me a couple of pairs of
> dark-coloured worsted stockings that will not dirty, or want much
> washing, which is an object onboard ship; and some warm, dark color'd
> waistcoat that will not show dirt or require to be put in the wash
> the whole voyage.[74]

He asked for them to be sent immediately or he would have to provide himself with them – and clearly his mother responded promptly because a week later he thanked her for the warm waistcoat, flannel jackets and stockings. In 1763 nineteen-year-old William Cornwallis left Britain for the West Indies where he served until 1766. On 20 May his mother wrote that if he remembered anything that he had forgotten no one could be more willing than she was to send these items on. She reminded him about the dangers of the climate and begged him for her sake to 'keep his blood cool'. Soon afterwards she wrote that she had sent the nine waistcoats he had asked for by coach to him in Portsmouth, and went on to say that she had been speaking to an acquaintance of hers who had lost her son in the East Indies and asked him again to take great care of his health. She added, 'I watch the wind all day long, and it has been with us so variable to Day you must have had some points that sail. But ye changes have been I am afraid too quick for you to make much way, is this last a proper sea term?'[75] Later Cornwallis wrote to ask her for boots, spurs and two pairs of white breeches to be fetched from his lodgings and sent out to him in Jamaica. At this period it was much less certain that parcels would reach individuals at such a distance; later, when his sister Molly offered to help him financially, she reasoned that he would probably prefer to buy what he needed in the West Indies.

Lady Cornwallis also supported her younger son financially. In April 1764 she wrote assuring him that he could be sure of £100 a year from her while she lived. When she died, of course, she would have no fortune of her own to leave him but in the meantime she took great pleasure and comfort from being able to do him some good through her influence. She nevertheless had to remind him that he needed to give her notice when he drew money on her account so that she could be sure to have funds in the right place to cover his bills.[76] Samuel Carteret's mother also offered financial support. In 1795 he wrote to her from Gibraltar about his debts: Gibraltar was a very expensive place because items were scarce, his equipment had cost a lot, and wine, porter and other things that he had bought to contribute to his health had cost more. Consequently, he was about £70 in debt. This worried him and three days later he wrote again to say that he was even more sorry to cause her additional expense because he knew that his brother had just been made a lieutenant and that she would also have to cover the cost of fitting him out for his new rank.[77]

Naval wives as consumers

Letters exchanged within naval families give an insight into what women were actually buying, and hint at the cultural significance of certain purchases. Everyday goods related to the running of the home were regarded as predominantly women's business, and in the 1770s the author of a popular conduct book noted that, 'the domestic economy of a family is entirely a woman's province, and furnishes a variety of subjects for the exertion both of good sense and good taste.'[78] However, a naval wife might be entrusted with purchases in her husband's absence that overstepped the boundaries of this conventional domestic role. In 1781 when Admiral Rodney took the fabulously wealthy West Indian island of St Eustatius from the Dutch in the War of American Independence and seemed to have repaired his fortunes at a stroke, he wrote to his wife Henny. He sent her a drawing of his coat of arms, as approved by the Herald's Office in London, asking her to ensure that her own arms were illuminated with his and then to purchase a coach and have the new Arms painted on it. He left it to her whether to buy a new or a second-hand coach, though he hinted that 'a seasoned one is certainly best'.[79] Alexander Hood was also prepared to entrust the business of sorting out his chaise to his second wife, Maria Sophia. He explained to her that he had offered the chaise to Admiral Jervis who was thinking of travelling from Portsmouth to London, and so possibly the chaise could be with his wife in Harley Street the very next day. He gave her the name of a man she could speak to about it and continued, 'If it is to be kept, My Love must order it to be painted, and put into proper condition. The wheels are good. If it is condemned a new one must be bespoke, but this merits due consideration.'[80] As recompense, he proposed filling the seat with the biscuits he knew she liked from a shop in Portsmouth.

Aristocratic women also contributed significantly to the market for commemoratives after naval victories. After the Battle of the First of June 1794, for example, Caroline Howe had a ring altered to commemorate her brother's victory, referring to it as her 'talisman' and aristocratic women set a fashion of wearing small gold anchors on chains round their necks.[81] The upper ranks set trends in the consumption of expensive items which manufacturers would then advertise as endorsed by the aristocracy and gentry. Elite families were particularly emulated in matters of dress and in the arrangement of their tables, which was linked to status-enhancing domestic hospitality. Tablecloths and table napkins made to commemorate battles, with designs woven into the white damask, allowed owners to demonstrate their patriotism. Commemorative silver, wine glasses and fine china added to the effect while deflecting possible criticism of luxurious taste, considered a sign, in this period, of moral decline. At balls, ladies sported topical fans, jewellery, silk purses and dress trimmings to show their support for naval heroes or mark the latest victory. As their lavish costumes were reported in magazines and newspapers, young women of more modest means could imitate the designs in simpler form.

Naval wives were in a position to set new trands, and it was some compensation that when their husbands were abroad that they often had opportunities to purchase luxury goods at cheaper prices for their families or re-sell them at a profit. In 1801, for example, while in the Baltic, Captain Tyler laid out £100 on goods that he was told were cheap there. Codrington was happy to make domestic purchases but needed his wife's guidance when buying items such as cloth and ribbon. At Middleburg in September 1809 he wrote, 'By the Bye tell me if I should buy Holland sheeting or linen, send me a pattern and say how much I should give.' Later he added with just a hint of condescension, 'I will get you more of the ribbons of which there are a great number similar but does it not occur to you that it would relieve me to be told how many yards of each answer the purpose for which you want them?'[82]

Shore leave

A key issue was how naval wives might actually manage to see their husbands if their ship put into port. Often they had to be prepared to travel at short notice and to alter their plans if the weather changed. Admiral Alexander Hood, for example, wrote to his wife from the Royal George cruising off Torbay in 1793, 'I have sent Captain Donnell's servant to meet my love on the Road to prevent her going to

Teignmouth as the weather is so rough that I cannot meet her there.'[83] Instead he thought it best if she took her carriage south to Brixham where he would be able to join her. In an undated letter, annotated by Sophia as having been received, 'after the Glorious First of June 1794' and written as he sailed home to Portsmouth, he sent her hurried instructions for joining him when he came ashore:

> If my love gets to Portsmouth, before the fleet arrives, at Spithead, and none of my family should be there, she will drive to the Crown Inn, and send a message of it to Mrs Cooper … We are now steering for the Channel with light wind fair … I judge we might reach Spithead on Friday as the wind is fair, and it blows rather fresh … Wednesday morning, 10 o' clock, we have made the Land, and the Fleet will be off Plymouth this evening, and I think to morrow it will be at St Helens, if not Spithead. My love will therefore come to Portsmouth, with all convenient speed, and I shall hope to see her either Saturday or Sunday, as I can hardly expect to find her there.

Similarly, on 27 December 1808 – the date of their wedding anniversary – Codrington sent Jane a mock order to put herself and the children into a carriage and get to Sheerness. He took advantage of the date to remind her of her marital promise to obey, and explained that he had arranged for a yacht to meet her at a certain inn at Chatham to speed her journey.

While at this period it was easy enough to get from London to Sheerness or Portsmouth, a journey to Plymouth presented more of a challenge. In 1809 Jane travelled there to meet Codrington, unfortunately leaving home before he could let her know that he had suddenly received his sailing orders. She arrived shortly after he had put to sea. Thereafter he was more cautious about asking her to travel to Plymouth, although in his letter of 14 May 1810, he regretted not asking her to join him there. He consoled himself by reflecting that he would have felt uncomfortable leaving her in a cabin, deprived of friends, while he went about on business – which throws light on the occasionally isolated situation of upper class wives who did follow their husbands around the country. Betsy Fremantle often scurried to Portsmouth with her children in tow and she too experienced the frustration of missing her husband when his plans changed. She recorded in her diary for 26 October 1806 that having received a letter from Fremantle written at sea in which he asked her to join him at Portsmouth, she eagerly travelled there with two children only to find that he had taken the overnight mail for London the moment he had landed.

Yet if Fremantle was to be in port for any length of time, Betsy's stay with him could seem like a holiday. On 24 July 1803 she wrote in her diary:

> I left Sunbury at seven o'clock and came into the Portsmouth Road at Ripley. I found it dreadfully dusty ... I suffered much from the heat and dust, as well as the poor children and arrived at Portsmouth quite fatigued at seven o'clock ... The house he [Fremantle] has taken is extremely small but tolerably clean and when we are a little settled we shall find it comfortable enough. We were not so on our arrival, the children being cross and tired.[84]

Though she travelled with a nursery nurse, twelve hours in a carriage with small children must have been trying. Once established at Portsmouth they visited the dockyard, and Haslar Naval Hospital, saw Porchester Castle, went on board Fremantle's ship, and visited the Sultana hulk, where French prisoners were kept, taking a close view of those on deck. The family had two months together before Fremantle was ordered back to sea on 25 September. Yet such brief interludes sometimes brought consequences that Betsy would rather have avoided. She recorded in her diary that on 1 November 1804 she received a note from Fremantle to join him in Portsmouth as he could not get leave of absence. She left home as soon as she could with two of her children, Tom and Emma, arriving at Liphook by 9 o' clock, where she stayed overnight, and reaching Portsmouth before noon the following day. By 20 January 1805 she was writing in her diary, 'I have not been at all well for this week past, being most wretchedly sick & sleepy – c'est un mauvais signe!' She gave birth to a girl the following September. Betsy was young and fit but aristocratic women did not always enjoy the health benefits that they might have expected, given their privileged station. Until around 1780, it was the custom for women of this class to employ wet-nurses for their children. Consequently, they did not benefit from the delayed conception that results when women breastfeed and their health often suffered from years of childbearing with very short birth intervals.[85] Rodney's first wife, Jenny, was weakened by bearing him three children in four years and when they both contracted a bilious complaint in the winter of 1757 she did not have the strength to withstand it and died after a short illness. In this respect aristocratic naval wives who saw their husbands rarely in wartime may actually have had some advantage over their peers.

Some officers of this class had an acute appreciation of the debt they owed their wives. When Codrington complained that his wife Jane had failed to send him a letter, he immediately regretted the reproach, 'well knowing that instead of failings in such cases I am indebted to you for a practical and well judged kindness in all that concerns my comfort and happiness'. His career and the long absences it necessitated meant that Jane shouldered heavy responsibilities; writing after nearly ten years of marriage, he assured her that not only was his love as strong as ever but that she had his esteem and confidence. Alluding to the stress his chosen career must have caused her, while still attempting to make light of the risks, he imputed her care of him to 'an unfounded anxiety of affection'. Yet however successful their marriage and whatever suggestions Jane may have made about their future, Codrington was committed to the navy, and cautioned, 'Do not fancy I am going to give up my ship, much as I wish I was a private gentleman in England.'[86] Jane's situation seems to have been a common one. Upper ranking naval officers were generally driven to make a success of their career, either because they were younger sons who would not inherit estates or because they came from families in financial difficulties. The navy offered such men the possibility of fame and fortune – not surprisingly in the circumstances, their families often came a poor third.

1. The aristocracy (peers, baronets and knights added together) made up only 0.0000857 per cent of the British population around 1800. See John Cannon, *Aristocratic Century: The Peerage of Eighteenth-Century England* (Cambridge, 1984), p. 33.

2. Marilyn Morris, 'Marital Litigation and English Tabloid Journalism', *British Journal for Eighteenth-Century Studies*, 28, no. 1 (2005), 33-54.

3. Jenny Skipp, 'Masculinity and Social Stratification: Eighteenth-Century Erotic Literature, 1700 – 1821', *British Journal for Eighteenth-Century Studies*, 29 (2006), 264.

4. Linda Colley, 'The Apotheosis of George III: Loyalty, Royalty and the British Nation 1760 – 1820', *Past and Present*, 102 (1984), 102 – 06.

5. *GM* (1795), 309.

6. Maxine Berg, *Luxury and Pleasure in Eighteenth-Century Britain* (Oxford, 2005), p. 207.

7. Middleton Papers, NMM X2003.039.1, no. 33, 27 Jan. 1807, Susanna Middleton to her sister, Miss Martin Leake.

8. *A New Collection of Trials for Adultery, by a civilian of Doctors' Commons* (London 1799), p. 70.

9. *ibid.,* p. 209.

10. Althorp Papers, BL 75644. vol. cccxliv. April – Nov. 1794. Caroline, wife of John Howe, to Lady Georgiana Spencer, 178.

11. *A New Collection of Trials for Adultery*, pp. 104, 105.

12. Staffordshire Record Office, D615/P(S)/1/3/G, 28 March 1749, Lady Anson to Mr Thomas Anson.

13. NMM AGC/12/10, 11 Dec. 1779, George Brydges Rodney to his wife Henrietta.

14. BL Add. MSS 37778 f 60, 17 Sept. 1812, Caroline Smith to Bickerton.

15. Elaine Chalus, 'Elite Women, Social Politics, and the Political World of Late Eighteenth-Century England', *The Historical Journal*, 43 (2000), 688. I owe this reference to Roger Knight.

16. NMM TYL/1 part 1, 2 Jan. 1792, Lady A. Dacre to Mrs Charles Tyler.

17. NMM TYL/1 part 1, 9 Feb 1798, Lady A. Dacre to Mrs Charles Tyler.

18. NMM TYL/1 part 1, 12 Sept. 1808, Emma Hamilton to Tyler.

19. Althorp Papers, BL 75643. vol. cccxliii, June 1793 – March 1794, Caroline Howe to Lady Georgiana Spencer, 146.

20. Cecil Aspinall-Oglander, *Admiral's Wife. Being the life and letters of The Hon. Mrs. Edward Boscawen from 1719 to 1761* (London, 1940), p. 70.

21. BL Add. MSS 54534, 12 Nov. 1801, Charlotte Emily Berkeley to Lt Charles J Napier.

22. BL Add. MSS 37200 f.90, Fri. 3rd n.d., Jane Codrington to C. Babbage.

23. NMM AGC/12/10, 1 April, 6 May and n.d. May 1778, Rodney to his wife Henrietta.

24. NMM AGC/12/1, 13 April 1782, Rodney to his wife Henrietta.

25. NMM COD 21/1a, 26 June 1810, Codrington to his wife Jane.

26. NMM COD 21/1a, 10 Sept. 1809, Codrington to his wife Jane.

27. NMM MKH/509, 11 Jan. 1783, Alexander Hood (1726 – 1814) to his wife Mary.

28. NMM MKH/510, 22 Jan. 1795, Alexander Hood (1726 – 1814) to his second wife Maria Sophia.

29. Anne Fremantle, ed., *The Wynne Diaries*, 3 vols (London, 1935 – 40), II, 194 – 5.

30. NMM NEP/4, 3 Sept. 1798, St Vincent to Nepean.

31. NMM Troubridge Papers, MS 84/070 [box 1], 23 May and 7 June 1801, Lady Amelia Calder to Sir Thomas Troubridge (incidently, the son of a London baker).

32. NMM COR/56, [2.15], 29 Aug. 1763, Lady Cornwallis to William Cornwallis.

33. NMM COR/56, [2.15], 17 July 1762, Lady Cornwallis to William Cornwallis.

34. NMM CRK/3/83 and 84, 28 Dec. 1800 and 21 March 1803, Lady Collier to Nelson.

35. NMM LBK/77, 11 Aug. 1805, Lord Barham to Lady Collier. I owe this reference to Roger Knight.

36. NMM CAR/8B3, n.d. Jan. 1795 and 6 Jan. 1795, Samuel Carteret to his mother Marie Rachel Carteret.

37. NMM RUSI/NM/235/5, 1 July and 6 Aug. 1790, Edward Riou to his mother Dorothy Riou.

38. Hardwicke Papers, BL Add. 35,376, fos. 132 – 5.

39. Althorp Papers, BL Add. 75644. vol. Cccxliv, April – Nov. 1794, Friday 5 Sept 1794, Caroline, wife of John Howe and sister of Richard, 1st Earl Howe, to Lady Georgiana Spencer.

40. Cecil Aspinall-Oglander, pp. 55 – 6.

41. NMM MKH/510, 18 Jan. 1795, Alexander Hood (1726 – 1814) to Maria Sophia.

42. NMM PRV/62/2, 29 August 1794, Purvis to his wife.

43. See T. H. McGuffie, 'The Walcheren Expedition and the Walcheren Fever', *The English Historical Review*, vol. 62, no.243 (1947), 191 – 202.

44. NMM COD 21/1a, 26 May 1809, Codrington to his wife Jane.

45. Cecil Aspinall-Oglander, p. 243.

46. *Morning Chronicle*, 16 August 1793, p.3 col. 3.

47. Althorp Papers, BL Add. 75643. vol. cccxliii, June 1793 – March 1794, Caroline Howe to Lady Georgiana Spencer, 158.

48. NMM HOW/4, 11 June 1794, George III to Lady Howe.

49. Anne Fremantle, ed., *The Wynne Diaries*, III, 216.

50. NMM TYL ms 52/014, 3 Nov. 1805, Tyler to his wife Margaret.

51. A.F. Scott, *Everyone a Witness. The Georgian Age* (London, 1970), p. 394.

52. Timothy Jenks, *Naval Engagements: Patriotism, Cultural Politics and the Royal Navy, 1793 – 1815* (Oxford, 2006), p. 28.

53. The Morning Post, 26 June 1794, p. 2.

54. Althorp Papers, BL Add. 75644. vol. cccxliv, April – Nov. 1794, Friday June 13 1794, 87, Caroline Howe to Lady Georgiana Spencer.

55. Cecil Aspinall-Oglander, p. 54.

56. NMM COD 21/1a, 15 June 1809, Codrington to his wife Jane.

57. NMM COD 21/1a, 28 Nov. 1810, Codrington to his wife Jane.

58. Troubridge Papers, NMM MS 84/070 [box 1], 9 Sept. 1809, Anna Maria Cochrane to her father.

59. Randolph Trumbach, *The Rise of the Egalitarian Family: Aristocratic Kinship and Domestic Relations in Eighteenth-Century England* (New York, 1978), p. 137.

60. Amanda Vickery, *The Gentleman's Daughter: Women's Lives in Georgian England* (New Haven and London, 1998), p. 166. Cf. Lydia Morris, *The Workings of the Household, A US – UK Comparison* (Oxford, 1990), p. 133.

61. Cecil Aspinall-Oglander, p. 72.

62. Cecil Aspinall-Oglander, p. 72.

63. David Syrett, ed., *The Rodney Papers. Selections from the Correspondence of Admiral Lord Rodney, Volume 1, 1742 – 1763*, Navy Records Society, 148 (Aldershot, Hants, 2005), pp. 211 – 22.

64. NMM COD 21/1a, 26 May 1810, Codrington to his wife Jane.

65. NMM MKH/510, Sunday morning [Oct. 1793], Alexander Hood to his wife Maria Sophia.

66. NMM MKH/510, Saturday evening [n.d.], Codrington to his wife Jane.

67. Susan Groag Bell, 'Women Create Gardens in Male Landscapes: A Revisionist Approach to Eighteenth-Century English Garden History', *Feminist Studies*, Vol. 16, No. 3 (1990), pp. 471 – 91.

68. NMM MKH/510, Thursday afternoon [n.d.], Alexander Hood (1726 – 1814) to his wife Maria Sophia.

69. NMM MKH/510, 18 January 1795, Alexander Hood (1726 – 1814) to his wife Maria Sophia.

70. BL Add. MSS 79200 ff 65, 27 Aug. 1812, Hon Frances Augusta Bentinck to Alexander Davison.

71. BL Add. MSS 79200 ff 66, n.d., 1812, Hon Frances Augusta Bentinck to Alexander Davison.

72. NMM COD 21/1a, 19 – 20 September 1809, Codrington to his wife Jane.

73. NMM MSS/87/053.3, 28 Dec. 1803, Emma to John Scott.

74. NMM CAR/8B, 21 Dec. 1794, Samuel Carteret to his mother Marie Rachel Carteret.

75. NMM COR/56, May 1763, Lady Cornwallis to her son William.

76. NMM COR/56, 11 Apr. 1764, 13 July 1762, Lady Cornwallis to her son Willliam.

77. NMM CAR/8B, 7 and 10 Dec. 1795, Carteret to his mother Marie Rachel Carteret.

78. John Gregory, *A Father's Legacy to His Daughters* (Dublin, 1774), p. 31.

79. NMM AGC/12/12, 23 April 1781, Rodney to his wife Henrietta.

80. NMM MKH/510, 22 Jan. 1795, Alexander Hood to his wife Maria Sophia.

81. BL Add. MSS 75643. vol. cccxliii, June 1793 – March 1794, 6 Oct. 1798, Caroline Howe to Lady Georgiana Spencer.

82. NMM COD 21/1a, 18 Sept. 1809, Codrington to his wife Jane.

83. NMM MKH/510, Sat. evening [n.d.], Alexander Hood to his wife Maria Sophia.

84. Anne Fremantle, ed., *The Wynne Diaries*, III, 84.

85. Judith Lewis, ""'Tis a Misfortune to Be a Great Ladie": Maternal Mortality in the British Aristocracy, 1558 – 1959', *The Journal of British Studies*, vol. 37, no. 1 (1998), 25 – 53; Randolph Trumbach, *The Rise of the Egalitarian Family*, pp. 197 – 208, 223.

86. NMM COD 21/1a, 20 June, 9 Aug. and 8 Dec. 1810, Codrington to his wife Jane.

Chapter Three
THE MIDDLING SORT

In 1794 when Nelson was in the Mediterranean, his wife Fanny wrote giving him a prudent account of her expenses, careful to reassure him that her economies had in no way compromised their social status, 'No stage coach I give you my honour do I travel in'.[1] Her concerns were common to many. In the course of the eighteenth century, growing numbers of people acquired wealth, cultural presence and an identifiable social status; they ranked below the country's elite but nevertheless occupied a social position that induced ambition and obtained respect. Today social historians generally call these people the 'middling sort' rather than the 'middle classes'. The latter term is more familiar but it was not prevalent in the eighteenth century and has since become loaded with connotations of Marxist ideology that is unhelpful when dealing with an earlier period. The precise nature of this social group is quite hard to define: people occupying the rank developed an identity and a stronger awareness of their social position during the eighteenth century but because increasing numbers laid claim to this status it was by no means homogenous. John Brewer described them as including:

> lawyers, land agents, apothecaries, and doctors; middlemen in the coal, textile, and grain trades; carters, carriers and innkeepers; booksellers, printers, schoolteachers, entertainers, and clerks; drapers, grocers, druggists, stationers, ironmongers, shopkeepers of every sort; the small masters in cutlery and toy making, or in all the various luxury trades of the metropolis.[2]

To these might be added substantial tenant farmers and comfortable freeholders. Other historians have defined the middling sort more generally as those who were mostly self-employed but 'who had to work for their income, trading with the products of their hands ... or with the skills of business or the professions for which they had trained'.[3] The upper tier of this middling rank often aspired to the manners and lifestyle of the gentry, with the result that social identities at the higher end remained muddled throughout the century.

If we turn towards the lower tier of this group, one way in which people differed from skilled artisans, socially just below them, is that the loyalties of highly skilled workers usually remained with their trade or craft. An artisan's security and sense of identity depended on the particular skill he possessed and on the supportive guild or network of others in the same line of work. The middling sort, on the other hand, showed a more marked loyalty to the extended family, which could generally be relied upon to offer help and advancement. It was this family network which could improve business interests by providing capital or standing surety for credit, and offer support in times of hardship or exert influence to benefit family members. Seamen's wives of middling status might rely on family support while their husbands were at sea. For example, the widow of Captain Charles Pelly wrote to the Charity for the Relief of Officers Widows in 1814 explaining that she had not applied to them before, 'as I have (from time to time) received pecuniary assistance from the Father of my late Husband'.[4] Family members often helped to set young people on a particular career path. For example, those with influence in the navy would be expected to promote the interests of their relations interested in military service, as happened with Nelson. His family were genteel country people: they had no wealth but were distantly related to the gentry and possessed useful connections through the Walpole and Suckling families. Most importantly, Nelson's uncle Maurice Suckling was a Comptroller of the Navy. These connections helped Nelson to rise quickly through the ranks in the early part of his career.

Naval officers were a prominent group among the socially mobile middle ranks. In wartime, many were able to acquire rank and fortune through rapid promotion and the acquisition of prize money, a fact that caused unease in some conservative quarters. A correspondent writing to the *Gentleman's Magazine* in 1810 to complain about the numbers of middle-ranking men claiming precedence over gentlemen by birth, specifically mentioned military officers:

> How should we like to see a man, perhaps the son of a tailor, a stonemason, or a lodging-house keeper, merely because he had attained a commission in the army or navy, rank before a man whose forefathers had been independently seated for many generations on an hereditary estate, and which forefathers may perhaps have partaken of the blood of the noblest families?[5]

By this time the navy had become a profession that attracted the minor gentry and impoverished younger sons from the nobility precisely because in wartime it offered the lure of prize money and opportunities for social advancement. The editor of the magazine could therefore respond with some authority that his correspondent seemed to have forgotten that most colonels in the army or post captains in the navy were actually the sons or relatives of the most noble and respectable families in the kingdom. And if this were not enough, he continued, the service these men had given to their country entitled them to the respect of society. Yet many from the upper classes continued to look down on officers who had risen quickly up the social hierarchy. Jane Austen, whose brothers were both officers in the navy, referred in her novel *Persuasion* to the snobbery that some encountered: the condescending Sir Walter Elliot complains that the navy is 'the means of bringing persons of obscure birth into undue distinction, and raising men to honour which their fathers and grandfathers never dreamt of'.[6] The wives of naval officers who did manage to advance up the social scale were naturally subject to a range of coded pressures.

Just as the actual composition of the middling sort needs careful consideration, so too does the relative status of women in this group, since this was far from homogenized. At the upper, wealthier, levels women in families who had long held that rank often had a fairly limited role in the family network, featuring chiefly as marriage partners though still expected to contribute to family stability and pass on shared values to their children. Yet if they did possess useful contacts, they were required to exercise what influence they could to further the careers of husbands and sons. For instance, William Webley-Parry, who entered the navy in 1779, was desperate to win promotion in order to improve his income. He made it to lieutenant by 1790 and thereafter did all he could to secure his own command. In his letters to his mother he was always urging her to write to people she knew who might recommend him to his superiors. He was finally made a commander in 1798 after nine years' war service. Lower down the social scale, middle-ranking wives who had rather more household duties to carry out were often accused of neglecting them to emulate the leisured lifestyle of their betters. In 1803 the *Gentleman's Magazine*, bemoaned the lack of economy to be found in tradesmen's wives: formerly such women had not been ashamed to bake their own bread and brew their own beer but apparently at this date not one in twenty did so: perhaps it may simply have become cheaper to purchase staple foodstuffs.[7] Ironically, tradesmen found that if their wives did live frugally, people suspected that their business was in trouble and refused to give them credit.

Women of the gentry and middling ranks were certainly expected to learn basic accounting, not least because it was the accepted duty of a wife to regulate domestic expenditure. A late eighteenth-century instruction book for children, written in the form of a conversation between a girl and her mother, explains that all daughters should learn to write a good hand and cast accounts well. When the girl demurs and suggests that accounting is something for boys, she is told that it is certainly the business of men to keep the accounts belonging to their trade or possession, or estate, 'but it is the business of their wives to keep all the household accounts: and a woman almost in any rank, unless perhaps some of the highest of all, is to blame if she does not take upon herself this necessary office'.[8] Even a humorous piece of the period which set out the mental and personal qualifications of a wife (while poking fun at male insecurities) admitted that although a woman might safely exhibit 'a little becoming deficiency' in spelling, she certainly needed 'a proper knowledge of *accounts* and arithmetic' – although by no means any sort of skill in fractions.[9] The expenditure of sizeable households, though not complex, still needed detailed attention. Women in middling families were more in touch with the world of business than has previously been thought, and probably this area of financial management has been under-valued because what would be called 'accounting' in a business context is termed 'budgeting' in a household.

The middling ranks were notable for their strong identification with moral virtue, sexual modesty and religious piety. Their women were expected to uphold these ideals and to exemplify them in their daily conduct. Since these values were regarded as 'feminine', female sexuality was rigorously policed to ensure social stability. By the early nineteenth century, this way of thinking had hardened. The ultra conservative writer, Jane West, in her conduct book *Letters to a Young Lady*, specifically addressed females of the 'middling classes' (and she counted herself as one of them), because she believed that dereliction of duty amongst this social order would herald national ruin. Consequently, she was disturbed by what she perceived to be a decline in their standards and strongly urged a return to virtue. Her peroration sets out an agenda for women: 'the political importance which this rank possess in England; the general information, sound sense, and unsophisticated manners, that were their marked characteristics; the blameless occupations, domestic tenderness, modesty, simplicity, and unaffected gentleness, that distinguished their wedded partners' were all strong reasons for women of this class to cleave strictly to respectability and turn their back on vain pursuits or any desire to ape the aristocracy.[10] Several other contemporary works, including the *Authentic and Interesting Memoirs of Ann Sheldon* (1790) and *The Woman of the Town* (1801), both tales of middle-ranking young girls who were enticed into prostitution, also warned readers of this class to avoid the corruptions of the elite. The *Memoirs of Ann Sheldon* featured the daughter of a London shipbuilder, engaged to the captain of a West Indiaman. When her father's business failed, baulking at the sudden need for economy, she allowed herself to be seduced by a corrupt aristocrat and became his mistress. The bawd who enticed her into this 'path to destruction' spoke strongly against the life of a sailor's wife, pointing to the absence of seamen for long periods and to their inconstancy when abroad. She warmly advised the girl to choose a rich husband instead who would keep a coach and always be at home. The heroine's subsequent downfall suggests that for the middling sort, at least, a seaman of some rank was a good catch and that a respectable woman ought to be content with the lifestyle such a man could provide. This moral tale features the captain of a merchant ship but at this period there was no firm distinction between merchant seamen and those serving in the navy: seamen regularly moved from one service to the other.

These and other moral publications underline the point that female reputation was an important commodity. Whenever women ventured beyond the boundaries of a domestic role, they placed their reputations at greater risk. Those from the landed classes with a good family name could look to their social position if their reputation were ever questioned, and to the men of the family for protection. Middle-ranking women could be compromised more easily. The navigator Matthew Flinders (see Plate 6) seems to have been keenly conscious of this. A long-term prisoner on Mauritius, accused by the French of being a spy, in 1806 he toyed with the idea of his wife travelling from England to be with him. They had been apart for five years by this time but he still had doubts, given the constraints placed on respectable women accompanying their men to sea. Apart from his fears for her health, she could not, he realised, travel unprotected, 'Let the conduct of a woman on board a ship, without her husband, be ever so prudent and circumspect, the tongue of slander will almost certainly find occasion, or it will create one, to embitter the future peace of her husband and family'.[11]

Naval wives whose sphere of activity had always tended towards the domestic and the genteel were vulnerable in widowhood, particularly if left with inadequate financial support. Those whose husbands had run businesses or been skilled artisans had more options. Writers advised such wives to take pains to understand their husband's business so that, if he died, they might continue with it for their own support. A correspondent to the *Gentleman's Magazine* in 1788 made the related point that women should be educated in useful employments, as well as accomplishments, so that they would be better able to deal with adversity. Women, by their 'oeconomical care', he wrote, should build up the confidence of others in their ability to handle money so that they might be entrusted with the disposal of their fortune on the death of their husbands.[12] A woman's reputation would be more particularly at risk if she entered the commercial world, yet ironically a good reputation would be important to the maintenance of her business – essential, if she wished to obtain credit.

Single women were always at liberty to take an active part in trade and may have helped to provide networks that other women could turn to, including naval wives and widows newly left to fend for themselves. Whereas a married woman was virtually deprived of a share in her husband's property, unmarried women had rights in law that were comparable to those of men, although they may not have enjoyed the social status of married women. There were limits and constraints on women's working lives but a range of trades and occupations remained open to them. For example, in 1788 the Court of the King's Bench determined that a woman was competent to serve in the office of Commissioner of the Sewers and Overseer of the Poor. The court judge even mentioned a parish where a woman had been chosen as a constable.[13]

Many businesswomen had links with the dockyards. In 1756, for instance, Mary Eastman wrote from Greenwich to the Navy Board asking if she could be allowed to continue with the contract to supply the Deptford and Woolwich yards with horn lanterns for powder rooms, storerooms and poop decks. She explained that her mother had had the contract for 40 years and that during the last 20 years while her mother had been in poor state of health, she had managed the business for her. Her mother had now died and Eastman claimed she would be largely unprovided for if the Board did not renew the contract. She promised to do the work well and assured the Board that she had good workmen for the purpose. Though she signed her letter, she employed a professional letter writer to set it out – probably to ensure that it was written in the correct style and would be well received. A note on the corner of the paper from the Board indicates that it did decide to continue the contract. The same year, a Mary Franklyn of Plymouth wrote to the Board to explain that her father, Mr Apollo Walker, for many years a contractor for various works at Plymouth Dockyard, had recently died. (Here the difference in surname suggests that Franklyn herself may have been widowed.) As his only daughter and executrix, she asked to be able to continue the contract for 'paviours work' (the laying and maintaining of pavements), having the proper workmen and materials. The Board granted this request also. Clearly the women here merely oversaw the business using an unchanged workforce, but the willingness of the navy, one of the largest single employers of civilian labour of the period, to employ women in this way is an indication that women of a certain class living in urban areas were not exactly subject to the constraining values advocated in contemporary conduct books.[14] There are also instances of widows running private shipyards. For example, Mrs Mary Ross actively ran her husband's shipbuilding yard at Rochester after his

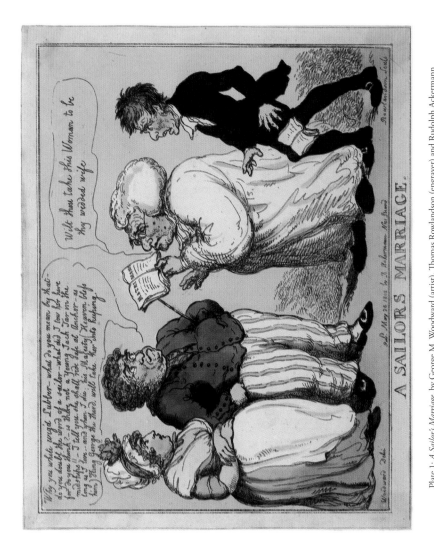

Plate 1: *A Sailor's Marriage*, by George M. Woodward (artist), Thomas Rowlandson (engraver) and Rudolph Ackermann (publisher), 25 May 1805. NMM Repro. ID PW3853.

Plate 2: *The Neglected Tar* (press gang), n. d., NMM Repro. ID PU4772.

Plate 3: *Rear-Admiral Fremantle*, by Domenico Pellegrini (artist), Charles Picart (engraver). NMM Repro. ID PU3287.

Plate 4: *Admiral George Brydges Rodney, 1st Baron Rodney, 1719 – 92*, oil painting by Jean-Laurent Mosnier, 1791.
NMM Repro. ID BHC2970.

Plate 5: *Alexander Hood, 1st Viscount Bridport (1726 – 1814)*, by Lemuel Francis Abbott (artist) and Samuel Freeman (engraver). Hope Collection. NMM Repro. ID PU3204.

CAPTAIN FLINDERS. R.N.
Autograph Copy of Parole on his release from six years Captivity
in the Isle of Mauritius.

I undersigned, captain in His Britannic Majesty's navy, having obtained leave of His Excellency the captain-general to return in my country by the way of Bengal, Promise on my word of honour not to act in any service which might be considered as directly or indirectly hostile to France or its Allies, during the course of the present war

Port Napoleon, Isle de France, 7th June 1810

(Signed) Matthw Flinders

Published by HARGROVE SAUNDERS. 34 Fishborne St. LONDON N
LITHO PHOTOGRAPHIC INST. 492, NEW OXFORD STREET

Plate 6: *Captain Flinders R. N.*, published by Hargrove Saunders.
NMM Repro. ID PW3511.

Plate 7: *Admiral Edward Boscawen (1711 – 1761)*, oil painting by Sir Joshua Reynolds. Greenwich Hospital Collection. NMM Repro. ID BHC2565.

Plate 8: *Captain the Honourable Augustus Keppel (1725 – 66)*, oil painting by Sir Joshua Reynolds, 1752 – 53. NMM Repro. ID BHC2823.

Plate 9: *Vice-Admiral Cuthbert Collingwood, 1st Baron Collingwood, 1748 – 1810*, oil painting by Henry Howard, Greenwich Hospital Collection. NMM Repro. ID BHC2625.

Plate 10: Fan commemorating the Battle of the Nile, 1798.
NMM Repro. ID D5541-2.

Plate 11: *Frances Nelson, 1761 – 1831, Viscountess Nelson*, British School, *c.*1800.
NMM Repro. ID BHC2883.

Plate 12: *A Mansion House Treat or Smoking Attitudes*, published by S.W. Fores, 18 November 1800.
NMM Repro. ID PW3887.

CAPTAIN INGLEFIELD,

of His Majesty's Ship

The Centaur,

Wrecked in 1782.

Engrav'd by B. Smith, from a Miniature painted in 1786 by Engleheart.

London, Pub Sep.r 14. 1815, by Thompson, Printseller, 26 S.t James's Street.

Plate 13: *Captain Inglefield of His Majesty's Ship The Centaur Wrecked in 1782*, by George Engleheart (artist) Benjamin Smith (engraver) and Thompson (publisher), 14 September 1815. NMM Repro. ID PU4608.

Plate 14: A copper commemorative coin, the obverse engraved with a sailor and his wife, and the legend 'JOHN AND MARTHA CROUCH', late eighteenth-century. NMM Repro. ID E3908-1.

Plate 15: *ACCOMMODATION or Lodgings to let at Portsmouth!!*, by T. Rowlandson and/or George M. Woodward (artist),
Thomas Rowlandson (engraver) and Thomas Tegg (publisher), 30 June 1808. Macpherson Collection.
NMM Repro. ID RM/66/340 or PX8580.

Plate 16: *Sweet Poll of Plymouth*, by H. W. Bunbury (artist), G. Shepheard (engraver) and T. Macklin (publisher), 10 June 1790. NMM Repro. ID PU4734.

Plate 17: *Shiver my Timbers Poll your grown out of Compass. I can scarcely embrace you*, by S. Jenner (artist), *c*.1820. Macpherson Collection. NMM Repro. ID PX8640.

MEN of WAR, BOUND for the PORT of PLEASURE.

Plate 18: *Men of War, Bound for the Port of Pleasure*, by Carrington Bowles (publisher), 25 April 1791. NMM Repro. ID PW4036.

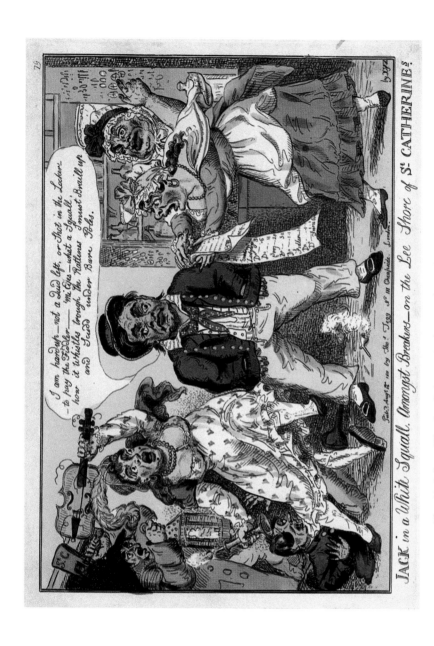

Plate 19: *Jack in a White Squall, Amongst Breakers – on the Lee Shore of St. Catherines*, published by Thomas Tegg, 16 August 1811. NMM Repro. ID PW3862.

The Sailor's Return.

Just on the Beach arriv'd, with great Surprize, } But **Molly's** Mother, more sagacious, opes }
Jack sees his **Molly**; Him too **Molly** Spies: } The wealthy Chest, on which She plac'd her hopes, }
What! is it Thou? with open Arms She cries. } And for the richest Prizes careful gropes. }
Then drops the brittle Goods She sells for Bread, } The settled Crew gay Mirth and Love proclaim, }
While all aghast beside stands Messmate **Ned**, } One leads aloft the mercenary Dame, }
And points where flows the Bowl, & Gen'rous Red.} Who drunk, returns her Load from whence it came.}

Contemning Wealth, which they with Risk obtain,}
Thus Sailors love, and then to Sea again. }

Printed for Carington Bowles   in S.t Pauls Church Yard, London.

Plate 20: *The Sailor's Return*, engraved by C. Mosley, *c.*1750.
NMM Repro. ID PW3801.

Plate 21: *Poll and my Partner Joe*, published by Robert Laurie & James Whittle, 12 May 1794. NMM Repro. ID PW4034.

Plate 22: Large creamware jug, transfer-printed in black and hand-coloured, Liverpool, Merseyside, England, after 1789. NMM Repro. ID E5680.

Plate 23: *Jack's Fidelity*, published by G. Thompson and I. Evans, 14 January 1796.
Repro. ID PW4042.

The TOKEN, or JACK safe RETURN'D to his TRUE LOVE NANCY.

Plate 24: *The Token, or Jack safe Return'd to his True Love Nancy*, published by
John Fairburn. NMM Repro. ID PW3798.

Plate 25: *Yo Heave Ho*, published by Laurie & Whittle, 24 April 1799.
NMM Repro ID PW4013.

Plate 26: An earthenware jug showing a sailor departing from his family, Sunderland, England, 1810. NMM Repro. ID E6064.

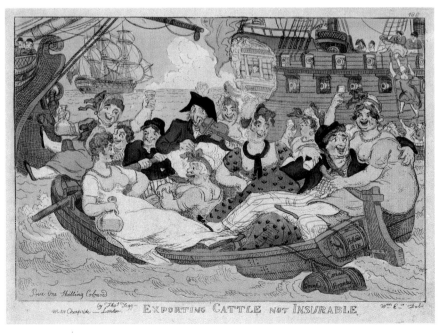

Plate 27: *Exporting Cattle Not Insurable*, by W. Elmes (artist), Thomas Tegg (publisher). NMM Repro. ID PW4163.

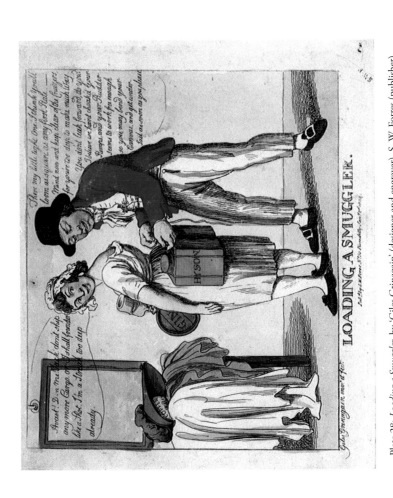

Plate 28: *Loading a Smuggler*, by 'Giles Grinagain' (designer and engraver), S. W. Forres (publisher). 2 January 1804. NMM Repro. ID PU4736.

Plate 29: *A Seaman's Wife's Reckoning*, by George M. Woodward (artist), Thomas Rowlandson (engraver), and Thomas Tegg (publisher). NMM Repro. ID PW3844.

Plate 30: *Wrecks of the Britannia, & Admiral Gardner, East Indiamen, on the Goodwin Sands*, 24 Jan, 1809. NMM Repro. ID PU6386.

Plate 31: A large porcelain jug painted below the lip with an oval portrait of Admiral Edward Boscawen (1711 – 1761), c.1760. NMM Repro. ID E5623.

Plate 32: *A Sailor's Return in Peace*, oil painting by Thomas Stothard.
NMM Repro. ID BHC1125.

Plate 33: A creamware mug, transfer-printed and hand-coloured with a portrait of an officer intended to represent Vice-Admiral Horatio Nelson, c.1800. NMM Repro. ID D5859.

Plate 34: A painted earthenware figure group depicting a sailor and his lass, early nineteenth century, (Fawssett Collection). NMM Repro. ID E6188.

Plate 35: *The interior of R. Ackermann's Repository of Arts, no. 101*, Strand, by Augustus Charles Pugin and Thomas Rowlandson, 1809. John Johnson Collection, © Bodleian Library.

Plate 36: *Wedgwood and Byerley in York Street, St. James's Square* in no. 2 of R. Ackermann's Repository
of Arts, Literature Fashions, Manufactures &c, published from 1809 until 1828. John Johnson Collection,
© Bodleian Library.

Plate 37: From 'Kettles to mend', by John Phillips (artist). John Johnson Collection, © Bodleian Library.

Plate 38: Oval patch box with a mirror inside the lid, from Bilston, West Midlands, England, commemorating the naval heroes of the French Revolutionary War, c.1800. NMM Repro. ID F4277.

death in 1808 and won five contracts from the Navy Board for ships when the naval yards were unable to keep up with demand in wartime.[15] Women who took over businesses from husbands or fathers were naturally anxious to keep existing clients and often issued trade cards or placed advertisements in the local press to ask for the continuance of custom. Their association with the navy, the country's largest industrial organisation, would have enhanced their commercial standing.

Source materials

Artefacts and archives open a window onto different worlds, lives and spaces. Unfortunately, any study of naval women from the lower middling ranks in this period suffers from a general lack of sources, so their contribution to the local economy and their everyday domestic circumstances are hard to recover. Such women seldom kept diaries or correspondence, and while those married to successful officers may have preserved the letters sent to them by their famous husbands, their own letters to their husbands no longer exist. Therefore the domestic circumstances of middle-ranking naval families often have to be deduced from just one side of the correspondence.

On rare occasions, a wife's situation does surface in the archival record, as in a surviving letter by Harriet Walker, the wife of Lieutenant John Walker in command of the *Cygnet*, a small sailing vessel or cutter. Harriet wrote to Admiral Nelson in the summer of 1801, when he was based at Deal occupied with measures to counter Napoleon's threatened invasion. She asked Nelson if he could help her husband to earn more money for his wife and family: she suffered from tuberculosis and her medical expenses were high; the couple had a daughter who could be educated at home to save expense but there was also a son who was of an age when he ought really to be sent to school. She explained that through influence her husband had secured a transfer to the *Cygnet* from a warship in which his fellow officers, all from noble families, maintained a standard of living he could not afford. The hope was that in the course of his new duties he would be able to capture enemy shipping and so supplement his income with prize money.[16] Yet after only a few months, the *Cygnet* had been commandeered to help supply the British ships blockading French ports. Once on supply service Lieutenant Walker had little chance of taking prizes and, even if he did, the action would be in sight of many other ships so that a prize would be subdivided into shares of little individual value. Harriet made it clear that her husband's pay as a lieutenant was insufficient to meet the family's needs, given wartime inflation: 'every article of subsistence is now so high, that had I not good friends – Mr

Walkers expences [*sic*] on Board, with the many suits of uniforms destroyed on this station, being deducted from our resources, we should want common comforts'.[17] She therefore asked Nelson if he would release him from the service of supplying the blockading fleet and allow him to cruise off the south coast, where he would have a better chance of taking prizes. This may sound unpatriotic and mercenary today but contemporaries accepted that, given low rates of pay, the opportunity to earn prize money was a sailor's due and a just recompense to men who put their lives on the line.

Harriet summoned every possible argument to support her request: she was able to claim that she was related to William Falconer, author of the famous poem, *The Shipwreck* and that, as an occasional author herself, she had written verses in praise of Nelson's victory at the Nile, which her husband had apparently presented to Nelson. She had even met Emma Hamilton at the house of an old friend, though she carefully explained that she would never presume to have any claim to Emma's attention. Her letter is a finely judged piece: she balances outright flattery with a claim to be treated with respect. She feels able to approach Nelson with confidence because he combines 'the charm of sensibility with the grace of politeness' but she also calls for the hearing that 'the solicitudes of a Wife and Mother' deserve. The letter neatly locates both parties within contemporary social constructs likely to prove most advantageous to her request. She intimates that Nelson, though battle hardened, still retaines the ability to empathize with the sufferings of others, and that he is blessed with the gentlemanly ease needed to be able to talk to people of all social ranks without any trace of discomfort. These civilizing qualities, she implies, will incline Britain's hero to give due weight to the arguments of a wife and mother whose vital domestic role justifies a direct approach. The letter shows how women of a certain rank could invoke contemporary social values when they looked for help, and demonstrates the importance of letter-writing skills at this period – although we do not know whether or not Nelson was able to oblige her.

Occasionally, the domestic circumstances of middle-ranking naval families in dire need were reported in newspapers, presumably because the navy was of such importance to the nation that cases of individual hardship excited sympathy. Naval families fell on hard times when the breadwinner became sick and was unable to continue in service. *The Portsmouth Gazette, and Weekly Advertiser* for 13 April 1795 carried the following item asking readers for charity:

The case of a distressed officer
A Lieutenant of the Navy, Son of a very respectable officer, who lost his life in the Tilbury Man of War, in the year 1757 … who from Illness

is obliged to remain unemployed, without the power of benefiting his Family by himself in the least, with a Wife far advanced in her pregnancy, and Five Children, almost wanting the common necessities of life. Subscriptions will be thankfully received at the DONALDSON's Library

The situation of this particular 'distressed officer' was exacerbated because his illness does not seem to have qualified him for any pension. Presumably the family preferred this course of action to asking for poor relief. Charitable giving to seamen and officers who had fallen on hard times was common. For example, the musician William Ayrton recorded in his account book that on 15 August 1805 he gave a 'distressed sailor' 1s, and in May 1808 he subscribed 10s 6d to a 'distressed officer'.[18] The wives of many officers living on half pay, with or without the addition of a disability pension, must have endured a kind of genteel poverty as they struggled to maintain appearances. Half pay provided the bare minimum to live on. Such economic realities may help to explain why other officers kept working although chronically ill. The *Gentleman's Magazine* reported the death of Captain John Huddart in 1805, explaining that he had been ill for some time. After a long career in the navy he was given command of the Townsend revenue cutter and died on the job, ferrying some officers, leaving 'utterly unprovided for, a wife and eight children'.[19]

Periodicals and magazines often published short biographies or obituaries of successful naval officers from the middling ranks. Such accounts focus on their public achievements but can also give and insight into family life, as their authors sometimes consulted the widows. Andrew Kippis in his biography of Captain Cook was able to say that Cook had married in 1762 and, according to Mrs Cook, had six children. (Elizabeth Cook had ample time to mourn her husband since she was still only 37 in 1778 when he was killed in Hawaii, during his third world voyage, and she would live to be 94.) The *Gentleman's Magazine* picked up on her subsequent misfortunes. In 1794 it reported that Cook's eldest and only surviving son, Captain Cook of the *Spitfire* had drowned in Poole Harbour. His brother had died of a fever in 1793 and another had drowned in the *Thunderer* in a storm. Two of Cook's daughters had married naval officers who also both drowned.[20] Such extracts give us tantalizing glimpses of the vicissitudes that naval wives and mothers had to endure.

Nor was the family network always able to respond to sudden changes in fortune, particularly in wartime. The *London Chronicle* reported in 1798 that one respectable woman, dressed in deep mourning, resorted to petitioning the King. She threw her petition into the King's coach where it fell onto the lap of the Princess Elizabeth. In it she explained that she had lost her husband on board the

Queen in the West Indies; that one of her sons, a lieutenant, had been murdered by the mutinous crew of the *Hermione*, that another had fallen in action, while serving on board the *Leviathan*, and that she was reduced to great distress.[21] The fact that the crew of the *Hermione* had mutinied while at sea – a rare occurrence – probably added to the interest in this woman's tragic plight. Newspaper and magazine reports indicate that when naval officers achieved success, their wives and relatives basked in reflected glory but in addition to those widowed, many women became carers to seamen discharged with broken constitutions resulting from the rigours of naval life. The *Gentleman's Magazine*, for example, reported that William Robinson, master and commander, had returned home after 25 years' service in broken health and that all the careful nursing of his mother and sisters could not save him.[22] The navigator Matthew Flinders was just one of many husbands who returned from the sea ill or maimed. He survived only a few years after returning in 1810, his health broken by his arduous voyage to Australia and subsequent imprisonment on Mauritius, though the immediate cause of his premature death was chronic cystitis and a kidney infection complicated by the effects of gonorrhoea, contracted on an earlier voyage. His wife Ann confided to a friend that in his last few weeks he was worn to a skeleton and looked 70 years of age, though still only 40.

Strain of separation

Women left at home were bound to worry about their loved ones at sea, although naval wives did what they could to alleviate this shared burden of anxiety by passing on news of other women's husbands. Fanny Nelson's anxiety is clear as, in November 1794, she faced the prospect of another winter without her husband and son (who had sailed together). She wrote to Nelson, 'This winter will be another anxious one. What did I not suffer in my mind last?' A fortnight later she complained, 'No end of my anxiety … My mind and poor heart are always on the rack'. In December she assured him that, 'I never hear the wind but my dear husband and child are fully in my thoughts indeed they are never never absent from my mind.'[23]

In this period many naval families from the middling and upper ranks took up residence at Bath and there Fanny Nelson made the acquaintance of Lady Saumarez. Sir James Saumarez was serving with Nelson in the Mediterranean, so Fanny was often able to pass on news of him to his wife. Unfortunately, the close networking between some naval wives meant that they were apt to compare notes about their husbands' behaviour and the frequency of their letters home.

After the battle off Cape St Vincent, fought on 14 February 1797, there was a lengthy silence from Nelson which made Fanny anxious. She wrote to him on 26 February 1797 explaining that she had just returned from calling on Lady Saumarez who had offered to send Fanny's letter to Nelson at no cost. She added, 'I have looked for a letter from you this age. The one from Gibraltar Decr 14th is almost worn out. I have it in my pocket.'[24] True to contemporary standards of conduct, Fanny did not wish to complain to her husband more overtly; instead she turned to Nelson's eldest brother Maurice who worked as a clerk in the Naval Office. He duly wrote to Nelson in blunter terms on 8 March:

> My Dear Brother
> I assure you I am exceedingly disappointed at not receiving a single line from you and I have also a letter this morning from Bath wherein Mrs Nelson complains heavily of not hearing from you particularly as Lady Saumarez who is there has had <u>five</u> letters since the action … I enclose you Mrs Nelson's letter by which you will perceive how uneasy she is.[25]

On 10 March Fanny received a letter from Nelson dated 16 February and, shortly afterwards another, dated 22 February, enclosing an account of the battle. He had also sent this account to others who helped to get it published and Fanny played her part in promoting Nelson's fame by circulating this exciting letter to her acquaintances, including Lord Hood. She had checked on protocol with her father-in-law before doing this but she still wrote diffidently to Nelson, 'I hope I have not done wrong. I have lived long enough to dread envy'.[26] Her excessively guarded words can be read as a mild rebuke to a husband who by now had made great efforts to get his name publicised. Their separation had already produced anxiety and resentment on her part, and the note of caution she struck in the face of his exuberance indicates how much separation had enhanced their natural tendency to view things differently.

The semi-public nature of contemporary letter writing prevented many couples from including explicit intimacies, adding to the strain that any prolonged absence placed on naval marriages. Captain Thomas Wells, who had relinquished the safe command of a prison ship in order to try his fortune with the fleet at sea, wrote rather incoherently to his wife from Göteborg on 2 July 1808, though he could simply have been drunk at the time:

> My Dearest Nancy,
> On this date two months you wrote to me I have it in my hand to view the superscription but dare not look to its contents because I well

remember the pain it gave me to think my dearest wife was in low spirits from my writing and had been otherways unwell, to see the anxiety I experienced yesterday when I had to distribute 2 sacks of letters which came by way of Yarmouth … I almost made certain I should find one and could hardly be prevailed upon to send them away to those they belonged something must be the matter it cannot be mere punishment that you are inflicting on me if so be assured [?] it has ceased to be bearable but I cannot bring myself but for a single moment to think you would willingly inflict pain then it changes into a thorough belief that you are unwell had I been in the West Indies letters would have come every fortnight at the Cape of Good Hope or Buenos Ayres … I hardly know to whom I am writing or I could say much more I dreamed of you 3 Nights ago in short you are never out of my mind. I could like to talk about my dear Children but it is to no purpose none will answer me … but why do I write so to whome who will take that trouble or perhaps they are not well trusting the Almightys Blessings on you and them with my love to your Brother I again subscribe myself your affectionate Husband.[27]

Wells afterwards began to prosper rather better with the fleet and in October he obtained an acting commission to command His Majesty's sloop of war, *Cruizer*, and went on to take a number of prizes. On 16 November he wrote to advise his wife to buy the weekly paper as he had captured a privateer and she would see his public letter about it in print. At the Nore on 19 December he wrote to her cheerfully, saying, 'well if you wont write will you come to an affectionate Husband who longs to see you so lose no time as I am ordered back to the same station & shall be gone in the course of a month'. He told her that he had bought her furs and a shawl, and that he believed that he had been confirmed in his command of the *Cruizer*, though he had not yet received formal notification. Travelling expenses did not seem to be a problem. He authorized his wife to bring with her as many of their family she could manage on the journey, 'you may do as you like', but added that he absolutely needed the maid to mend his 'rags' and sew buttons on the ten shirts he had inherited from a dead member of the crew. If she needed assistance she was to write to a Mr Wheatley at the Prince George, and he hoped that her mother would now think he had acted rightly in quitting the 'temporary comforts of the Prison Ship' in order to secure a better income for his family. His gamble seems to have paid off: Thomas Wells survived the war and died in 1825.

Surviving correspondence between William and Ann Young also demonstrates the anguish of separation. Ann's father owned an established firm of shipbuilders and shipowners in London. She married William in 1789 and they set up home in Torrington Street, off Ratcliff Highway. They had a large family of five sons and four daughters, and when William went to sea the couple found separation difficult, though both were devout and took comfort from religion. Their correspondence was often irregular. For example, on 4 April 1801, Young (serving under Lord Keith on his expedition to Egypt) wrote to say that he had not heard from Ann since the previous November, partly because a brig carrying mail had been captured off Gibraltar. He certainly thought that the long absence from his family was a sacrifice, hardly rewarded in monetary terms, but he reasoned that it was unavoidable given that he was a sailor, an officer, and it was wartime. At this stage in his career he had taken a decision to make a push for preferment, promising Ann that if it did not succeed he would find alternative employment. As it turned out, he was promoted and wrote to reassure his wife that their sons also stood to benefit if he continued to be successful:

> You know, my love, my sentiments respecting the service I am engag'd in, as a publick man, having gone thus far, it appears to me I must go further, and if I get no good from it, probably one day or other our dear Boys may, as they seem so determined, if they are spar'd to follow the Sea Life.[28]

As he had received orders to sail only a short time after his latest child was born, he did not know for a long time whether or not the baby, who had been born sickly, had survived or what name Ann had given it. She herself had been in such a weak state that he had written from Portsmouth to ask his mother-in-law to break the news of his sailing to his wife, rather than write directly to her himself. It is clear from their correspondence that Ann was eager for him to find employment ashore that would allow him to spend more time at home. In October 1805 he finally managed to secure a shore job as resident agent of transports at Deptford, where he remained until he retired.

Pain is obvious, also, in the correspondence between the Grant sisters and their father Samuel, a purser. Their mother, Jeanie Grant, suffered from some affliction that affected her sight and when Samuel Grant left to take up his post on the *Goliath* in 1801, the task of letter writing mostly fell to their middle daughter, Jean. She promptly wrote, 'My mother is as well as you left her she cryed all the time we was away for the first day that did her no good but she is very composed now but we all think it very od [*sic*] without you already only since the morning but I hope you will be home soon again.' Later Mrs Grant heard from a female friend whose husband was also serving on the *Goliath* that

Samuel had been ill. Worried at not receiving a letter, she instructed her daughter Jean to write saying, 'if you are not able to write yourself she desires you will get some one els [*sic*] to write as soon as possible and let her know what is the matter with you.' Gradually, Jeanie's eyes improved sufficiently to let her write short postscripts to her daughter's letters. Passionate and religious, these postscripts assuring Grant of her love, fidelity and trust in providence, contrast oddly with her daughter's careful prose. Examples include: 'my Dear life and soul my eyes is something better thank God fir it com hom [*sic*] soon as you can God bless you Jennie Grant', and 'I ever shall be yours for ever till Deth'. These brief notes assured Grant of her love, fidelity and trust in providence. Otherwise she relied on her daughters to help maintain their relationship, and they dutifully reported the state of her health and state of mind often with humorous naivety assuring their father, for example, that she was, 'always dying yet never dead'. The family had a strong Welsh identity and the daughters often sent their best wishes to the other Welshmen serving with their father. There was also the comforting fact that the family had strong connections with naval officers in Pembrokeshire (including Captains Tyler and Foley), to whom they could turn if in trouble.[29]

Some wives endured years of absence. Cuthbert Collingwood's (see Plate 9) career was so demanding that his wife hardly ever saw him. The son of an insolvent Newcastle trader, Collingwood joined the navy when he was twelve, serving under his mother's cousin (a frigate captain), and slowly working his way up. Though his family was impoverished, he came from old Northumbrian stock, and allied himself firmly to values of respectability and selflessness. In 1791 when he was 42 and well established, he married Sarah Blackett, the daughter of John Erasmus Blackett, Mayor of Newcastle. The couple had two daughters: Sarah born in 1792, and Mary Patience in 1793; then war with France broke out. From 1793 until 1810, except for a short break during the Peace of Amiens in 1802 – 3, the dutiful Collingwood was continuously on active service. He served first with the Channel Fleet, then in the Mediterranean from 1795 – 98, then back with the Channel Fleet again blockading Brest from 1799 – 1802. By 1801 he had been absent from his family so long that Sarah was prepared to travel 500 miles to Plymouth from the family home in Morpeth, outside Newcastle in order to see him – even though it was mid-January. On this occasion, she left her younger daughter in the care of her family and travelled with eight-year-old Sarah or 'Little Sall'. On the very day after their arrival, Collingwood had to go to sea again and was unable to put into port until mid-March. Sarah settled in lodgings and wrote to her father that at least in Plymouth she had the satisfaction of seeing how much her husband was respected; people were very attentive and she received more invitations than she could accept, not wishing to leave her daughter too much on her own. In March Collingwood took his wife and daughter to sea but unluckily a storm blew up which made them both seasick, though at least they were able to experience something of what his life was like when he was away from them. During the short Peace of Amiens he was able to spend some time at home but in 1803 he was once more summoned to sea. He reported to a family friend, 'Sarah is bearing this event like a British lady, who far prefers her husband's honour to her own comforts'.[30]

Collingwood had served without a break since June 1803, and at the close of 1807, he sent Sarah his portrait, painted at Syracuse by the artist Giuseppe Sorcevani. She had not seen him for over five years and far from being pleased with the gift, the painting proved a great shock to her. Nor could she have been reassured by his next letter in which he remonstrated, 'The painter represented me as I am; not as once I was. It is time and toil that have worked the change, and not his want of skill.'[31] Sarah confessed in turn that she had grown 'moderately fat' but Collingwood gallantly averred he was glad of it since this suggested that she was at ease and not worn down with care and worry. In March 1808 he wrote to her with enthusiasm at the prospect of battling with the French one more time, 'what my heart is most bent on (I hope you will excuse me) is the glory of my country'.[32] By this time his priorities could have come as no surprise, though later that year, as his health failed, he repeatedly asked to be relieved so that he could come home. He died in 1810, without having seen his wife or family once in the last six years of his life.

Children

The education of children often proved another source of stress and anxiety since seamen with families often returned in their letters to the question of how their children were being educated at home during their absence. Collingwood wrote frequently to his wife Sarah, urging her to keep their daughters constantly employed. They were to read serious books, not throw away their time on novels and nonsense, and she was to make sure that they read aloud to her – not 'trifles' but history. He admitted that he could not advise her in detail on their daughters' education at such a distance but that did not prevent him from frequently returning to the topic. He was concerned that they might become too provincial in their speech and be socially disadvantaged by their accent and use of dialect words. In 1803, back at sea after some months with his family during the Peace of Amiens, he wrote that his chief anxiety was to see his daughters well and virtuously educated. Nothing, he thought, would be too good for them, if they proved wise and good-tempered. He particularly wanted the girls to be taught geometry, mathematics and astronomy. After the victory at Trafalgar when Sarah and their daughters were preparing to make the journey to London to be presented at court, he wrote to encourage the girls to make a note of the geography of the landscape they passed through and to find time to see everything of interest in the capital. Having witnessed at first hand the plight of women in war-ravaged Spain, and seen that they had fought with muskets alongside men, he toyed with the idea of having his girls learn to shoot in case England was ever invaded, and taught to swim in case they needed to flee across rivers as poor villagers in Spain had had to do. Later, close to death, he wrote to his daughter Sarah, emphasizing that his girls' future happiness and respectability depended on the application of their knowledge, manners and accomplishments, 'Never forget for one moment that you are a gentlewoman', he wrote.[33]

Captain Thomas Wells was also concerned about the welfare and education of his children. In 1805 he wrote to his wife Nancy, at home with her mother in Plymouth, explaining that now their daughter Anna Maria was beginning to speak, he wanted his wife to do all she could to prevent her learning the provincial dialect of the West of England from playmates and servants. He also told her to have their son vaccinated and warned that she should be, 'careful of washing him in the Kitchen as the draft from the Door is so great'.[34] His wife's reactions to such needless advice are not recorded. For a long while their correspondence was irregular because Wells was posted to Scandinavian waters where there were few means of conveying letters to England so his comments on the children's welfare were bound to be random. Captain Thomas Young wrote in similar sententious vein to his wife Ann, explaining that he wanted his sons to apply themselves to French and Latin, as it would be useful to them when they entered the navy and were posted abroad, and he also wanted them to learn how to draw. For long periods it was Ann's responsibility to ensure that the sons were properly educated for their future career, though she was also able turn to her own family for support.

At times wives sought advice from absent husbands – particularly if their children's education required additional expenditure. Jeanie Grant, though often unwell, seems to have kept a careful eye on her daughters' schooling: her middle daughter Jean explained breathlessly in a letter to her father, 'My mother desires me to tell you that she has taken Peggy from Thomases Skool there is such rude children at it that if she be there much longer she will be as bad as they and she can not think of letting her go there any longer but there is a very good school at Tinby we hear for £20 a year if you like to bestow that on her my mother will put her to it'.[35] Jean was learning fast and before bringing up the question of school fees she was careful to give her father the good news: one of their three cows had calved, which was a welcome New Year's present. Even though the day-to-day responsibility for bringing up children rested with wives at home, husbands were still expected to be able to make key decisions, and wives had to meet expectations as best they could.

Managing finances

The wives of seamen, left alone to run households and oversee family finances for long periods, needed to be adept at accounts and were sometimes required to be able to invest sensibly the lump sums their husbands accrued from prize money. Wives could turn to male relatives and to their husband's agents for financial advice but as many men from the middling sort hoped to make their fortune in wartime, or at least enough to confirm their middling status, husbands, anxious about their financial affairs, wanted to be able to depend on their wives' good sense.

If wives borrowed, they had to borrow wisely. Jeanie Grant, still suffering from poor eyesight, asked her daughter Jean to explain to her husband Samuel that she had borrowed money from a respectable member of their social circle in Pembroke. Grant duly received this rather incoherent account, 'My mother desires me to tell you that she has been forced to borrow ten pounds from Mr Leach also all the money that is in the house besides she has had so many things to pay that you does not think any thing about'.[36] While Jean seems to have accurately reproduced the tenor of her mother's grumblings, Grant might have received a more tactful account if his wife had been able to write in person. As a purser, Grant could be paid several years in arrears when his accounts were approved; his livelihood therefore depended on meticulous bookkeeping and his family had to be careful with money. An income tax bill, found with Grant's correspondence, indicates that his declared income for the year ending 5 April 1801 was just under £100.00, although bank statements from Coutts show that he was worth much more than this. Some of his financial business also seems to be tallied in an account under his wife's name. Grant's painstaking accounting obviously registered with his wife and daughters: when they were unable to draw fully on the bill he send them from Jamaica in 1802, they wrote giving full details which they repeated in subsequent letters, presumably in case the first went astray.

Matthew Flinders had hoped to win financial independence after Sir Joseph Banks supported his appointment to survey the Australian coastline in 1801. He also hoped to avoid a long separation from his sweetheart Ann, so married her quietly and tried to take her with him to Port Jackson. His plan was discovered, however, and the Admiralty refused her permission to travel with him. Ann returned to her family with a miniature of her husband, few instructions about his finances and no means of corresponding regularly with him as he headed for the other side of the world. When Ann complained that his leaving her to go on such a long voyage of discovery was proof that he cared more for his profession than he did for her, he wrote that they could barely have existed in England on his naval pay, that they would have been deprived even of necessaries, and that he depended on this risky employment to secure them a comfortable life. He always presented his personal struggle between love and ambition in this apparently logical way, maybe hoping to secure the best of both worlds: Ann and fame. Yet in fairness he could not have guessed that the French would accuse him of spying and imprison him on Mauritius, keeping him from her six years longer.

Flinders sent bills home to his agent and Ann was permitted to draw £40 annually from this fund. This was hardly enough to live on comfortably, and though Flinders authorized her to write to obtain an increase if the allowance proved inadequate, in reality he was expecting her family to help support her. Yet he remained status conscious: not only did he want his wife to send him newspaper reports of his exploits, he also instructed her to dress and behave in a manner suitable to his station. In his letters he asked Ann to obtain statements of his affairs from his agent and from his brother who was helping to arrange transactions with the agent. In time Ann became more active in her husband's financial affairs, tactfully suggesting that she should be permitted to pay an annual sum for board and lodging to her stepfather, Mr Tyler, a clergyman of only modest means. Flinders duly wrote to Tyler, proposing an annual sum of £30 – £40, and also to his agent to double his wife's annual allowance so that she could pay the sum. Yet he expected his wife to take the initiative and inform the agent of the date when the change should take place and later deal with his investments, although she could turn to her stepfather for advice. She was loyal to Flinders, though when he married her he had misrepresented their situation and should certainly have taken the precaution of consulting with the influential Sir Joseph Banks before trying to take her to Australia. During their long separation, she did all she could to maintain Banks's interest in her husband's career, writing to him when it seemed as if Flinders might be returning home, and copying extracts from her husband's letters for Banks's information. This produced some financial benefit: when Flinders returned, Banks helped to get him an advance from the Admiralty towards the costs of producing a full account of his voyage.

Not all women were so reliable when their husbands were away for years at a time. Admiral Collingwood's wife, Sarah, proved disappointingly inept at managing his financial affairs. While Collingwood praised Sarah's patience and equanimity during his absence as proof of her wisdom and resignation to the inevitable situation of a naval wife in wartime, he became increasingly frustrated at her inability to manage money. Collingwood set duty and honour above mere wealth and believed at first that his wife held the same views. When, in 1799, a family friend wrote to congratulate him on winning some prize money, he replied that although it was comforting not to have financial worries, he did not think wealth had anything to do with happiness, and neither, he believed, did his Sarah:

> Your sentiments of her brought a pleasure to my heart that the prizes never did. It is that calm and wise temperament of mind that can adapt itself to our circumstances, whatever they may be, that makes my wealth. I am persuaded were they more confined she would possess a peaceful composure under them, and if ever our good fortune advances them, no body will use them more creditably to themselves or more beneficially to their society than she will.[37]

Yet as Collingwood's career advanced, Sarah grew increasingly worldly – and who could begrudge her some pleasure since her husband was never at her side? She busied herself with home improvements, and accompanying her daughters as she introduced them to society. Collingwood's pay as an admiral was £1000 per annum but after Trafalgar he began to accumulate more money. At first he was pleased that Sarah should be enjoying a better social life on the strength of his fame and increasing popularity but then she began to outspend his income. On 27 April 1806 Collingwood, newly awarded a peerage, wrote to his wife explaining that his sister had told him he should come home to supervise his affairs. He believed, however, that it was his duty to remain at sea, where he was needed more, and airily wrote that he had too little information to offer any guidance on the subject; he trusted that his brother would take care of everything. All the same, typically of the middling sort, he evinced an anxiety about getting into debt:

> My bankers tell me that all my money in their hands is exhausted by fees on the peerage, and that I am in their debt, which is a new epoch in my life, for it is the first time I was ever in debt since I was a Midshipman. Here I get nothing; but then my expenses are nothing, and I do not want it, particularly now that I have got my knives, forks, teapot, and the things you were so kind as to send me.[38]

Sarah spent the summer of 1808 in Brighton with her daughters, dancing at the Prince of Wales's fancy balls, which some members of the family thought reprehensible when her husband was away serving his country. By 1809 Collingwood could ignore his domestic affairs no longer. Unfortunately, his wife was now under great pressure from her father, Blackett, an extravagant man who had begun to use Collingwood's money as his own in order to settle debts and entertain lavishly. In earlier years, before Blackett got into financial trouble, he had been a great support to Sarah while her husband was away at sea. In 1795 Collingwood had written to thank his father-in-law for looking after his wife and baby daughters, 'They do not know the want of a father's care while your protection is over them'.[39] He did not wholly blame his wife: he understood that she would gladly obey him if she were able to resist her father. Yet he now took strong measures to preserve his fortune for his two daughters, considering it his first duty to provide for them. He wrote to his agent to explain that in future his wife could only draw bills in her own name for £2000 a year, and that if she exceeded that sum the bills would not be honoured. His daughters' bills would be paid in London, where they were at school, and the account would be sent to him. The funds for his wife and children were now quite distinct and if his wife chose to be extravagant, less would remain for her to spend in future. He conjectured that since his elevation to the peerage, the newspapers had carried exaggerated reports of his fortune and that perhaps his wider family had felt that economy was unnecessary. Privately, he believed that no one had been so long at sea for so little proportionate reward.

What particularly enraged Collingwood was that his father-in-law had borrowed £2200 from him in order to pay off debts and then, without his knowledge, repaid the sum with shares in a fire insurance company without 'any more question than if I had been a bit of sea weed'.[40] The association with low commerce involved in this transaction touched directly on Collingwood's social pretensions; he ordered that his name be erased immediately from the company records. When Collingwood had been made a lord, Walter Spencer Stanhope, Member of Parliament for Carlisle, had moved in the House of Commons that a pension be granted to Lady Collingwood and her daughters so that she would be better able to support the peerage – the implication being that her husband's income alone would be inadequate. As Collingwood became more depressed and unwell at sea, he reflected on the embarrassment of this interference, and on the apparent slight when the government in 1809 promoted more admirals but stopped short of making senior vice-admirals full admirals. Collingwood now saw that he would never fly a full admiral's flag at his main top, and he thought he knew the reason why. The fire insurance business, he confided in a letter to his sister, established his character as a 'mercantile jobber'. How could the King respect someone who dealt in insurance? He surmised that his Majesty, protecting the dignity of his flag, could not 'be very anxious to have it an insurance beacon'.[41]

Certainly Sarah's financial mismanagement helped to embitter the final months of Collingwood's life. The extravagance of his wife and daughters proved a great disappointment – but then, he had built up high expectations of them and had never been able to spend enough time at home to ensure that they all absorbed his own strict principles. Just months before his death he wrote with bitter humour to a family friend, 'Don't you think Lady Collingwood is well prepared for her widowhood: she will make an admirable widow. I suppose she must go through the ceremony just as if she had a husband all this time.'[42] He left over £163,000 on his death and Sarah, who survived him by nine years, found herself comfortably off. She moved with her daughters to Tynemouth and there they enjoyed a social round to which her husband's fame and comparative wealth had admitted them.

Opportunities and benefits

Naval wives from the middling sort were generally aware of the figure they cut in society and understood that they needed to exercise judgement in their patterns of consumption. They often benefited from their husband's ability to buy expensive goods more cheaply overseas, and sometimes husbands could trade these goods to boost their domestic income. William Wilkinson, master on the warship *Minotaur*, wrote to his wife Sally from the Elsinore Roads on 14 August 1807 explaining that he had been on shore and bought about 34 lbs of tea for £5 2s. He anticipated that the tea would last them a long time if he could get it home safely. She replied in November that she had, 'got the trunk home and the tea is very good'. Wilkinson also purchased alcohol, some of which the couple sold and some they kept for themselves. In similar vein, Thomas Young asked his wife to tell her father that he had bought two pipes of good wine from Oporto but that he would keep it on board and bring it back himself to avoid paying freight. Naval wives had other opportunities to enhance their social standing that were largely denied to other women of their class. For example, they were sometimes able to display exotic presents that their husbands sent them from abroad. Fanny wrote diffidently to Nelson in Leghorn, 'If you can get a little cambric for ruffles and pocket handkerchiefs well and good but prey don't load yourself with presents thank you.' Later she was happy to thank him for sending gold chains that she had had made up into beautiful bracelets, and explained with satisfaction that she had now worn in public the Italian flowers he had sent her, 'which were much noticed'.[43]

Fanny's early married life with Nelson from 1788 had been dogged by money worries when he was out of favour with the Admiralty and unable to get a ship. The couple lived in Burnham Thorpe, Norfolk, on Nelson's half-pay of £100 a year, supplemented by allowances of £100 a year to each of them from their respective uncles. When Nelson married Fanny, he may have expected that she would inherit considerable wealth from her uncle, the president of Nevis, but no such inheritance materialized and this may have added to her anxiety not to waste money. Fanny never really lost the habit of economy, even after Nelson reckoned that his station in life needed to be marked by a certain standard of conspicuous consumption. Fanny, coming from the West Indies, may have been schooled in the narrow-minded, precise etiquette that women from the colonial ruling class there were careful to maintain. Janet Schaw, for example, travelling from Scotland to Antigua in 1774, recorded that it was the custom for young ladies there to touch nothing stronger than limejuice and water.[44]

Yet if Fanny's social life in Norfolk had been mostly limited to her husband's family circle, in some respects her lifestyle actually improved once he returned to active service in 1793, although she was left to care for his ailing father. During 1794 she indulged in a round of social visits at various places so that Nelson was often unsure where he should address his letters to her. Afterwards, she travelled with her father-in-law to stay in Bath until 1797, though she also took short breaks in London and Bristol. Nelson's father was grateful for her company: he would not let her contribute towards the housekeeping, only to the house rent. Not only did Fanny's social circle become more varied; she also resumed piano lessons and enjoyed a greater choice of polite entertainments, including plays and concerts. Occasionally, naval captains who knew Nelson called on her to pay courtesy visits. Yet during this time she remained extremely attentive to Nelson's interests. For example, in 1794, at Nelson's request, she paid her respects to his patron Admiral Viscount Samuel Hood when he returned from command of the Mediterranean fleet. Eager to please, Fanny wrote to say that Lord and Lady Hood had made her very welcome; she was anxious to assure her husband that she had not let him down, 'I dined with them was cheerful and well dressed'.[45] In the same letter Fanny assured him that she did nothing in his absence that she thought would give him cause to say that he wished it had been otherwise. 'No, not for the world.' As Nelson had by now taken a long-term mistress at Leghorn, Fanny's warm assurances that she regarded his feelings above all else may have made him feel just a little uncomfortable.

Officers' wives could generally command a degree of social deference, particularly during invasion scares, since the public was well aware that the navy was vital to the nation's safety and also supposed that naval wives possessed more authoritative information from the combat zone than that printed in the newspapers. Those whose husbands became famous enjoyed much greater social attention. Once Nelson's exploits at the battle of St Vincent in February 1797 were publicized, Fanny discovered that prominent people favoured her with their notice and sent her newspaper reports of her husband. By the time Nelson was granted a knighthood, in May 1797, Fanny was able to comment that her new title sat as easy on her as if she had been born to it. After Nelson's promotion to rear-admiral, she was jubilant when an acquaintance was able to procure for her a much prized ticket for Bath's Catch Club on Ladies' night (there was only one such event a year and everybody of title or fashion in the town was present.) In her letters to Nelson she took delight in relating the general admiration for him and repeated the praise that she had heard from various individuals. Yet while she appreciated all the marks of respect she now received, the sensitivity with which she registered her heightened social status suggests that she was not perfectly comfortable in her new role.

If it was already difficult to draw a line between the upper tier of the middling ranks and the gentry, successful naval officers added to this difficulty because those from the middling sort might be rewarded with promotion to aristocratic rank. Their social elevation could be a mixed blessing for their wives. On the one hand, while their husbands were at sea they might have great freedom in choosing and decorating new homes. After her husband was made a baron, Sarah Collingwood decided to move from their small house at Morpeth in order to take up residence at Chirton, an estate which Collingwood's cousin had bequeathed him for life. Although Collingwood much preferred the Morpeth countryside to coal-polluted Chirton, he was resigned to the fact that the new house befitted a gentleman more. Once his fortune improved sufficiently for them to think of purchasing, Nelson's wife, Fanny, was also entrusted to choose a new home. He wrote to Fanny in February 1797 to say that she could buy a house near Norwich or anywhere else, and that he would like it if she did. In the event, nothing was decided until later in 1797 when, as a Rear-Admiral, he was in England recuperating from the loss of his arm. He then purchased Roundwood, a substantial house two miles north of Ipswich, though he had no time to view it before returning to sea. Fanny was left to manage the improvements and decoration of the house during 1798 – 9. The couple never lived there and, once Nelson had separated from Fanny, he allowed Emma Hamilton to find an alternative house for him in England. She chose Merton Place and decorated it to her own flamboyant taste. Emma's husband, Sir William, commented that, 'a seaman alone could have given a fine woman full power to chuse & fit up a residence without seeing it himself', and in fact a seaman's peripatetic lifestyle meant that this was not uncommon. [46]

On the other hand, if their husbands became famous, naval wives had to deal with a certain loss of privacy. In 1799, for example, the *Gentleman's Magazine* printed an alleged extract from Nelson's letter to his wife Fanny after the Battle of the Nile (see Plate 10). In 1800 the *London Chronicle* reported that, 'Lord Nelson has transmitted to his Lady a Variety of seeds from the Coast of Egypt, which her Ladyship has sent to a gardener at Ipswich, in order to be raised.'[47] In 1801 a full account of Nelson's Christmas visit to William Beckford at his gothic folly, Fonthill Abbey, appeared in the *Gentleman's Magazine*. As Nelson travelled with Sir William and Emma Hamilton, leaving Fanny at home, the increasing publicity that surrounded their marriage must have been unwelcome to her (see Plate 12).

Marital indiscretions

As with high ranking naval wives, we learn more about the marriages and relationships of the middling sort if contemporaries found good cause to report irregularities. Long absences put a strain on naval marriages at all levels of society and during the wars against France, 1793 – 1815, the more efficient the navy became in keeping men healthy at sea for long periods in order to win the war, the greater the damage. *A New Collection of Trials for Adultery*, published in 1799, contains a number of crim. con. cases relating to absent naval officers from this social group. Titillating stories are recounted in detail, with scant reference to any underlying moral message. For example, Lieutenant George Hayes accused Joseph Carter, an opulent dealer in gold and silver lace, of having an affair with his wife. Hayes had command of the lugger *Experiment*, employed in the Channel service. When he was sent on a longer voyage with dispatches to Admiral St Vincent, he placed his wife and child in the care of her father and his sisters in Deptford, London. She began an affair with Carter and when she found herself pregnant she told her maid that she was going to post a letter and absconded to Hoxton where she and Carter lived as man and wife. After the birth, the child was sent away to be nursed and she returned to her Deptford home explaining that she had been abducted but, against all odds, had managed to retain her virtue. While her father was prepared to believe her story, her husband on his return was not so credulous. However, he had no proof of misconduct until he received a letter from an acquaintance who had spotted the adulterous pair in Hoxton (it had been misdirected to the *Experiment* and so did not reach him for a year). He sued for divorce and won damages of £400 while Carter was held up to ridicule in the press and in prints.

Another case, reported in the *Morning Chronicle* for Tuesday 20 July 1802 carries an explicit moral judgement:

> A Young woman who had only been married ten months summoned her husband for violently threatening to shoot her and her mother. The Defender said, that he had only just returned from sea, when, to his great surprise, he found her living in quality of a mistress with a gentleman of fortune, who had wrote to him several letters to commute with him for the injury he had occasioned to the young man, which he rejected with scorn. It appeared that the mother of the young woman was very criminal in encouraging the vices of her daughter.

The husband was released on promise of preserving the peace.

One of the most publicized divorce cases of the period concerned Captain Inglefield who had already gained notoriety in 1782 for having escaped the wreck of his ship, the *Centaur* with just a few officers (see Plate 13). Back on shore, he published a self-justifying account of his ordeal. Subsequently his conduct was fully vindicated at court martial and he was appointed to the command of the guard ship *Scipio* at Chatham. In 1785, while still a public figure, he accused his wife Ann of adultery with their black servant, James Webb. The racial element added to public interest and was widely reported. All early accounts assumed that Ann Inglefield was guilty. *The Morning Herald, and Daily Advertiser* for 20 July 1785 noted:

> The Captain of a guardship, at this time in commission, is said to have lately charged his lady with infidelity, and the suspected gallant is a *Negro* servant, -- They have in consequence agreed secretly to a separation, without the formality of writings; as the husband says there has already been *black and white* enough on the subject! [48]

Webb, who was on the crew list of Inglefield's ship and received no separate wages as a domestic servant, was ready to swear that his mistress had taken various sexual liberties with him. Yet when the full significance of taking an oath was explained to him, he became agitated and refused to swear any evidence against her. Webb's inconsistency meant that the case collapsed since, although Inglefield seems to have tried earlier to amass additional evidence, he had no other means of proving his wife's infidelity. Inglefield claimed that he had moved his wife to Singlewell, near Gravesend, so that they could be together, and he had taken her on board the *Scipio* with no other attendant than Webb. He alleged that rumours about her conduct caused him to ask his steward, McCarthy, to keep a special watch on his wife and on her relations with Webb while they were on board. In due course, McCarthy reported that, 'upon a certain day he did hear the boy called into the cabin to empty a basin of water, which he accordingly did'. He heard Webb return to the cabin afterwards, then the door being fastened on the inside and, 'presently afterwards he heard great struggling, and such a noise, that he concluded adultery had been committed between them'.[49] Yet Webb always denied the allegation as did Ann Inglefield, making the point that on the *Scipio* once she and her husband got up in the morning their bed was always stashed away and that it would take 20 minutes to get it ready again.

The truth of the case remains obscure. Either Inglefield was consumed with jealousy and over-sensitive about his wife's relations with her servant or, maybe, he had simply grown tired of his wife and wished to be rid of her. But Inglefield was not on trial. The Court blamed Webb for the collapse of the couple's conjugal happiness since there was no doubt that he had initially lied. In the subsequent pamphlet war between husband and wife there was a strong hint that Inglefield had formed another attachment. Certainly, Ann found supporters in the close-knit naval community at Greenwich, notably Mrs William Parker and her husband Captain Parker, then appointed to a guardship in the Medway, who refused to side with Inglefield as a brother officer, much to his chagrin. There were also other naval officers who disliked Inglefield and sneered at his social standing. Thomas Fremantle, for example, complained in 1794 of 'his hectoring manner, more like the bully of a bawdy house than a Gentleman'.[50]

The Inglefields' divorce proceedings were taken down in shorthand and published and, since both parties afterwards rushed into print with accusation and counter-accusation, some circumstances of Ann Inglefield's married life can be pieced together. Putting aside the sordid details of the divorce proceedings, they give a helpful indication of the typical preoccupations of a naval wife at this social level. Ann did not bring enough money in marriage to advance the ambitions of her husband and ultimately she failed to secure his loyalty. As the daughter of the shipbuilder Sir Thomas Slade, she had the interest of £3000 annually for the first ten years after her father's death, and then the interest of £1000 more. Yet the capital sum went to her children. On the death of her mother, the remainder of the family estate would be bequeathed in the same manner. Inglefield was therefore disappointed in the terms attached to his wife's modest fortune and ungallantly stated that he would not have married such 'an exceeding plain and awkward woman' if he had found them out before becoming too entangled in the relationship to retreat with honour.[51] His own father, a quarterman in Deptford dockyard, had died insolvent leaving a wife in distressed circumstances, so Inglefield was certainly in need of money to help support his elderly mother. He married Ann when a lieutenant on half pay, and Ann's mother let them live rent-free in one of the four cottages she owned in Greenwich. Inglefield then began to make his way in the world and later they were able to rent a house, which they furnished themselves.

When Inglefield became captain, he left instructions with his agent to let his wife have what money she needed while he was at sea. Yet during the divorce proceedings he declared that he was surprised on his return to discover how much she had spent when, as he said, it was common knowledge that if a captain were to appear with credit he would need all his pay to support the expense of entertaining on board. A pushy officer, he clearly expected that his wife would help him network in the social arena. On her own admission, Ann was shy and retiring and in any case had four children to bring up; but Inglefield roundly claimed that his wife did not share his wish to move up the social ladder, that his advancement actually depressed her and that he could never get her to take her proper place in society. Ann countered this by stating disingenuously that she did not have the clothes to appear in her proper station. Money seems to have been a root cause of the couple's differences but Ann denied in the strongest terms that her husband could ever accuse her of extravagance. Her defence reveals the kind of household accounting she would need to undertake when he was at sea. She wrote:

> Captain Inglefield was absent from Greenwich, two Years, two Months, and ten Days; on his Return to England, he had not, to the best of my Recollection, a Sixpence to pay on my Account, except one Quarter's Rent, and one Quarter's schooling for my eldest Daughter, the Quarters being nearly expired when he came home.

> From this faithful Relation of our Circumstances it is clear, that from the Time Captain Inglefield left me, I had to pay House Rent and Taxes, Repairs, and the Expences incidental to moving, together with new Furniture, and Household Linen (Articles we were much in want of) also to maintain my two eldest Children in Board and Education, and my youngest at Nurse; to these Expences are to be added, Servant's Wages and Cloaths for myself and three Children, two of whom were fitted up to appear suitable to Captain Inglefield's Rank, and sent, for the first Time, to a Boarding School.[52]

Ann was also entrusted to invest wisely. When Inglefield was in the West Indies, he sent her £200. She added to the sum and bought £300 worth of New South Sea Annuities in their joint names – which he sold and disposed of on his return.

After the couple separated, Ann tried to send her children into hiding when it became clear that she might lose custody of them. She was put under a court order to produce the children and later by the terms of the divorce settlement it was decreed that they should be brought up by their father – though she could visit them and receive their visits. Yet since Inglefield put the children to school in France (according to his wife because he could not afford to have them educated in England), regular visits would have been difficult. He gave his wife a parsimonious settlement of one fourth of his pay and the interest of her own fortune.

Frances Nelson's letters to her husband's prize agent, Alexander Davison, similarly reveal the social tightrope she had to walk during the break-up of her marriage. Her position was delicate: financially dependent on her husband, and facing the machinations of certain members of his family who decided that it was in their interest to support Nelson, the hero, rather than the unwanted wife, she had to work hard to safeguard her position. First, she had to be circumspect and ensure that Nelson could have no cause for complaint: if she had to make a domestic decision of any importance, she sought the approval of Davison and other advisors. Second, she had to indicate (to those aware of the marital rift) that she had no wish to antagonize Nelson further, and would take him back (as she may genuinely have wished to do), without recrimination. Third, she had to keep up appearances in order to salvage her social position, pride and self-respect. The career prospects of Josiah Nisbet, her son by her first marriage, would be affected by her success in this regard. Her letters therefore reveal a web of motives and a sly manipulation that her uncomfortable position encouraged.

After the Battle of the Nile in 1798, Fanny was largely dependent on newspapers and acquaintances for news of her husband because he wrote so rarely.[53] By April 1799, reports of her husband's behaviour with Lady Hamilton had filtered back to London. Fanny was critical of the situation but in her letters she shrewdly suggested that Nelson's ailing father suffered more, 'Mr Nelson made sure, of my Lord's coming home, there you may suppose how very much he feels it – two or three month absence [...] . Lord Hood always expressed his fears "that Sir W & Lady Hamilton would use <u>their influence</u>, to keep Lord Nelson with them: they have succeeded – ["]'[54] Gradually, references to her ill health became frequent, 'I have not been well for some time anziety [sic] will shake the strongest – and I never had to bost much of that good thing – I think a slow fever teizes one'.[55] She added that Nelson had hardly written for months. Later, she explained that she had heard from Lady Hamilton who reported that Nelson had recovered his health but still needed a good deal of nourishing. Fanny wrote of her fears for him, but her own health seems affected by an unvoiced jealousy, 'My head acks [*sic*] so very much I cannot write to my Lord – today'.[56] A postscript indicates further cause for irritation: Lady Hamilton had written kindly of Fanny's son, Josiah, who had promised to write to her *when he had time.*

In October 1800, Nelson finally told Fanny he was coming home and that he had asked Davison to take a house or good lodgings in London. Fanny communicated the news to Davison, adding 'Read the letter carefully and I think you will see it is best for us to go to an Hotel – it is impossible for me to send linen etc – to London our stock being too scanty to divide – and the expence of the servants travelling amounts to a large sum'.[57] She expressed a very proper diffidence, 'Now I have given you my opinion – you must say what you think I had better do – and I will do it.' But then she added, 'I wrote to my Husband yesterday both to Yarmouth & Harwich telling him I had just received his letter of Sept 20th – and ... therefore it was impossible for me to be in town, no house could be taken and got ready in a few days. I likewise mentioned the convenience of an Hotel'.[58] So she had pre-empted Davison's advice even as she requested it. However, when Davison apparently advised her to carry out Nelson's wishes, she duly departed for London.

If Nelson expected his wife to accept complacently his relationship with Emma, he was disappointed. His marriage disintegrated and in January 1801 Nelson left Fanny, granting her a generous settlement: half his income paid quarterly in advance. Fanny gave up their London house for Brighton and there she learnt from servants that Emma Hamilton had tried to hire the butler she had just dismissed. Emma allegedly said, 'I am extremely surprised at Lady Nelson's leaving London at this time of the year, giving up the house, and parting <u>with all the servants</u> – I cannot think the reason of it, to my knowledge Lord Nelson allows her 2000 a year and with that she might make a pretty [?] appearance – it looks very <u>odd</u>.' Fanny, clearly bitter, is quick to justify herself to Davison:

> none of us I believe like the servants to know our incomes – I can only say no Woman can feel the least attentions from a husband more than I do – and I will say I never will [*substituted for would, crossed out*] withhold from the world any thing that will [*'would' crossed out*] add to his credit – altho' mentioning the sum particularly I did not think right.[59]

During this time, Fanny emphasized that she lived 'very retired' – 'if possible I am more circumspect and cautious than any young miss of 16 '.[60] After Nelson's victory at Copenhagen, she considered taking a London house again but feared the expense. Typically, she presented this to Davison indirectly, quoting her father-in-law who believed that Nelson would give Fanny more money if she asked. 'I told him my spirits were so truly broken I dare not ask'.[61]

In 1801 Fanny travelled to London to make an appearance at court since honours had been conferred on her husband, but London made her bilious.[62] She mentioned this to Davison, writing that she had received news of Nelson's ill health and that his 'good father' wished him 'to have W. Hume and Dr Baillie – in short what the World call the best advice'. In a telling juxtaposition, she continued that she herself had been obliged to send for Dr Falconer by the desire of the apothecary. Dr Falconer had diagnosed 'great debility' and fever. The contrived contrast between what she thinks is due to herself (the attentions of an apothecary until, at his insistence, she called for a doctor), and due to her husband (the best available advice), invites the reader's pity even as she affects stoicism.[63]

Fanny kept the way open for a reconciliation. In March she explained to Davison, 'I am just returned from receiving the sacrament – and I now say if at any future time my Husband will make my home his home – I will receive him with joy; and whatever has passed shall never pass my lips'.[64] In June she wrote, 'If you have an opportunity – you may assure him that I never had any other wish than to please him I am ready willing & desirous [*last two words inserted*] to live with him, and will do every thing in my power to oblige him – I think I cannot say more If I cd.'[65] Yet she seems chiefly determined to repress bitterness and anger; the words '& desirous', added as an afterthought, do not convey deep love. Fanny was constrained by etiquette but her earlier words, 'A conscious rectitude will carry me through, let what await me', seem most convincingly indicative of her character.[66] She may have been physically weak but these letters reveal a strong-minded, manipulative woman.

Other naval wives learnt that their husbands had been unfaithful or bigamous only when they claimed a pension on his death. For example, the papers of the Charity for the Relief of Officers' Widows record the case of Mrs Ann Barnard, who was placed on the pension list as the widow of Lieutenant Thomas Barnard of the *Cordelia* in July 1809. Subsequently another person signing herself Helen Barnard claimed the pension and investigations proved that when Thomas married Ann, he was indeed already married to Helen. The charity had no option but to substitute Helen for Ann on the pension list.

Two other series of letters are illuminating: those from William Wilkinson, a ship's master, to his wife between 1807 and 1809, giving an insight into domestic life at the lower tier of this middle rank and, in contrast, a series of

56 letters from Susanna Middleton to her sister between 1805 and 1808. These throw light on the life of a naval wife further up the middling ranks and one, moreover, who was able to accompany her husband abroad for a period of three years while he was based in Gibraltar.

The lovesick master

Wilkinson served as ship's master, first on the *Minotaur* under Captain Mansfield and then on a captured Danish ship *Christian VII* in the Channel Fleet. The master was the most senior of the warrant officers, responsible for the navigation of the ship and entitled to mess with the senior officers in the wardroom on a two-decker, so that his social status would have been a little unsure. A master's annual pay varied according to the rate of the ship, from just over £151 in a first rate in 1808 to just over £88 in a sixth-rate. Wilkinson was at Copenhagen Roads during the bombardment of the city and the capture of the Danish navy by Lord Gambier in 1807. During this period he wrote regularly to his wife Sally at their lodgings in Church Street, Kensington. He retired from the Navy in 1810 due to persistent ill health and was appointed Master-Attendant of the Royal Victualling Yard in Deptford. He died aged 80 in 1857. Sally Wilkinson was not well educated: her only surviving letter is poorly punctuated and written in a blotchy script. At the time of writing, she had a young baby girl – also called Sally – and later there was a son called Billy, already keenly anticipated by his parents.

When the couple married Wilkinson had already gone to sea, otherwise, as he writes in his letters, he would have taken any employment ashore to be with his wife. Since he lived to a ripe old age, his ill health at sea was probably a symptom of his unhappiness at their separation. Polished writers from the upper ranks often began family letters in an informal way (Admiral Codrington, for example, often inserted his wife's name in the first conversational sentence), but Wilkinson always began his letters with 'My Dear Wife', at once more proprietorial and suggestive of his concern with personal status. Many details in his letters indicate that he was both deferential and anxious to get on in the world. For example, on 8 July 1807 he reported that on board ship, 'I dined with Captain Mansfield who drank your health – and you may be sure I very politely drank the health of his family in return for his civility.' Wilkinson was continually urging his wife to improve her skills and particularly to practise writing in a small, regular hand. On 29 Jan 1809 he wrote, 'Try all you can to please me, by improving your mind, by reading and writing.' He imagined that when he returned, they would go regularly to church and he clearly envisaged a shared lifestyle of hard work, self-restraint and respectability. His letters reflect how delicately poised the social position of masters in the navy was.[67] They were the earliest warrant officers to rise in social and professional standing: in 1808, they were officially recognised as 'Warrant Officers of Commissioned Rank' and afterwards generally accepted among the wardroom officers – which was the social test of gentility. By 1814 when the widows of masters at Plymouth petitioned the Charity for the Relief of Officers' Widows for an increase in their pensions, they felt entitled to base their claim on rank, explaining that due to the respectable rank their husbands had held in the navy, they had been classed with lieutenants in respect of half pay, and so they hoped no distinction would be made in respect of widows' pensions.

Sally Wilkinson hoped to see her husband whenever his ship was in port, but her travel arrangements had to be economical. In November 1807 she wrote, 'I was thinking as you cannot come to see us, our dear little babe and myself must come to see you, should it be likely you stay at St Helens any time, in less than three weeks I should be able if you think you could afford it.' In June 1808, Wilkinson (now serving with the Channel Fleet on HMS *King Christian VII*, a captured Danish ship) wrote to Sally from Portsmouth explaining how she should travel from London to meet him. The morning coach from Fetter Lane would pick her up at Kensington and then he would be at the India Arms in Portsmouth to meet her. She must book a place for the baby when she booked one for herself, and if not all her things were ready they could be sent on afterwards. He added that as she was not fond of writing there was no need for her to reply. Meanwhile, he would go on shore to take lodgings for her and to hire a girl who would help look after the baby; he hoped they would live 'tolerable cheap and comfortable'. A year later, in April 1809, he was at sea off Torbay and wrote explaining that his ship would put in at Plymouth. As he was likely to be there only a fortnight, he did not think he could visit her because the distance was too great. One difficulty in arranging to meet was specifying the day on which the ship might come into port so that his wife knew when to book lodgings and did not waste money by arriving too early.

Money was always a concern for Wilkinson. Sally had to be extremely careful with money and sometimes relied on her relations, Mary and Fanny, or on Wilkinson's uncle. When Wilkinson was recuperating at the naval hospital in Portsmouth, he wrote to Sally on 19 December 1807, 'I recollect you said that the Doctors Bill will come in about Christmas – I shall enclose a Ten pound note (a Portsmouth one) but you will see it is payable in London, you can pay Mary and Fanny out of it – but pray be carefull [sic] and write down every thing for money is very scarce – and write by return of Post to say you have received it.' He was increasingly determined not to go to sea again if he could help it because of his health, and because of the travelling expenses incurred when his ship put into port and they tried to see each other. In this letter he gloomily sets out their finances taking her into his confidence if only to explain the reason for economy. His uniform cost him £60 a year; she could not live on less than £60, making their joint needs of £120 a year. They paid another £20 a year in rent, making total of £140 but at this time his annual income was only £146 in pay and dividends from stocks, leaving barely £6 a year for clothes.[68] On this calculation they would find it impossible to see each other, as there would be no money to pay for coach hire or lodging etc. – or even for the posting of letters. He was owed a period of half-pay but was concerned to find that he was in debt to his agent to the sum of £7.15s. On 18 September 1808 he wrote to explain that he had been forced to draw on her for a bill of £25 and when it was claimed she must get the money to pay it. Their money troubles continued into 1809. Early that year Sally wrote to Wilkinson complaining that he had sent only £5 when she had expected at least £10. He replied on 20 February explaining that he had not been able send more as he lacked money to pay for his food and washing, although since receiving her letter he had sold his flute for two and a half guineas. By his reckoning she ought to have had money in hand so he was hurt at her reproach and reassured her that their interests were as one and that everything he owned was as much hers as his – he would send her another £5 soon. On 17 July 1809 he wrote, 'I see in the paper that part of the Copenhagen Prize money began paying last Wednesday. We must try all we can not to brake into it but keep it as a reserve.'

Wilkinson encouraged his wife to be happy that their child was not a boy since boys were so unmanageable, especially in the absence of a father – the prevalent opinion echoed in Captain Codrington's letters. He wrote in 1807 describing the contemporary approach to education for both boys and girls: 'I hope you read and write a great deal, for mind you, I never intend that Sally shall go to school, her dear mother must teach her every thing. Billy [as yet unborn] I shall teach myself if please God I am at home, if not he may (when old enough) go to school – but by that time I hope I shall be home with my sweet wife never to leave her again, and then I shall take delight in instructing both, if God is pleased to send us them.'[69]

Sally's letter demonstrates that naval wives were avid readers of newspaper items that gave news of the fleet. She wrote, 'I see by the paper Captain M has left your ship and McVicar made commander Mr Bell of course is First Lieutenant', and then she enquired if he was due any prize money. Such public topics were fairly safe and must have helped give seamen the sense they were making history, but letters often went astray or were delayed. Wilkinson frequently complained to his wife that she did not write often enough and suggested, rather patronizingly, that she should be more systematic, preparing letters for the post before receiving his, only leaving a space on the paper to answer particular queries he might have. From Elsinore roads he wrote on 14 August 1807 explaining that he had made particular arrangements to get his letters to London from Yarmouth. After she had received his first, she was to be sure to make it a rule to drop a letter to the post office on the same day of every week whether she had heard from him or not. When there was a possibility they could meet at Yarmouth, he wrote to say he thought he would have to send for her as he could not do without her but added, 'so if you don't wish to come you must say you are very ill, and yet I know you wont like to tell a story'.[70] Obviously it was always a possibility that wives would not want to travel just to spend a few days with their husbands.

Wilkinson was also concerned about how his wife amused herself in his absence and worried about her spending time with new friends, arguing that visiting their relatives ought to be amusement enough. He wrote:

> I am afraid that you cannot find enough to do, when one's mind is not
> employed or we have nothing to do, we are apt to get low … I hope
> you will not get too fond of visitings or making new acquaintants,
> which cannot be done without expence [*sic*] – you can take your
> walks with Fanny for the good of your health, and visiting our relatives
> and being visited by them ought to satisfy us – when I am home I shall
> always find amusement enough within the circle of our relations.[71]

Wilkinson realized that this advice might not be welcome and asked his wife not to take offence as it was meant for their mutual welfare. Yet later, when Sally again complained that she found life at home tiresome, he returned to his theme and commented that he was sure she had too little to do. He continued that he was beginning to think that her uncle had been right and that it would have been better if she and Fanny had found some employment after their marriage – although such a course of action would probably have had an impact on their social pretensions. Similarly, we know from Matthew Flinders' letters that while he encouraged his wife to visit friends so that gloomy fears for his safety would not prey upon her mind, he too did not assume she would cultivate a wider circle of acquaintances. But Sally Wilkinson had her own fears for their marriage. Early in 1809 she wrote to her husband asking if there were any 'bad ladies' on board his ship. Happily, he was able to reply that two days after his ship had joined the fleet under the command of Admiral Lord Gambier, the admiral, 'a very good and strict religious man', had issued an order saying that no such women should be permitted to come on board the ships of the fleet as it was 'to the great annoyance of married men and against all decency and morality'. Wilkinson added that if any officer broke the order, his name was to be passed up to Gambier and he did not doubt that the officer would be punished. Although the Evangelical Gambier was unpopular with the fleet, as crews resented his determination to impose his own narrow code on them, his pious reputation had its uses in letters home.[72]

Wilkinson's plan was to earn sufficient money to be able to maintain his wife in domestic ease but in the first instance it was more important to him that they should be together. He wrote that if he found that he could only quit the sea by going on half pay, he would have to make ends meet by finding a supplementary job on shore. She might be able to help boost their income by finding a job as well – they should not, he thought, sacrifice their comforts to a little false pride about status.

The dockyard commissioner's wife

In 1805, Susanna Middleton sailed for Gibraltar with her husband, Captain Robert Gambier Middleton, who was on his way to take up his post as Commissioner of the dockyard there. She took her maids, Betty and Drivers, and at once began a regular correspondence with her sister, Miss Martin Leake, still living at the family town house in Harley Street, London. Her description of their convoy's difficult passage across the Bay of Biscay helps to explain why so many officers were reluctant to take their wives to sea with them. On 4 September, 12 days into their passage, she wrote:

> I think if we are a fortnight longer we shall not only be made distress'd for clean linen, but for provision, the water is getting now almost black, which makes the tea & coffee so bad at breakfast, that it is really difficult to get it down.[73]

The eggs, she admitted were tolerable but supplies were running low. Dinner was not bad, though the cook was 'one of the nastiest creatures you ever saw' and one of the worst cooks, too, not ashamed to serve pieces of stinking meat.

> At supper I generally eat some biscuit and drink some wine & water soon after eight and go to bed at nine, for if I sit in any of the cabins below it makes me half sick, there are such a collection of dreadful nasty smells, in short we are all completely sick of living on board a ship.[74]

Then the convoy met with equinoctial gales. After a lengthy passage of five weeks, the family party finally arrived in Gibraltar where new perils awaited them. On 28 September Susanna wrote to her sister:

> We are all of us eat up almost with nats or mouskitoes, poor Drivers beauty is quite spoil'd for the present, & my hands & arms are quite in a fever, but I hope they will get tired of us soon, or that when the rain comes on there will be fewer of them.[75]

But even in November she was sleeping in a gauze mask and wearing gloves to avoid insect bites.

In Gibraltar Susanna had to make her own amusements. Her husband rose at first light, tended to his garden and then got to the dockyard by 9 a.m. He was sometimes back by 1 or 2 p.m. when the couple took a walk before dining at 4 p.m. They might entertain one or two naval officers at dinner but the guests left promptly when the evening gun fired at 8 p.m. Susanna explained to her sister that she was determined to find a great deal of amusement in her farmyard because she was left much by herself. It would seem, however, that it was to view it rather than to tend the animals herself, though some middle-ranking women of the time seem to have taken pride in caring for their poultry themselves. In 1794 a woman called Hannah wrote to the *Gentleman's Magazine* explaining that her poultry gave her great pleasure and asking if readers knew of a guide to treat the distempers that fowls were prone to catch. Susanna also kept poultry and was fattening up two turkeys for Christmas. When tired of reading she would go and observe her ten little pigs, one of which was also destined to grace the festive season's table. Again, other remarks in her letters suggest that it was actually her maids who did all the work.

Few people in Gibraltar could entertain, Susannah wrote, because they had neither the facilities to give a dinner nor the food to offer. Her sister sent her food packages via naval ships to avoid paying freight. Susanna asked for sheep from England because mutton, however bad, was expensive in Gibraltar; also baskets of salt, beef, casks of butter and, on one occasion, muslin gowns and hats, nankeen bonnets and gingerbread. When finally this shipment arrived, the bonnets were covered in mould and cobwebs and the gingerbread was wet but Susanna was optimistic that the hats would brush up well and the gingerbread only needed to be put in the oven. Gibraltar, she reported, was a place to save money, as there was simply nothing to buy. Yet because she could obtain goods cheaply from England, she was able to support Middleton's career when she did entertain. All the same, the lack of consumer goods in Gibraltar meant that she and her maid Driver were forced to make her husband's shirts and even stuff a mattress and pillows with the wool from their sheep. Her self-conscious account of these domestic labours are a gesture towards an earlier tradition of housekeeping, now disappearing as the middling ranks aspired to greater gentility. However, her husband's posting allowed Susanna to engage more actively with the world. She took up an interest in botany and exchanged plant seeds with acquaintances in England. Captain Berry, a keen botanist, spent time with them in Gibraltar and on his return to England asked Susanna to send him specimens of indigenous plants for Lady Cavendish. Susanna worried in subsequent letters about the exact meaning of 'indigenous plants'. Were they a separate species or simply plants native to the country? She wished to get it right because her husband's posting now offered her an opportunity to be of service to a member of the aristocracy and therefore extend her social influence. Middleton later asked his wife's sister to send seeds out to Gibraltar for his own use. To show her appreciation, Susanna was able to send home to her family oranges, lemons and a drum of Smyrna figs.

Susanna's letters also throw light on the ways in which some women from the middling ranks were able to help their social inferiors. She and her sister were the means of ensuring that the wife of Captain Middleton's clerk, Mrs Reeves, obtained regular support for herself and her family. She had been left in England with the children but although Reeves was paid £150 p.a. and received an allowance of food, he rarely sent money home. The sisters arranged for Reeves to remit quarterly payments to his wife by means of Susanna's sister in Harley Street. On 13 March 1807, Susanna explained that her husband only kept Reeves on as his clerk for the sake of his poor wife because Reeves had sworn that if for any reason he left the captain, his wife would not get a farthing more. Later that year, on 15 June, Susanna revealed that Reeves had sold all his furniture, absconded, and had last been seen in a vessel bound in convoy for England. This was sad news for Mrs Reeves because her regular income would cease. Susanna confided to her sister, 'I fear'd he would not long submit to paying his wife ten pounds a quarter. ... I only hope he will not go to his wife and get the little money she has poor woman, all Capt M: can now do for her is to send her all the wages due to him.'[76] On 28 July she wrote again to explain that all the money Captain Middleton could collect for Mrs Reeves amounted to £7 5s 4½d and she asked her sister to pay this sum to her.

Susanna's accounts of her livestock and ingenious housekeeping give the impression of a resourceful, indefatigable wife, well able to cope with the rigours of her husband's service abroad. In fact her health seems to have been delicate and her maids seem to have done most of the work she claimed occupied her own time. While in Gibraltar, she suffered recurrent bouts of a mysterious complaint and a miscarriage – her second. In April 1808, having been advised by doctors not to spend another summer abroad, she returned to England. Her husband had long hoped to be posted to the dockyards of Woolwich or Deptford, but when she sailed she was forced to leave him behind.

Widows' pensions

When tragedy did strike naval families, what help was at hand? The wives of naval heroes who died in battle might have honours heaped upon them. Admittedly, the honours awarded to Nelson's family after Trafalgar were unprecedented but Fanny gained a pension of £2000 even though Nelson had abandoned her in 1801. In contrast, the Establishment ignored Emma Hamilton's public appeals for financial compensation after Nelson's death, though they caused Fanny considerable embarrassment. For more ordinary people there were various charities, including the Charity for the Relief of Officers' Widows, which largely supported middle-ranking naval wives. When ships were thought to have been lost, it seems that some officers' wives waited a considerable time, hoping for better news, before applying for a pension from the Charity. For example, Lieutenant Adam Scott's ship sailed from Exeter for Newfoundland in March 1755 and was never heard of again. His wife applied for a pension only in October 1757. Her request was granted and the pension backdated to June 1755 since it was reasonable to conclude that the ship had foundered about that time. Elizabeth Ann Baker, married to the purser of the sloop *Peregrine*, supposed lost in January 1762, applied for a pension only in June 1763, 'being in hopes of hearing more favourable accounts of the sloop'. Unfortunately, by this time one Martha Baker had already claimed the widow's pension, and investigation proved that she was legally married to the purser before Elizabeth Ann. The pension went to Martha, even though she too had allowed more than a year to elapse before putting in her request.

The Charity administrators recognised that in cases of shipwreck there was sometimes no certainty that a ship had been lost until many months after the event.[77] Officers' widows stood to benefit from an additional income by seeking charity, so it appears that the act of actually applying for a pension operated as a form of closure after a period of grieving. How did such women survive in the meantime? An exchange of correspondence in the papers of the Charity for the Relief of Officers' Widows gives us a clue. The Charity would not grant widows a pension if they were already receiving one equivalent to that due in respect of their husband's rank from another charity. Nor were they granted a pension if their annual personal income already amounted to double the sum they would receive. Widows had to take an oath regularly that their income was within this limit and, typically, some were troubled in conscience as to whether the income they earned 'by keeping a shop – by teaching Drawing, Music, etc.' exceeded the limit. They wrote to the Charity and the officials, who appreciating any sign of self-help, replied that they had no doubt that the income resulting from a widow's labour should not be taken into account or disable her from receiving a pension. Perhaps the Charity's attitude was influenced by the fact that the widows of army officers received a pension whatever their private income happened to be.[78]

Yet not all widows were in a position to work. Ann Butler, a lieutenant's widow, petitioned the *Queen* in 1801 to be put on the charity list. Her husband had been wrecked in the sloop *Weazel* leaving her with five small children. Her petition was passed to the Charity for the Relief of Officers' Widows who found that she had been on their list since 1799. Clearly, the widow was still in distress, having so many children, and hoped that there might be an additional source of charitable income. In contrast, Elizabeth Hammond, the widow of a gunner who died in 1788 leaving her with three children, was more resourceful and managed to bring them up entirely 'by her own industry'. She applied to the Charity only on 12 January 1802, fourteen years after his death, explaining that only now did she find herself in great want and distress.[79] Even after pensions were increased in 1814 in response to the higher cost of living, the awards were modest and did not cover unforeseen, expenses. Margaret Tucker, a surgeon's widow in Aberdeen, asked at this time for another £10 annually to make her pension equal to that of a lieutenant's widow. She explained that her only child, a son of 19, had just died and that she had been forced to sell all her furniture in order to pay medical bills and funeral costs, before moving into furnished lodgings.[80] The records indicate that, as a rule, officers' widows on a fixed income found themselves in the position of having to manage more frugally each year as living costs increased.

Not all officers' widows were virtuous. At a meeting on 13 September 1813, the Charity's Court of Assistants discussed the cases of two widows living in Plymouth. John Smale, an official at the dockyard there, had reported that Mrs Jane Namby, who received a pension as the widow of Lieutenant Robert Namby, 'was committing various acts of swindling & had had two children since the death of her husband who were then in the Poor House, she having abandoned them'. The birth of the children had been confirmed by a warrant of bastardy in which Mrs Namby had sworn that their father was a man named Matthew Nosworthy, whom Smale described as 'a cunning, artful, designing fellow, living without any employ and I have no doubt assisted by this base woman'. At the time Mrs Namby was receiving £40 p.a. from the Charity, but also £25 p.a. from the Patriotic Fund and another £25 p.a. from the King's Bounty Fund at the

Navy Pay Office. The Court considered Mrs Namby as wholly undeserving the benefit of charity and resolved that she should be deprived of her pension.

Another case concerned Mrs Martha Hay, who had sworn each quarter that she was the widow of Lieutenant John Hay and had received a pension as such, but who had in fact re-married in 1808 by the name of Amelia Jenkins to a man who also went under an assumed name. The Consistory Court had decreed the marriage null and void due to the man's minority (he was under 18 years of age). Though the widow had two children, the Court was unsympathetic. It wrote to the Admiralty, asking it to lay both cases before the law officers of the Crown to see if they had the right to deprive 'these depraved women' of their pensions.[81] Sometimes widows were simply tempted to bend the truth a little. In 1802 Henrietta McMillan, Widow of Neal McMillan, acting master of the *Pallas*, wrote to the Admiralty to explain that her husband had died after long service, leaving her without dependents. She had petitioned the Admiralty before, in 1800, to ask if she could be admitted as a nurse to Greenwich Hospital. Now she had learnt that vacancies were about to come up in the hospital and earnestly asked to be considered because she had no other means of earning a living. The officials who received her petition were uncertain: they noted that her husband had only *acted* as master, doubted whether he had ever passed his examination, and wondered if she was eligible for such a position.[82] This may seem over-scrupulous; but records suggest that charity officials, having limited resources at their disposal and faced with numbers of women in need, usually took refuge in strict attention to the rulebook.

Life for naval wives was unpredictable. Fanny Palmer, wife of Jane Austen's naval brother Charles, wrote in 1814, 'You well know the uncertainty of Naval people, & that their private arrangements must yield to public duty; indeed I find there is little use in planning.'[83] She was acknowledging that a captain's duty to his country had to take precedence over his inclination to chase valuable prizes for his personal interest. Yet within a few months Fanny was dead, giving her words particular resonance. To save money Charles had taken his family to live on board with him. These domestic arrangements led to his wife's death, a few weeks after the birth of their fourth child: the birth had not gone smoothly but with expert help ashore her life might have been saved. For all naval wives, the outcome of their husband's career and therefore their own future was something of a lottery. Yet for those of the middling sort perhaps the turns of fortune had the greatest potential effect.

1. George P. B. Naish, ed., *Nelson's Letters to his Wife and Other Documents 1785 – 1831*, Navy Records Society, 100 (London and Colchester, 1958), p. 261, 10 Dec. 1794, Fanny to Nelson.

2. John Brewer, 'English Radicalism in the Age of George III', in *Three British Revolutions*, J. G. A. Pocock ed. (Princeton, N.J., 1980), p. 333.

3. Jonathan Barry and Christopher Brooks, *The Middling Sort of People: Culture, Society and Politics in England, 1550 – 1800* (Basingstoke, 1994), p. 2.

4. TNA ADM6 387.

5. *GM*, 80 pt II (1810), 14. Cf. 308.

6. Jane Austen, *Persuasion* (1818), ed. D. W. Harding (Harmondsworth, 1965), p. 49.

7. *GM*, 73 (1803), 216.

8. John Aiken, *Evenings at Home; or, the Juvenile Budget Opened*, 2nd edn, 6 vols (London, 1794 – 98).

9. *GM*, 31 (1761), 36.

10. Jane West, *Letters to a Young Lady*, 3 vols (London, 1806), p. 192.

11. www.nmm.ac.uk/flinders accessed 18 Jan. 2007, 16 August 1806, Matthew Flinders to Ann Flinders.

12. *GM*, 58 (1788), 864.

13. *GM*, 58 (1788), 361.

14. TNA ADM 106/1118/287 and ADM 106/1118/339.

15. Helen Doe, 'Challenging Images: Mrs Mary Ross of Rochester, Nineteenth-Century Businesswoman and Warship Builder', *Journal for Maritime Research* (May, 2006), <jmr@nmm.ac.uk> accessed 18 Jan. 2007.

16. See W. Spavens, *The Narrative of William Spavens a Chatham Pensioner Written by Himself* (London, 1998), p. 59 for an explanation of how prize money was shared.

17. NMM CRK/13/122, Harriet Walker to Nelson. [n.d.].

18. BL Add. MSS 60361, 60364.

19. *GM*, 75 (1805), 85.

20. *GM*, 64 (1794), 182.

21. *The London Chronicle*, 21 – 23 June 1798, p. 597.

22. *GM*, 76 (1806), 1076.

23. Naish, p. 256, 2 Nov. 1794, Fanny to Nelson; p. 248, 17 Nov. 1794, F. to N.; p. 262, 10 Dec 1794, F. to N.

24. Naish, p. 350, 26 Feb. 1797, Fanny to Nelson.

25. BL Add. MSS 34988, 8 March 1797, Maurice Nelson to Nelson.

26. Naish, p. 353, 20 March 1797, Fanny to Nelson.

27. NMM MSS/86/051, 2 July 1808, Wells to his wife.

28. BL Add. MSS 46712, 17 Aug. 1800, Young to Ann.

29. NMM GRT/23, 29 April 1801, 14 Oct. 1801, August 1802, 16 July 1801, Jean Grant to her father.

30. Edward Hughes, ed., *The Private Correspondence of Admiral Lord Collingwood*, Navy Records Society, 98 (London and Colchester, 1957), p. 147, 16 March 1803, Collingwood to Dr Alexander Carlyle.

31. C. L. Newnham Collingwood, ed., *A Selection from the Public and Private Correspondence of Vice-Admiral Lord Collingwood*, 2nd edn, 2 vols (London, 1828), II, 196 – 7, 28 July 1808, Collingwood to his wife Sarah.

32. Newnham Collingwood, II, 108, 9 March 1808, Collingwood to his wife Sarah.

33. Newnham Collingwood, II, 306, 5 Feb. 1809, Collingwood to his daughter Sarah.

34. NMM MSS/86/051, 10 May 1808, Wells to his wife Nancy.

35. NMM GRT/23, 1 Jan. 1802, Jean Grant to her father Samuel.

36. NMM GRT/23, 5 Oct. 1801, Jean Grant to her father Samuel.

37. Hughes, pp. 107 – 8, 5 Dec. 1799, Collingwood to Dr Alexander Carlyle.

38. Newnham Collingwood, I, 318, Collingwood to his wife Sarah, 16 June 1806.

39. Oliver Warner, *The Life and Letters of Vice-Admiral Lord Collingwood* (London, 1968), p. 63.

40. Hughes, p. 300, 19 October 1809, Collingwood to his sister Mary.

41. Hughes, p. 311, 28 Dec. 1809, Collingwood to his sister Mary.

42. Warner, p. 245.

43. Naish, p. 347, 10 Dec 1794, Fanny to Nelson; p. 262, 15 Feb 1797, Fanny to Nelson.

44. Janet Schaw *Journal of a Lady of Quality; Being the Narrative of a Journey from Scotland to the West Indies, North Carolina, and Portugal, in the years 1774 to 1776* (New Haven, 1934), p. 80.

45. Naish, p. 261, 10 Dec. 1794, Fanny to Nelson.

46. Alfred Morrison, *The Collections of Autograph Letters and Historical Documents Formed by Alfred Morrison: The Hamilton and Nelson Papers*, 2 vols (privately printed, 1893 – 4), II, 175.

47. *London Chronicle*, 22 – 25 March 1800, p. 6, col. 2.

48. *Morning Herald, and Daily Advertiser*, 20 July 1785, p. 2, col. 3.

49. Anon., *The Arguments of Counsel in the Ecclesiastical Court in the Cause of Inglefield ... on the twenty-second of July, 1786, at giving judgement.* (London, 1786), p. 99.

50. Anne Fremantle, ed., *The Wynne Diaries: the Adventures of Two Sisters in Napoleonic Europe*, (Oxford, 1982), p. 253. I owe this reference to Roger Knight.

51. J. Inglefield, *Captain Inglefield's Vindication of his conduct: or, a reply to a pamphlet intitled Mrs. Inglefield's Justification* (London, 1787), p. 5.

52. Ann Inglefield, *Mrs. Inglefield's Justification, containing the proceedings in the Ecclesiastical Court ... on July 11 and 17, 1785* (London, 1787), p. ix.

53. NMM DAV/2/1, 18 December 1798, and NMM DAV/2/20, Tuesday, n.d., Fanny to Davison.

54. NMM DAV/2/7, 11 April 1799, Fanny to Davison.

55. NMM DAV/2/13, 8 May 1799, Fanny to Davison.

56. NMM DAV/2/3, n.d.1799, Fanny to Davison.

57. NMM DAV/2/24, 20 October 1800, Fanny to Davison.

58. NMM DAV/2/25, 22 October 1800, Fanny to Davison.

59. NMM DAV/2/27, 5 February 1801, Fanny to Davison.

60. NMM DAV/2/41, 1 May 1801, Fanny to Davison.

61. NMM DAV/2/44, 7 May 1801, Fanny to Davison.

62. NMM DAV/2/46, 24 May 1801. See also NMM DAV/2/48, Fanny to Davison.

63. NMM DAV/2/48, 15 June 1801, Fanny to Davison.

64. NMM DAV/2/32, 15 March 1801, Fanny to Davison.

65. NMM DAV/2/49, 22 June 1801, Fanny to Davison.

66. NMM DAV/2/30, 24 February 1801, Fanny to Davison.

67. Cf. Hannah Barker and Elaine Chalus, eds, *Gender in Eighteenth-Century England* (London and New York, 1997), pp. 19ff.

68. An annual income of £200 to £300 is thought to have secured a place within the middling sort in urban areas. See Leonore Davidoff and Catherine Hall, *Family Fortunes. Men and women of the English middle class, 1780 – 1850* (London, 1987), p. 23.

69. NMM WIL/1/4, 29 Aug. 1807 and WIL/1/12, 19 Dec. 1807, Wilkinson to his wife Sally.

70. NMM WIL/1/3, 8 July 1807, Wilkinson to his wife Sally.

71. NMM WIL/1/34, 17 July 1809, Wilkinson to his wife Sally.

72. NMM WIL/1/21, 3 Feb. 1809, Wilkinson to his wife Sally.

73. Middleton Papers, NMM MDT/2, 4 Sept. 1805, Susanna Maria Middleton to her sister Miss Martin Leake.

74. Ibid.

75. NMM MDT/3, 28 Sept. 1805, Susanna Middleton to her sister.

76. NMM MDT/41, 15 June 1807, Susanna Middleton to her sister.

77. TNA ADM6/388.

78. TNA ADM6/386.

79. TNA ADM6/339.

80. TNA ADM 6/388.

81. TNA ADM6/386.

82. TNA ADM6/339.

83. Park Honan, *Jane Austen: Her Life* (London, 1987), p. 331.

Chapter Four
LABOURING AND CRIMINAL CLASSES

On 13 August 1810 the front page of *The Times* carried the following small advertisement: 'If the NEXT of KIN of ABRAHAM PATTINGER, late a Seaman belonging to his Majesty's ships Blenheim and Lion, deceased, will apply at the Office of the Inspector of Seamen's Wills, at the Navy Pay Office, London, they may hear of something to their advantage'. Such notices recur during newspapers of the Napoleonic War period. They indicate how easy it was for a common seaman, perhaps pressed into service and then deprived of shore leave for years on end, to lose touch with his family.

This chapter looks at the wives and women associated with the common seaman, including men pressed unwillingly into the navy, and at the wives of some warrant officers such as gunners, boatswains and ships carpenters. It deals with the respectable, labouring poor, but also with those who belonged to the criminal classes. Newspaper accounts, local records and Old Bailey trial records can provide an insight into the experience of sailors' women living in poverty on the fringes of society. Yet since the lower classes left so few records of their own, we only see them through the eyes of others. Notably, working class women were still often depicted as savage or depraved even in the 1780s and 90s, and gained a degree of social acceptance only if they complied with the standards of domesticity set for them by their betters.

The labouring poor were largely occupied with the staples of life: feeding and clothing their families, and putting their children in the way of earning a living. Professional seamen in this class sometimes found places for their sons on board ship in the hope of earning more money for the family or getting sons started on a career at sea. In Jane Austen's *Mansfield Park*, even the family of a lieutenant of marines on half pay expected to sew the shirts their menfolk needed to take to sea. The wives of common seamen would have needed to undertake such functional needlework, though seamen could also buy working clothes, or 'slops' from sellers ashore or from the purser on board ship. There is some indication that wives may have tried to equip their men with clothes designed to protect them from the elements. The *Gentlemen's Magazine* for 1766 offers thrifty readers a cheap method of making a 'watch coat' for soldiers, claiming that it would be 'equally serviceable to sailors at sea, in rainy weather'. Readers were instructed to take a large checked shirt, unpick any small darts, and then paint the whole garment with warm linseed oil. Afterwards they had to hang the shirt carefully out to dry so that no surfaces were touching, and then give it a second coat of oil. This messy business was supposedly worth the effort because the magazine insisted that the general use of such shirts would save many lives.[1]

Most of the information about domestic relationships of seamen at this end of the social scale come from instances when they or their womenfolk broke the law and were arrested, or when one partner actually brought charges against the other. Occasionally episodes from their domestic lives might be reported in newspapers but throughout the period such events would have needed to be extremely bizarre to make it into print, and over-reliance on such sources would certainly produce an unbalanced picture. For example, on 10 March 1763 *The St. James's Chronicle; or the British Evening-Post* reported that a sailor had returned home to his wife in Newington, Surrey, with £100 in pay and prize money and the next morning, for reasons unknown, hanged himself. After the end of the Napoleonic War, on the 4 December 1818, *The Times* carried the strange story of a man who took his own wife to court. He returned home with over £50 in pay, which he put under the bed for safekeeping. Next morning, having made the bed, his wife offered to take care of the money, then left the house. The husband grew suspicious, 'from certain tricks she had played him before' and hearing a rumour that she had gone to the country, he quickly found an officer and caught up with her just as she had taken her place in the Plymouth coach. Questioned by the Alderman, she innocently claimed to have lost the money. He was about to consign her to jail for a few days in the hope that the salutary experience would jog her memory, when the officer knowingly suggested searching the woman. She was led off to a private room where a body search soon produced the money. The Alderman, we are told, let her off with a strong warning but her husband determined to return his wife to her parents in Ireland and have nothing more to do with her.

Social studies of port towns offer insights based more firmly on statistics. A study of marital violence in eighteenth-century Portsmouth has shown that wife beatings tended to rise when soldiers and sailors were demobilized since peacetime was usually accompanied by unemployment and a decline in real wages.[2] When peace was declared, sailors, often brutalized by war or just accustomed to shipboard routine and naval discipline, returned to households that might have been headed by women for several years. The period of adjustment often proved uncomfortable and economic hardship increased the strain. Statistically it appears that a high percentage of wife beaters were sailors even though, as a rule, they did not live with their wives all year round. Their numbers were probably also underestimated since poor women could not afford to take their husbands to court. Portsmouth seems to have been an exceptionally violent town, although most seaport towns at the time had a reputation as places of drunkenness, profanity and riot: men beat their wives but many women were also prosecuted for beating men. Those cases that came to court, certainly until the end of the eighteenth century, reveal low literacy levels in both sexes, although by the early nineteenth century it has been estimated that just over 50 per cent of common seamen were literate. Couples of this class would therefore have found regular communication by letter difficult when the man was at sea, even if circumstances permitted the exchange of letters. In times of family crisis, women employed the services of professional letter writers. For example, widows used scribes to petition the Admiralty for the release of under-age children who had been pressed into the navy or who had been retained on board ship after the death of fathers who had taken sons with them to sea.

Couples facing a long separation often exchanged love tokens.[3] Almost any article could be used, but coins were common (see Plate 14). These were polished flat and then engraved with a personal message. Some were exquisitely crafted and clearly engraved professionally; others, belonging to the humbler classes, were home-made – possibly by the sailors themselves. Some tokens were pierced so that they could be worn around the neck. In other cases coins were cut in half, one piece to be retained by the giver, the other carried by the husband or sweetheart to be matched up later. For ordinary people, the giving of tokens, especially a coin or ring split in two, was significant and popularly believed to imply a formal contract of marriage. The Church did not recognise the custom, and no verbal contract without witnesses was likely to be upheld in court, but the custom still persisted. Engraved ships were popular motifs on sailors' love tokens. One token of 1781 shows the *Foudroyant* on one side and, on the other, a circular inscription: 'When this you see Remember me'. The names 'Jn° [John] Walsh' and 'Elisabeth Manah' are engraved in the centre of the inscription, above twin hearts pierced with arrows. These tokens survive because they were treasured and they show how some couples tried to come to terms emotionally with the long periods of absence imposed by naval service.[4]

Some seamen did manage to write home or they were able to find scribes among their more literate shipmates. In wartime, when the country's resources were stretched, parodies of letters from the lower deck were published in newspapers to help convince those of higher social status that the navy remained loyal and in good heart. *The Times* of 24 October 1795 carried what purported to be a copy of a letter from a sailor on board the warship *Fortitude* to his wife in Wapping, giving an account of a skirmish with the French off Cape St Vincent. Malapropisms, poor spelling and national stereotyping make what was probably a desperate engagement seem quite humorous.

> *Monshire* did not like the shell, do you see, Chickey, but hove a-back in less time than a frog would have jumped down a Frenchman's gullet. The other five, as they saw the van shaking with an ague, hung an-arse; so we kept on our course, and came home to tell the Lords of the Admiralty all about it.

He concludes, 'So no more at present, from Your loving husband to command, TIM HARDY'.[5] The seaman's envoi reassuringly suggests that he and his wife enjoy a permanent and faithful relationship that will be resumed at the end of the war.

Popular guides to communication found a ready market, since letter writing was the only option available. *The Newest Young Man's Companion*, published in 1754, offered examples of how a sailor should write to his sweetheart and also how she should reply, suggesting that this was a familiar situation where people needed help. The two sample letters were reprinted with minor alterations in *The Accomplished Letter-Writer; or, universal correspondent. Containing familiar letters on the most common occasions of life*, published in 1779. The reference to love tokens demonstrate how prevalent the custom was:

> My dear Peggy
> I constantly dream of my dear *Peggy.* I wear my Half-Bit of Gold always at my Heart, ty'd to a blue ribband round my Neck; for *true blue*, my dearest love, is the colour of colours to me. Where, my dearest, do *you* put *your's*? I hope you are careful of it: for it would be a bad omen to lose it.

The sailor explains that he will now give the letter to an acquaintance, who happens to be in a ship bound for England and who promises to deliver it by hand. The next model letter in the manual gives Peggy's answer. Her mother has given her permission to begin her letter 'Dear Andrew', since they now regard themselves as engaged, but in describing to him the reaction of women friends to the news, Peggy touches on what must have been a common female fear:

These sailors run such sad chances, said one that you and I both know. *They may eturn, and they may not*. Well, I will trust in God for that, who had return'd safe to his friends, their dear *Andrew*, so many a time, and often. *They will have a mistress in every land they come to*, said they. All are not such naughty men, said I; and I'll trust *Andrew Trusty* all the world over. For why cannot *men* be as faithful as *Women*, too? And for *me*, I'm sure no love shall every touch my heart but *yours*.

Your faithful, &c.

P.S. I had this Letter writ in Readiness to send you, as I had an Opportunity And the Captain's Lady undertakes to send it with hers. That's very kind and condescending, is it not?[6]

The difficulty people of this class encountered when sending letter is borne out in correspondence between Lady Georgiana Spencer and her friend Caroline, wife of John Howe and sister of William, 1st Earl Howe 1759 – 1814, who was feted for winning a victory against the French at the Battle of the Glorious First of June, 1794. In November 1794, Lady Spencer wrote from St Albans to Caroline Howe in London enclosing a letter for Thomas Lemon on board the *Culloden* under Captain Troubridge from Lemon's wife, who was very anxious that the letter should reach him. Caroline Howe made enquiries and discovered from Lady Pitt in Portsmouth that there was a ship of that name at Spithead but that it was due to sail on convoy duty with one of the outward bound fleets. She was not certain that Troubridge still commanded the *Culloden* nor that Lemon was still on board, but she forwarded the letter to Lady Pitt and let Lady Spencer know that she could 'acquaint the poor woman that her letter is gone to Spithead, & that when I can be certain it has reached her husband she shall know it'.[7] A few days later, Lady Spencer sent another letter to her friend from Lemon's wife. Caroline Howe had meanwhile consulted her navy books and discovered that the *Culloden* was at sea with Howe's fleet. She said she would keep the letter until the ship came in and send it on the best way she could. Lady Spencer replied on 25 November, 'You have been very good my Dear Howey in taking so much pains about the letter, the poor woman will be very thankful when she knows that her letter will reach her Husband if he is not gone.' Finally, on 26 November, Caroline Howe was able to reply:

I am rejoiced to have it in my power to tell you my dear Lady Spencer, that you may give Mrs Lemon the pleasure of knowing that her husband is perfectly well & is in the possession of her letter, Lady Pitt gave it into his own hands yesterday morning. She employed a Captain of her acquaintance to speak to Capt Troubridge to enquire after him, & to desire he might be sent to her if found to be on board the Culloden, he gave him the character of being a very good man; & she says he is a very clean and well looking man, he told her he had not heard from his wife for the last six months; and Lady Pitt offered to send his answer to her, to you.

Lady Spencer wrote back on 29 November, 'Thanks for your account of Lemon it rained so hard that I could not get at his wife yesterday but I expect to see her to day.'

The *Culloden's* muster book for that period shows that Thomas Lemon came from Wells in Somerset and that he was 21 when he joined the ship as an ordinary seaman on 1 January 1794. He seems to have impressed his officers since he was made an able seaman on 1 June 1794.[8] The correspondence shows the pains that some fashionable ladies would take to convey to seamen their wives' letters.

The sample letters relating to seamen in correspondence manuals give the impression of faithful, long-term relationships. In reality, most sailors' women at the lower levels of society lived very differently. With their men absent for long periods, few could survive economically without forming other ties or resorting to occasional prostitution to make ends meet. Often the 'marriages' that seamen contracted in the first place were not strictly legal according to Hardwicke's 1753 Marriage Act. Sailors often 'married' prostitutes in ceremonies of dubious legality. A comic print of 1808, *Accommodations. Or Lodgings to Let at Portsmouth!!* (see Plate 15), depicts a sailor and his woman outside a house that offered 'lodgings for single men and their wives'. The man exclaims, 'Why Nan – this is the very birth [*sic*] we have been so long looking after'. The joke depends on the common knowledge that irregular arrangements between sailors and their women existed; but also suggests that arrangements, though irregular, did not necessarily preclude long-term relationships. Again, this panders to a sentimental attitude towards the common sailor, which may not have been very near the truth.

Cases that came to court reveal a more mercenary and casual attitude to relationships among the lowest sort. *The St. James's Chronicle; or the British Evening-Post* for 2 – 4 April 1763 reported that:

A few Days since one of the Men belonging to the Active, which took the Hermione, who had for some Time past fixed his Quarters at a

Public House at Portsmouth, came to Town Yesterday se'nnight with his Landlord, in Search of his Wife, from whom he had been absent about five Years, and after some Enquiry, found she had been married to another Man the preceding Thursday; the Tar pleaded his prior Right, and insisted on having his Wife back again, which the new Husband readily agreed to. The Sailor putting his Hand into his Pocket, said, "Here, Friend, accept of a couple of Guineas for the Service you have done my Wife;" and afterwards set out with her and his Landlord, in a Landau and Four for Portsmouth.

The story would have attracted more attention because the capture of the Spanish frigate, *Hermione*, in 1762 netted £485 in prize money for each seaman. The anecdote illustrates both the extravagant lifestyle that ordinary sailors could afford if they were lucky enough to capture such rich prizes, and the consequences of the long separations they might endure in the process.

A woman sentenced to seven years' transportation for bigamy in 1826 explained to the judge that ten years earlier her first husband had sold her to a sailor called George Bligh for just 5 shillings and a bottle of wine. Wife sales were common among the poorer classes who could not afford more expensive means of public separation: recorded cases were still rising at this period and did not peak until the 1830s. Men commonly escaped failed marriages by joining the military forces, and the long periods of separation in wartime made it easier for individuals to strike up other relationships. *The Times* for 20 November 1820 reported the bigamy of Thomas Gordon, a gunner on board the frigate *Venus*. Gordon married Harriet Cole in 1809 but in 1818, while Harriet was still living, he married a second woman, Frances Elizabeth Lawes. Frances was already in an infirm state of body and mind but Gordon married her for her settlement of between £200 and £300 a year. By 1820 both wives had died but his second wife's relations were determined to prosecute him in order to recover the money. Gordon's defence throws further light on the marital relations of common seamen. His first wife, he argued, became a common prostitute and died in Magdalen Ward of St Thomas's Hospital on 8 July 1815. The witness willing to swear to this was one Elizabeth Millington, with whom he had cohabited on board the *Pomona* frigate when it was lying at Portsmouth in July 1815. Gordon was nevertheless found guilty as the court was satisfied that his first wife was living when he married the second. The uncertain legal status of many sailor's marriages made desertion an easy option for them, and while many men died abroad, others whose wives never heard of them again simply started new lives and families elsewhere.

Prostitutes

Once the fleet had anchored, hundreds of so-called wives and prostitutes were ferried out to each warship. When the *Royal George* tragically sank in 1782 as it was being hauled to one side in order to clean the hull, there were 400 prostitutes on board and many children. The women shared the men's hammocks and when hands were called on deck in the morning, the women were allowed to lie in – which is where the boatswain's call 'show a leg' originates since if the owner of the leg appeared to be female she was left to sleep on in peace. Prostitutes were tolerated on the lower decks, particularly in wartime, because captains were reluctant to grant shore leave as men were so liable to desert. However, when the women were put ashore men often attempted to desert hidden underneath their petticoats.[9] The scale of the desertion problem is evident from *The Hue and Cry, and Police Gazette*, the eighteenth-century equivalent of the television programme *Crime Watch*. This official publication appeared once every three weeks and listed deserters with a brief description of each man, as well as publicising other crimes in the hope of receiving information useful to the police. The problem of desertion was well understood; that prostitutes were allowed on board ships was no secret either. When the London paper, The *Morning Post and Fashionable World*, informed readers on 25 August 1794 that the fleet was expected to sail any day, the reporter was explicit: 'As the seamen are allowed to have women on board, which *they call wives*, there is an order just come on board from Earl *Howe*, to order every woman out of the ships of the fleet, which I conclude is a proof of sailing soon.'[10] Some evangelical captains took a tough line, notably James Gambier (1756 – 1833), who, as captain of the *Defiance* in the 1790s, refused to allow any woman without a marriage certificate to remain on board.[11] Once the war had ended, in the 1820s, there was more widespread outrage at the 'immoral practices' permitted on board British warships in port.

The term 'prostitute' comprised a range of women from high-class courtesans to streetwalkers, but those who serviced the fleet were among the most desperate of their kind. They were exposed to every infection present on the ship and there would have been a strong likelihood that any partner would also be suffering from a sexually transmitted disease. Before 1795 seamen who found themselves in this situation had to pay the surgeon 15 shillings for a cure, so they had a strong incentive to avoid treatment if they could. After 1795, treatment was free but medical examinations were irregular and in any case the diseases themselves were poorly understood so that symptoms went unnoticed. Secondary syphilis is not so contagious as primary, and most seamen probably died of other causes before tertiary syphilis set in. The usual treatment was mercury – itself dangerous to health and not always effective. There was little women could do to protect themselves. Prostitutes operating from a bawdy house might have had treatment if the owner was willing to help pay for it, but those working the streets or servicing the fleet would have found access to medical care difficult. Some newspapers of the time openly advertised cures for venereal diseases on the front page (at this period, the front and back pages of newspapers were often pre-printed with small advertisements so that the latest news could be printed on the inside pages as it came in, enabling newspapers to meet a tight deadline). But many of these patent medicines appear to have been of dubious worth. For example, *The Portsmouth Gazette, and Weekly Advertiser* in April 1795 advised those about to marry to dose themselves with a course of Dr Brodum's botanical syrup if they feared that, having consorted with 'unclean people' in the past, they might be about to communicate disease to their partners and offspring. The syrup allegedly acted through perspiration to cleanse the blood and was recommended as a gentler substitute for mercury.

Many of the prostitutes working in port towns seem to have been little more than adolescents. They were recruited from the slums or came fresh from the countryside in times of economic hardship when work and food were scarce. Most migrants entering towns at this period were young women hoping to be employed in service, although the supply always exceeded demand. Female migration from the countryside meant that most towns contained more women than men. Studies of London prostitutes have shown that invariably these women were born into poverty, had never had the chance to acquire the skills that would help them to earn a living, and that many had suffered the death or desertion of one or both parents.[12] (This may also be true of prostitutes in other major towns.) The majority took up the life in their late teens or early twenties and seem to have left the streets after a few years. Contemporary critics harshly implied that at this point they left the world altogether, a prey to early death, but many may just have returned to casual labour or even married. Those who did continue as prostitutes until they became too old or ill to ply their trade ended up in the workhouse or in prison. Contemporaries offer conflicting images of prostitutes: they were sometimes depicted collectively as wicked harlots, a corrosive and corrupting force in society, leaving a trail of broken hopes and diseased bodies in their wake; at other times they were presented as victims who had unintentionally entered a life of vice and who were more properly objects of pity and philanthropy. This latter attitude helps to explain why special provision was eventually made for them: significantly the women discharged from the Magdalen Hospital in London, which opened in 1758, were generally under 20 years old. Similar asylums for prostitutes and destitute women were later set up in other major towns, including the Female Penitentiary for Penitent Prostitutes founded in Stonehouse in 1808, which later moved to Plymouth. The dockyard towns of Portsmouth and Plymouth could apparently summon 1000 or so prostitutes with ease when the fleet returned to its anchorage. A week or so onboard ship with food and drink probably compared favourably with walking the streets, however unpleasant the atmosphere on the lower deck, but some women may have combined occasional prostitution with other work. There is little reliable information about their way of life: descriptions in contemporary accounts and prints aim to be cautionary or merely humorous.

Representations of seamen's women

George Pinckard, a genteel visitor to Portsmouth in the early 1800s, was taken aback by the aggressive quality of the town's hardened and hard-drinking prostitutes. He asked readers to imagine:

> The warlike features of two wounded cheeks, a tumid nose, scarred and battered brows, and a pair of blackened eyes, with balls of red; then add to her sides a pair of brawny arms, fit to encounter a Colossus, and set her upon two ancles [sic] like the fix supporters of a gate. Afterwards, by way of apparel, put upon her a loose flying cap, a man's black hat, a torn neckerchief, stone rings on her fingers, and a dirty white, or tawdry flowered gown, with a short apron, and a pink petticoat; and thus you will have something very like the figure of a "*Portsmouth Poll*".[13]

The hyperbolic tone of this passage suggests that Pinckard was describing a well-known type. The common prostitutes of port towns were depicted as Amazonian, often the worse for drink but still able to take care of themselves: an object of humour rather than of pity. This is true of the print ironically titled *Sweet Poll of Plymouth* (1790), which shows that it needs two well-meaning seamen to navigate the drunken Poll safely through the dockyard town (see Plate 16). This popular print was re-issued in 1819. Over the years representations of Poll increased in size, as in *Shiver my Timbers Poll your grown out of Compass. I can scarcely embrace you* (see Plate 17). This particular print may be alluding to the fact that sailors' women often became pregnant while their partner was absent on a long voyage, but the gargantuan, unrealistic Poll may also be a sign that such a rumbustious image was itself becoming untenable in a new century with a new, more moral tone.

Naval prints featuring prostitutes were meant to be entertaining and were often produced to bolster the war effort. Many depict sailors carousing with women in public houses and spending their money freely on securing a good time during their brief period ashore (see jacket illustration).[14] Moderately priced, they were published in London and then disseminated through print sellers' catalogues and by travelling salesmen, achieving a relatively wide circulation although print runs were modest and would have ranged from several hundred to just a few thousand. Mezzotints of similar subjects were more expensive and aimed at a more privileged market. An example is *Men of War, Bound for the Port of Pleasure* (1791), which shows a scene of comforting harmony: sailors bent on sexual gratification and prostitutes happily fleecing them of their money (see Plate 18).

At times the prints allude lightly to typical misfortunes. *Jack in a White Squall, Amongst Breakers – on the Lee Shore of St. Catherines* (1811), shows a seaman fending off a group of angry women demanding the money he owes them. The women of St Catherine's Dock, London, befriended the seaman when he came ashore but are quick to turn on him once his money has run out (see Plate 19). One holds a list of expenses – an indication of the way in which women might manage a sailor's finances while he was on shore. Numerous prints depicted the sailor's return and these could also be ambiguous. C. Moseley's version dating from the 1750s suggests that the sailor's sweetheart, a street seller, has not exactly waited faithfully for his return. She drops one of her eggs – a familiar symbol for loss of virtue (see Plate 20). Here the visual language allows the artist to present a darker side to a theme that was a popular subject in ballads, songs and the theatre and also reproduced on ceramics. Occasionally the dangers of a seaman's absence are represented openly, as in the print *Poll and my Partner Joe* (1794), which illustrates a popular ballad by Dibdin: in this case Jack returns home only to find that his Poll has taken another lover (see Plate 21).

Comic or sentimental prints often glossed over the exact status of sailors' women. Many of those depicted were clearly prostitutes but they appear to be jolly rather than degraded (see Plate 22). They may have been portrayed more favourably than other common prostitutes because by servicing sailors' needs they were somehow contributing to the country's war effort. Yet sailors were widely regarded as being kinder to their women than soldiers: the surviving visual commentary indicates that their relationships with women were largely enjoyable and happy, which conforms to the prevailing image of the generous and benevolent Jack Tar. Prints of seduction scenes, such as 'Jack got safe into Port with his Prize' (1780), a coloured mezzotint depicting a seaman and a high class prostitute dallying on a sofa, show the prostitute as healthy and well dressed.

Prints often show the sailor making the first advances but here it seems clear that the woman is leading him on. Similarly, in other prints when couples are shown walking by themselves in a garden or park, there is often no suggestion that the woman's alluring glances could be directed at any one other than the seaman or that he is other than unattached, since presumably this would have offended contemporary sensibilities and made the prints unsaleable.

Yet increasingly during the period of the French Wars 1793 – 1815, the image of the young Jack Tar in contemporary prints was that of a sailor faithful to his one true love at home. Such ideologically charged works include *Jack's Fidelity* (1796), and *The Token, or Jack safe Return'd to his True Love Nancy* (see Plates 23 and 24). These images of domestic bliss idealized the impact of naval conflict on society and served to counteract the view that sailors lived on the margins of society and morality. They would have been produced as commercial ventures and presumably found a ready market. Mezzotints of the time could be mawkish. *Yo Heave Ho* (1799) shows a wife with her son and daughter bidding a tearful farewell to her husband's ship. The ballad printed underneath the design helps to reinforce an ideal of patriotic sacrifice, making good use of an additional form of popular entertainment to help depict conventional view of the war. Such sentimental images were also replicated on ceramics and tableware (see Plates 25 and 26).

A very few contemporary prints showing sailors' women have a sardonic twist. The caricature *Exporting Cattle Not Insurable* (see Plate 27), depicts sailors ferrying a boatful of rowdy women to a warship at anchor where a number of others are already clambering aboard. The caption compares the women to cattle and more particularly to beasts that cannot be insured because they have been brought on board unofficially. The ex-seaman William Robinson, writing an account of his life on board a man o' war for a more moral readership in the 1830s, described how prostitutes were formerly ferried to the fleet at anchor. He also compared them to cattle being taken to market, concluding, 'Of all the human race, these poor young creatures are the most pitiable; the ill-usage and the degradation they are driven to submit to, are indescribable.'[15] He did admit that from habit these women had become callous and indifferent to any delicacy of speech or behaviour, and were totally lost to all sense of shame but he thought that the blame rested with those responsible for their abject condition: largely the seamen themselves. Yet in the earlier period, this is not how prostitutes were generally depicted, although accounts exist which suggest that many of their relationships with seamen were violent. Robert Wilson, impressed into the navy in 1805, relates one such episode when women were allowed on board his ship as stores were being taken on at Spithead. He noticed that one young woman was heavily pregnant and tried to persuade his shipmate to leave her alone, but the man assumed that Wilson's solicitude stemmed from his wish to keep the girl to himself which made him even more determined to have his way with her. The next morning the girl was seized with labour pains, at which the First and Second Lieutenants each gave her a guinea and sent her ashore. Wilson also gave her what cash he could spare, and later heard that she had safely given birth and expected to rejoin old friends who had decided to overlook her errors and help her in this time of trouble.[16]

Except for such brief glimpses, the maritime subcultures of port towns remain largely hidden from view, part of a shadowy underworld that had its own networks. Women in this world, engaged in prostitution, laundering, ballad mongering or operating bumboats to supply ships near port were scraping a living in desperate circumstances. On the River Thames, the goods sold by the bumboat women were often foreign produce, pilfered from merchant ships at anchor, although under the Bumboat Act, the women could be imprisoned if caught. Prostitutes were often implicated in theft from these vessels: many were involved in smuggling and the common perception was that seamen smuggled tea and spirits ashore hidden in their women's voluminous clothing (see Plate 28). Their livelihoods were often inter-dependent and many preyed on each other. None hesitated to fleece seamen of their money once they were ashore. Yet there is evidence that prostitutes could be instrumental to others making a more respectable living; for example, they were welcomed in some public houses because they attracted customers.

Despite the sanitized version of the seaman's relationship with women offered by most prints of the period, after 1820, in an age increasingly concerned with moral reformation, more critical evidence against these women emerged. One report to the Admiralty, *Statement respecting the Prevalence of Certain Immoral Practices in His Majesty's Navy* (1821), noted that some of the women who had recently been living in a warship for the six weeks it was in harbour, 'sung openly the most grossly indecent parodies on the Lord's Prayer and the Creed' that were of too coarse a nature to bear repetition. Their behaviour was roundly condemned as tending to promote disloyalty among the crew and consequently their presence on board warships was deemed to be a political as well as moral issue. The moral reformation of the navy now became a matter of urgency. The same report stated that such women were implicated in the mutiny of the Nore, 'When an admiral, then commanding a fleet on a foreign station, interrupted and examined the letters addressed to the sailors on that station, it was found that the greater portions of them were written by women with whom they had cohabited in British ports, urging them in the strongest manner to join the mutineers.'[17]

Making ends meet

Some women had more long-standing relationships with seamen. How did they cope when their men were at sea? At the lowest social level, those with children had a precarious existence especially if they had no family or friends to fall back on. Many took temporary, unskilled work such as harvesting (particularly in wartime when male labour was scarce), taking in washing, cleaning, and buying and selling common wares. The statements of women who were taken before justices for vagrancy or trading without a licence suggests that many who were left destitute after their husbands died or enlisted during wartime took to the roads with goods to sell in the hope of making a living.[18] Women had always been employed in low-paid jobs and small trades that yielded meagre profits. Now rapid urban growth led to a proliferation of part-time and casual jobs concentrated in traditional areas of female employment, which included sewing, washing, street vending, nursing and helping out in shops and public houses. Whereas men might be regarded with suspicion if they failed to hold down a steady job, it was accepted that lower class women would take on a range of employments that could be fitted around their domestic duties, particularly as many of the jobs open to them were seasonal and low paid. The welfare of poor, labouring families depended on the wages of wives and children, even though many would have earned far less than a man. Women were also prompted to take on casual work because any waged employment counted in their favour if they were forced to apply for poor relief (in contrast to today's practice). They might find more permanent jobs in towns, particularly if the towns supported larger-scale industries such as clothing trades which depended on women's work as seamstresses (regarded as a respectable trade), coat-makers and milliners. The wife of a boatswain, Martha Veasey, who married in 1791 at Gosport, worked as a weaver in Spitalfields, London, and seems to have taken on piece work at home when she lived for a time with her husband at Deptford in 1802. When he died she was recommended for a pension as 'a sober, honest, industrious, chaste woman'.[19] In towns, single, working women might share rented accommodation, which was more plentiful than in the country, and though their existence was insecure, arguably towns afforded them a wider safety net of charities since in the countryside able-bodied, single women might be denied any poor relief at all. Widows and women deserted by their husbands might go into service and trade the loss of independence for security it brought; but many lacked the necessary references for this work and those with children might find this route wholly closed to them. At times the labour market was simply over-stocked as thousands of women flocked to the towns in search of jobs.[20] Young girls who had left their families were particularly vulnerable in these circumstances and many ended up in prostitution. Yet even those who found work might remain vulnerable: contemporaries saw a connection between prostitution and commerce, suggesting that women who sold goods would be prepared to sell themselves, and many male customers seem to have regarded shop assistants as fair game. Matthew Flinders was dismayed when his sister Susan was to be sent away to be a millener's journeywoman. He regretted that his father's finances seemed to require such a step and was concerned that his sister would be 'subjected to such snares as I shudder to think what would be consequence had she fallen into them'.[21] Even women trying to make an honest living by selling wares outdoors were regarded as potential prostitutes.

There were often immediate dangers for women who consorted with seamen. The trial of James Carse, for the murder of Sarah Hayes in 1787 was widely reported. Carse had been a cooper on board the frigate *Boreas* stationed in the West Indies under Captain Nelson. He fell ill with sunstroke in 1784 and was sent ashore to recover but some kind of mental disorder remained even though he recovered sufficiently to be able to return to his ship: friends noted that his former 'humane disposition' had left him. The *Boreas* returned to England and Carse received wages amounting to 40 guineas. On 30 November he was paid off at Sheerness, receiving ten guineas as the remainder of his pay, and around 10p.m. that evening he picked up a prostitute called Mary Mills in the neighbourhood of St Catherine's. The couple went to a public house in Wapping aptly called 'The Ship in Distress'. Mary lodged with Sarah Hayes, and having persuaded Carse to sleep with her that night she took him back to her lodging. Sarah Hayes was at home and she showed them into a room, where Carse drank some more and lay down on the bed. He had scarcely been there two minutes before he jumped up with an open clasp knife in his hand, seized Sarah Hayes by the neck and muttering 'I will, I must, I must, I must', he forced her back against the table where she was sitting and slit her throat. Mary, who had not yet got undressed, escaped and raised the alarm. Carse, soon caught, made no attempt to deny what he had done and was found guilty of murder but escaped execution because he was judged insane.[22]

Even the more respectable wives of lowly seamen could be vulnerable in their husband's absence. In July 1787 Ann Johnson, whose husband was at sea, was robbed of her silk handkerchief and earrings. She had just returned from sending a parcel by road to her child in the country and stopped at a public house for a meal of beer, bread and cheese. That day she had been trying to pawn the handkerchief but no pawnshop would it take because it was of Indian make.

As she was leaving the public house, two women followed her. One called out 'Mistress, do you know your hair is down?' and as she stood still a moment for the woman to pin it up, the stranger snatched the handkerchief from her shoulders. At that moment the woman's accomplice came up and said, 'D—n your eyes, you bitch, if you say a word I'll knock your brains out.'[23] With that, the accomplice gave her a blow with her fist, knocked her to the ground and ran away. Ann Johnson complained that she had never been well since.

If women could afford regular subscriptions, they set up friendly societies so that they would have some assistance in times of hardship. These societies provided financial relief during illness, or covered the expense of a funeral. Advice books aimed at the lower orders strongly recommended friendly societies to all young women who had nothing to trust but their labour and whose labour depended on their health. These societies do seem to have grown in popularity after the first decade of the nineteenth century and won favour among the propertied classes too – not least because they eased the burden on rich of contributing towards the relief of the poor.

In these difficult times, some women of the poorer classes proved to be formidable. Women were active in food riots in times of scarcity when the price of bread was high, and they were often key figures in any mob that formed to resist press gangs and release the men that had been snared. Opposition to press gangs naturally hardened in wartime. *True – Blue; or, the Press Gang* was revived at the Theatre Royal in Covent Garden as a musical interlude in 1770 but the action of the press gang in the piece seemed to cause only temporary difficulty. Nancy's lover, True-Blue, is press-ganged but her father says she is too young to marry anyway and her lover appears quite happy to venture his life at sea. He promises to be true and to return 'with a Load of Doubloons'. Yet when the same situation was replicated in a broadsheet ballad called *True blue, or, the press gang. A favourite song* (1790?), the tone was quite different: the woman was left inconsolable and the press gang implicitly condemned. Many women of the time whose husbands were pressed wrote to the Admiralty explaining that their men had wives and children to support but such pleas were invariably ignored. On the other hand some men voluntarily joined the forces if conditions at home were so bad that they could not find work.

Women were also active in mobs that formed against known crimps, although women were also implicated in crimping themselves. Gangs of crimps got seamen drunk and delivered them to the press gang on payment of head money. In Britain it was an offence that could lead to a prison sentence. Crimps or kidnappers were so despised that riots could break out if their whereabouts were revealed, and the mob would try to pull down the buildings they used. In

1794 there was an outcry in the press over a gang of vagrants who had infested the area of Charing Cross, London, in order to kidnap the unwary. These 'traders in human flesh' apparently loitered in the area in the hope of seizing men newly arrived in London on the outside of coaches. Crimps often used women of the town to decoy weary travellers and had even been known to seize tradesmen and other decent people once it was dusk, gagging them, then torturing them until they agreed to enlist in the army or could be handed over to press gangs. On 18 August 1794, *The Morning Post and Fashionable World* reported that a mob had torn down the premises of Sarah Ann Hannah, a notorious crimp who owned seven houses in the same court in Charing Cross. She was arrested and tried at the Westminster Quarter Sessions that October but the case against her collapsed due to lack of evidence. On 20 August, the same paper noted that the riots against crimps had spread to a house in Whitcomb Street. It was alleged that a poor woman, with five children, and far advanced in pregnancy, had lost her husband and suspecting that crimps had decoyed him, she watched the house, and by chance saw her husband chained in the cellar. She collected a crowd and they stormed the premises so that soldiers had to be called to keep the peace. Many such attacks may have been the result of rumour stirred up by malice because in this particular case other publications offered different versions of the story.

The Bon Ton Magazine for August 1794 also reported the riots:

> A warrant had been issued for apprehending Kerr, the master of the White Horse public-house in Whitcomb Street, together with one of his accomplices, on the deposition of *Edward Barret*, a sailor, who had been trepanned, confined, and robbed there. The case of Barret was peculiarly hard and distressing. After standing forth the guardian of his native isle; after being wounded in its defence on the memorable and glorious First of June; he had the misfortune to fall into the clutches of these harpies near London Bridge, from whence he was conveyed to the rendezvous in Whitcomb Street; where, after experiencing the most cruel and inhuman treatment, the marks of which were still visible, he was at length compelled to sign his attestation before a sham justice with a wooden leg ….This done, as the last part of the discipline which he was doomed to undergo, the miscreants robbed him of his watch, silver buckles, and sundry other articles.[24]

On this occasion the rioting was so fierce it lasted into the night and a troop of horse had to be sent to reinforce the Guards.

During wartime, the number of crimes committed by women, particularly single women and widows, increased substantially, especially if the harvest was bad and cereal prices rose. With so many men serving in the forces, there were fewer male vagrants and petty criminals on the streets but dependent women committed more thefts particularly in urban areas as they struggled to provide for themselves and their families. Life in the city was especially difficult as poor relief was often less generous and less well managed although it afforded more opportunity and there were fewer paternalistic controls to restrict behaviour. If the theft could be proved, punishment was severe but evidence suggests that the risk was worth taking. In 1748, Elizabeth Kerr, who had a child and whose husband was at sea, was successfully prosecuted and transported for stealing a watch and chain from a person that she and the man she was currently living with had plied with drink and lured to their lodging. Yet in 1752 Mary Scott, also the wife of a seaman, was more fortunate: she was indicted for stealing a linen sheet worth 5s but acquitted because her prosecutor did not appear in court. At the end of a war crime rates tended to increase alarmingly. An approaching peace was often viewed, after the initial jubilation had worn off, with trepidation, as the number of petty criminals at large was swelled by indigent seamen. Seamen would be paid off as quickly as possible but thousands of these might be kept waiting for their pay, as would the widows of those who had not survived.

Some naval women relied on poor relief in the absence of their men. Funds for the poor were obtained by taxing those with property. The poor could claim relief only in their home parishes (their place or birth or last place of residence), and only women with strong local connections were allowed to stay in a parish. Parish records, particularly those of seafaring counties such as Devon, include frequent orders for removing single women and their children to other parishes in order to avoid the expense of supporting such families. The itinerant life of such women, forced to claim charity at every turn, must have been both stressful and demeaning. The offspring in their care were invariably very young since any children would be apprenticed by their early teens. Poor relief consisted of regular cash payments, supplemented by other allowances for rent, funeral expenses, nursing and other miscellaneous items. Not everyone got the same amount across the country because parishes varied in size, some were richer than others and some had a disproportionate number of people claiming relief. Records of their interviews with officials show that a high proportion of the women heading families and dealing with local bureaucracy claimed to be the wives or widows of serving seamen. The burden of poor naval wives could be considerable in some parishes. For example, in 1801 the Deputy Town Clerk of Plymouth wrote to alert the authorities about the lack of subscriptions for the maintenance of the 'casual poor' in the area, which then, as he explained, consisted chiefly of the wives and children of seamen and soldiers in His Majesty's Service. Parishes tried to recoup their expenditure on naval families whenever they could: records show that in 1791 the overseers in Modbury Parish, Devon, managed to secure a bond from John Burch, a seaman on board the *Cambridge*, that he would pay 2s 6d each month from his wages to the parish for as long as his family was receiving poor relief there.

The 1790s and 1800s were a particularly harsh time for families and lone parents; payments from the poor relief may only have been supplementary and people were urged to be charitable. For example, a broadsheet ballad of about 1800 called *The Lamentation of the Sailor's and Soldier's Wives for the Loss of their Husbands* contains the verse:

> Poor wives they think a month more longer,
> Than they us'd to think a year,
> Because they've lost husbands and fathers,
> And can't their pretty children rear;
> If they ask relief, the parish grumble,
> It is the truth you really know
> When they can't keep a house any longer,
> Then to the Workhouse they must go.

The final verse of the ballad concludes, 'I hope the rich they will consider, | And take compassion on the poor'.[25] Seamen's families were also sent to the workhouse when awaiting transportation to home parishes where they could claim poor relief. The death rate in these institutions was very high because all inmates, sick and well, were housed together in unsanitary conditions. Most women would take any work rather than expose their children to the dangers of the workhouse. However, if they begged on the streets, they could be arrested under vagrancy laws. It is reasonable to assume that friends and relatives also helped seaman's families but almost impossible from surviving evidence to discover the supportive, social networks that existed between relatives and neighbours. Also, wives whose husbands were peremptorily seized by the press gang before they could make provision for their families may well have been in an even worse economic position.

Slightly higher in the social scale, the wives of warrant officers might also be left for long periods to look after their husbands' interests at home; although entitled to accompany their husbands on board ship, some stayed ashore if they had children to bring up. Warrant officers were in skilled employment and their status on board was higher than that of the common seaman, but although they may have been industrious and taken a pride in their craftsmanship, their families were not necessarily comfortably off. Their wives often had to take an active role in preserving their family interest with the Navy Office. For example, Sarah Barker, wife of a ship's carpenter at Plymouth Dockyard, wrote to the Commissioners on 4 July 1756 to explain that her husband's apprentice had served his time and had now entered Plymouth Dockyard as a carpenter in his own right. She continued:

> I am humbly to beg your honours favourably that William Howell, who has serv'd above half his time in Plymouth Ordinary and is said to be a good Workman may serve the remaining part of his apprenticeship as Extra Servant to my husband in the form of the other, my husband being from this port I humbly hope will excuse my presuming to make this humble request.[26]

This letter was written by a scribe and Sarah Barker merely signed her name. We do not know whether this was all she could write, or whether she employed a scribe for this important letter because she was anxious to get the wording correct and to show due respect to the Commissioners. It is evident from other surviving letters from the wives of ship's carpenters that the work of apprentices helped to maintain the wife and children in a reasonable standard of living if the family were left at home. For example, Updalia Beverstock of Chatham Dockyard, wrote to the Commissioners on 19 August 1756 in similar vein to explain that her husband Daniel was serving at sea in the *Magnanime*. His apprentice had been involved in a riot the previous June, arrested and sent to sea as a punishment, 'to the great Injury of myself and children'.[27] As he had been near the end of his apprenticeship, she humbly requested the Commissioners to send orders to Chatham for a replacement servant.

In general naval officials, when making apointments, seem to have taken into consideration the welfare of the families of warrant officers. For example, in 1767 Chatham Dockyard wrote to the Navy Board explaining, 'John Lester Cook of His Majesty's Ship the Falkland at this Port, died here the 4th instant; Charles Mathers late Cook of the Hampshire, who is a sober good Seaman, with a large family, will be very thankful, if the Board would be pleased to appoint him to that Ship.'[28] Yet naval regulations had to be observed. For instance, the wives of warrant officers had a free berth if they went with their husbands to sea but once the ship was taken out of commission they became homeless and had to make other provision. In September 1767 Thomas Hanway, then Commissioner of Chatham Dockyard, was embarrassed to receive a note from the Navy Board, responsible for management of all naval dockyards, to the effect that warrant officers' wives were apparently still living on board some ships put into reserve at Chatham. Hanway replied promptly, assuring members that he had carried out a search and had indeed found the wives of gunners, carpenters, boatswains and cooks on the various ships. He explained that he planned to inform the officers of these vessels that they would be instantly suspended if any woman were found on board in future. Three days later he was able to assure his superiors that all the women had been ordered ashore.[29]

Relief for widows

If seamen failed to return at all, charitable assistance for their dependents was sporadic. After major battles, campaigns, or even naval disasters, subscription funds might be set up to relieve victims' families. These would be advertised in newspapers or by means of public notices. Wealthy institutions and individuals often gave ostentatiously and their names would be printed in promotional literature to encourage similar generosity in others. Printed copies of sermons preached after battles might also be sold for the benefit of widows and orphans. Theatres would hold benefit nights: after the Battle of the Glorious First of June in 1794, the Theatre Royal in Drury Lane promptly held a benefit night on 1 July and all proceeds went to the fund. It was the same in the provinces: after this battle, the theatre at Buxton held a benefit night for 'the Widows and Orphans of the gallant Tars who fell gloriously fighting'. *The Times* reported on 6 August that local dignitaries had supported the initiative – no doubt eager to find any means of easing the burden on the poor relief. After the 1799 expedition to Holland, newspapers explained that widows wishing to claim from the fund would have to present a certificate from their husband's commanding officer and also one from the clergy or parish officers in the place where they lived. To save families travelling from the country to claim in person, certificates were to be distributed to officers for completion then sent to the clergy of respective parishes to identify the claimants. This was a cumbersome procedure at best, likely not only to produce long delays but also to by-pass those families who were 'invisible' to the local clergy.

Poor relief for elderly naval widows was erratic. Pensions did not automatically start at a certain age but were set according to the parish officer's perception of an individual's needs. The person's ability to work was taken into account and payments might be conditional on good behaviour, though funding could be supplemented by other charitable donations – such as gifts from the Lloyd's Patriotic Fund. In general, parish officers were more willing to give poor relief to those who appeared 'deserving' rather than feckless and idle. The Charity for the Relief of Officers' Widows paid pensions to the wives of warrant as well as commissioned officers and the papers of the Charity offers insights into married life for naval women at this level of society. For example, Elizabeth Gough, wife of a gunner of the sloop *Falcon*, was granted a pension on 25 January 1815 even though her husband had died years before on 22 May 1811 when his ship was in Ordinary (reserve dock) at Sheerness. As she explained in her letter to the Charity, 'he left me about four years ago without even informing me where he was going Except it was abroad in some ship'. He had not sent her any allowance for some years and she knew that she should have applied to the Charity sooner but was not sure how to go about it. She lived in Webber Row, off Blackfriars Road in south London and had during this time 'been a great Burthen on my friends'. When a poor widow applied to the Charity, as we have seen with the middling sort, she sometimes discovered that her husband had had two wives. There are several instances where a second widow turned up as long as two years after another had applied for relief. If the later widow could prove she had been the deceased's first wife, the pension was transferred to her whatever the hardship it caused the second. If the husband had found it expedient to change his name at any point (and often seamen did sign up for duty under an assumed name in case they found an opportunity to desert), then the wife could find it difficult to prove she was legally married. In 1809 the wife of James Nelson, who had been warranted a gunner under the assumed name of Charles Johnson, was fortunate to be able to find proof that he was the same man. The widow of William Moore Sullivan, Carpenter of the sloop *Antour*, supposed to have foundered about August 1813, had a slightly easier task. She was able to present letters that he had written home to her in Plymouth explaining that he had merely dropt the 'Sullivan', becoming plain 'William Moore' (after deserting from an East Indiaman) and she should be careful to write to him under his new name in future. Their correspondence extended over years of separation but Sullivan's letters show that poor communication led him to doubt his wife's fidelity. He wrote to her on 25 July 1811:

> Dr Susan, I am very uneasy by not hearing from you, I have sent several letters to you but never received any answer, the frigate that I am home in, is paid off at Deptford. I understand that you live at Howe, so I dow [*sic*] not know where to direct to you. I suppose that your thoughts are otherwise Engag'd at present, if that is the Case let me know Immediately, then I shall better judge how to act.[30]

However, they stayed together some years longer: he was still writing to her from Barbados in July 1813. The widows of some warrant officers could turn to the captain of their husband's ship for help. In July 1802 Elenor Broderick, a boatswain's widow living in Plymouth, asked Captain Rowley, her husband's former captain, to petition the Charity to put her on the pension list. She assured him that she was, 'in the midst of the greatest distress and Poverty that ever was Experienced by myself & three small children'. He duly wrote to the Admiralty explaining that the boatswain had been a good officer and that his widow was a deserving case.[31]

The administration of the Charity was fallible, which added to some widows' distress. Ann Atkinson, a carpenter's widow in Sunderland, wrote to complain that her pension for the year ending 31 May 1810 had been paid to a different woman of the same name. The charity officials duly investigated and found that:

> The woman who has either fraudulently or ignorantly received the pension of the legal widow of Thos Atkinson late carpenter of the star, states that her Husband died eleven years ago after having served many years as Carpenter of several of his Majesty's ships, the last of which is stated to have been the Prince William; However it does not appear that any man of that name was ever carpenter of the Prince William, & therefore it does not appear as present, that she is entitled to any Pension whatever: and the Court will be pleased to determine whether the woman shall be prosecuted or what other steps shall be taken.

The Court urged that all steps be taken to recover the money and noted that the woman should be asked to supply details of the other ships her husband had belonged to, since he did not appear to have ever served on the *Prince William*.

Further investigation indicated that the mistake had occurred because the real widow had moved house and the postmaster in Sunderland had looked for her under surname rather than address. Edward Hatton, the charity's paymaster, reported to his superiors that such mistakes must sometimes happen due to the obscurity of the residences where many of the widows were forced to live and their frequent changes of habitation – presumably due to financial difficulties. He drew the Charity's attention to a similar mistake earlier in the year. The widow who should have received the money wrote to the Charity again in October of the same year explaining that the other woman had stated that she had been robbed of the whole £25.00 on the day after receipt. The first widow believed that the other woman had accepted the money in ignorance, having a husband of the same name who had also been a carpenter and had three sons in the service. Her letter continued, 'she is certainly verry poor so that it is imposable for her to repay the money and to punish her according to law would be croule as all her family is serving his magesty & her left alone to want & poverty – this is a plain statement of facts, Nevertheless I must have my pension as my necessity is urgent theirfore I hope you will send me an order to receive my years pension at the Custom house'. There is also a letter from the other widow, explaining that she had applied for a pension only the previous May, though her husband had been dead eleven years, since she had not understood that as the widow of a warrant officer she was entitled to any pension. She was worried that now she would be prosecuted for fraud and earnestly asked for advice on how to clear herself of the charge. Patiently, the official wrote back to ask her to state the names of the other ships her husband had served in.[32]

When the widows themselves died, relatives or debtors often wrote to the Charity asking for the arrears of the pension owing, either to cover funeral expenses or medical bills. These sums were paid as a matter of routine on production of a certificate of burial. Ann Cooper, a spinster with the same name as her mother, went one step further and concealed her mother's death so that she could continue to receive the pension of a carpenter's widow. In due course, the Charity decided that the daughter should be sued for the money but declined to prosecute her for fraud.[33]

Pay and fraud

During this period successive acts of Parliament made it easier for men at sea to remit money to their wives and families but this provision also made naval women more liable to be preyed upon by the unscrupulous. In 1811 an elderly widow who went to the Navy Pay Office at Somerset House in London to claim the money her son had remitted to her was robbed in the Strand. As she walked off with her half a guinea, a man tricked her into thinking that she was also due 30s prize money and snatched her half guinea as change for a two pound note which he never gave her anyway. The man was caught because he regularly tried the same trick and the widow was able to identify him as he loitered outside the Navy Office the next day. As he had been transported for seven years for the same crime in 1802, this time he was sentenced to death. Since poor women were often illiterate, they were easily defrauded when faced with banknotes.

Because seamen's wives and families were known to be able to claim money through the intervention of the Navy Office, there was scope for other kinds of fraud. Some women swore oaths to the effect that they were the sole surviving kin of some deceased seaman in order to benefit from their will. If these women were unlucky, particularly if the dead man happened to have a wife living, they could be found out and prosecuted. Other women went further and actually presented forged wills in order to claim a dead seaman's effects. *The Penny London Post; or, Morning Advertiser* for 11 – 13 February 1751 reported that the Lord Mayor had committed a certain Mary Carney to the Poultry Compter for impersonating the widow of George Bell, a seaman on the *Exeter*, 'by which Means she fraudulently obtained a Ticket to receive his Wages'. In March of the same year Carney was sentenced to death at the Old Bailey. In 1765 Elizabeth Dunn was convicted of fraud at the Old Bailey after passing herself off as wife of the seaman John Wallace in order to receive the prize money and wages due to him. She was sentenced to death but fortunately for her the court recommended mercy. In 1780 Catharine Dicks attempted to collect the wages of Richard Wallather, claiming that she was his surviving sister, but it was discovered that he had a wife living who should receive the money. Dicks had been put up to the fraud by her husband, who had served in the same ship as Wallather before being discharged as an invalid. The wife had last heard from her husband three years previously from the West Indies, although by the time of the trial he had been dead just eighteen months, which again demonstrates just how long wives might have to wait without news. In another case, on 13 May 1812, Catherine Foster was sentenced to death for perjury and trying to claim a dead seaman's wages. In this instance, the death of the breadwinner (who had been pressed into the navy) had already affected his family: his wife had disappeared, having put her son into the navy and leaving her daughter to be cared for in her sister's household. Such break-ups were not unusual. A correspondent to the *Gentleman's Magazine* in 1800 decried the effect that a seaman's death could have on his children and explained that although the orphans of a seaman's family could be placed at the London Foundling Hospital, another kind of asylum ought to be set up because even when the mother survived she was often unable to care for the children, due to emotional or financial distress.[34] In 1803 the Paddington naval asylum was duly set up for the orphans of seamen. This was a charity supported by subscription that took both boys and girls (the boys all being intended for naval service).

Women who attempted to claim the wages of deceased seamen by presenting forged documents, often became involved in such crimes through relationships with hardened forgers. Contemporary manuals for letter-writing usually contained samples of seamen's wills and letters assigning power of attorney, making this kind of fraud easier. David Fordyce's *The New and Complete*

Letter Writer, dating from the 1790s, contained a sample 'Letter of Attorney by a Seaman'. Such letters gave the bearer the power to act as the seaman's agent and to ask for and receive from the paymaster of the navy and from commissioners for prize money all wages, bounty money and prize money that might be due to the seaman.

The navy did try to introduce systems that would reduce fraud and help genuine naval widows. On 16 February 1751 *Read's Weekly Journal, or British Gazeteer* carried the following notice:

> All Petty Officers and common Seamen's Widows, whose Husbands were killed or drowned in his Majesty's Service, since the 18th Day of November 1740, are forthwith desired to bring or send Certificates, under the Hands of the Minister, Churchwardens, and Overseers of the Parish where they live, that they are the real Widows, to Mr Francis Reynolds, at the Great Tower-Hill Coffee House, on Great Tower Hill, London, on or before the 30th Day of March ext, otherwise they will be too late, as Mr. Reynolds will not apply to Parliament only for such Widows as will apply to him, either by themselves or Agents, of which this Notice is given, in order that they may not miss this Opportunity. All Letters Post paid, will be duly answered.

What is striking about this notice is that these families had already had to wait ten years for compensation. Yet, the naval officials do show some signs of conscience. The notice was followed by a short appendix:

> N.B. If Mr. James Johnston, who was Surgeon of his Majesty's Ship Canterbury, in the Year 1748, will signify by a Line directed as above, where he may be sent to, in order to sign Captain Clarke's Certificate for a poor Woman, of her Husband's being killed on board the said Ship, in an Engagement with a Spanish Fleet in the Havannah, he will have the Prayers of the Widows and Orphans, as they cannot recover the Bounty paid in that case without.

Similarly, in 1763, several newspapers carried notices from the Navy Pay Office in Broad Street explaining that widows of seamen who had died in service often ignorantly applied to their nearest ecclesiastical court to obtain administrations or probates for their husband's wills. The notice explained that wages due could only be paid legally once the wills had been proved by the Prerogative Court of the See of Canterbury, held at Doctors Commons, London. This was very difficult for those seamen's families who lived in the country because the journey to London might be costly. Often widows failed to prove a seaman's Will, thinking that the expense of seeking legal advice probably outweighed any financial benefit. The Pay Office was anxious to disabuse them of this thought and the notice included a table showing that a scale of charges applied, depending on amount of wages to be paid out. For example, if the wages owed amounted to less than £5, the charge of proving the will was just 6s or, including commission, 12s (when all stamps, office and proctors fees were taken into account). But although the Pay Office tried to make the bureaucracy easier to understand, the legal process must have seemed intimidating to those with little education. Nor was the Pay Office particularly successful in preventing fraud. In 1816 the *Gentleman's Magazine* was still complaining that the easy and frequent forging of seamen's wills was 'a national disgrace'. It was suggested that the captain of every ship should keep a register of his sailors' wills, and that once a will had been registered, no alteration should be valid, unless made in the presence of the captain or a specified officer. But this arrangement, too, would have been cumbersome to administer.

Seamen received tickets instead of wages if they were turned over to another ship or sent to hospital at the time when their ship was paid off. Men could, legally, with their captain's consent, assign their tickets in favour of a named individual, usually a ticket broker or innkeeper. The tickets could be cashed in by the navy or by private individuals at a discount. However, seamen could easily be defrauded by this process, and captains usually discouraged it, or forced those who now owned the seamen's tickets to accept lower rates of discount when they were presented for payment. However, seamen could use the same method to make over their pay to their relatives, if they wished, giving their women considerable economic authority as tickets were often traded locally among friends and acquaintances. A dead seaman's family might also be defrauded of the man's wages because the spiritual court at Doctor's Commons regularly granted administrations to his creditors, or pretended creditors. Publicans, in particular, often bought tickets entitling them to seamen's wages on terms hugely advantageous to them. In this way they would gain possession of the deceased's wages and prize money, or at least of his tickets, before the widow or family heard anything of the man's death. The judgement of the court might be revoked if the next of kin protested later but once the money was in the hands of the publican or dealer it was not easily retrieved. Although the sums earned on each ticket might be small, cumulatively purchasers were dealing in large sums. The *Gentleman's Magazine* for 1758 reported that Mrs Swan, the wife of a purser, cashed in one thousand pounds of tickets in a week. These dealers in seamen's wages effectively prevented many seamen from saving for their old age or for a time when they were unable to work.

Prize agents were often also dishonest. A letter to *The Times* of 24 July 1787 criticizes them for telling claimants that their books were made up and that any unclaimed money was forfeit to Greenwich Hospital when in fact they were keeping the money themselves. The correspondent cited the case of one prize agent in Antigua who had no intention of living in Britain to help claimants. People who claimed he owed them money often had to travel to the West Indies if they sought a resolution. The widow of the boatswain of the *Vengeance* asked someone in the West Indies trade to act on her behalf but the agent refused to deal with him, 'though the poor woman was in the utmost distress, and still continues so'. The correspondent, purporting to be 'an old seaman', calls upon the directors managing this unclaimed money to put a stop to such proceedings in order to prevent 'such mercenary rogues as navy agents, from plundering the poor seamen and their families'.

There were also frequent attempts to defraud Greenwich Hospital by claiming prize money owed to deceased seamen. Often male accomplices put women up to claiming that they were sole surviving kin of the deceased. For example, in 1767, Mary Peck, wife of the cook of the *Infanta* at Portsmouth, received half a year's pay from him to travel to London and obtain sworn documents that she was the widow of the deceased seaman Richard Walker, whom she may indeed have known before her marriage to Peck but to whom she was never married. Those who were caught and found guilty were hanged or imprisoned: Mary Peck was recommended for the death penalty though she claimed that she was innocent and that others had tricked her into the affair.

Coming ashore

There were many temptations and dangers in the way of seamen intent on bringing their wages home to their dependents. When the fleet returned, it was important for a wife to try to meet her husband as soon as his ship anchored in order to be with him on shore when he was paid. In all the principal commercial towns there were people ready to advance seamen money against wages due, or to purchase certificates of prize money due to them at rates greatly to the disadvantage of the seamen and always injurious to their families. Yet wives seldom knew in advance when their husband's ship would arrive, and so relied on word of mouth or scanned the columns of ship news printed in newspapers for early intelligence. Naval women may not have needed to pay the full price of the newspaper: some hawkers illegally hired newspapers from house to house.[35] Once wives were sure that a ship was due in a particular port, they would have to travel there on foot, having no money for a stagecoach or coastal vessel. Often by the time they arrived, prostitutes (to whom their husbands might already owe money) would already have been ferried out to the ship. Once on board, there was no privacy, and wives and any children with them might have to mix with crowds of prostitutes and other women on board.

The kinds of seamen's women involved in separating a seaman from his money were little better than common thieves. *The St. James's Chronicle; or the British Evening-Post* for 12 – 15 February 1763 noted one such occurrence after ships were paid off at the end of the war:

> On Saturday Morning a Man well dressed belonging to the Sea, was found almost smothered, in a muddy Place at Greenwich; by proper Care, in a few Hours, he recovered, so as to give the following Account how he came there: That he was much in Liquor, and was met by a Woman, who offered her Service to see him to his Lodgings, which he accepted; that in going along she took the Opportunity of picking his Pocket of 27 Guineas; and on his charging her with the Robbery, she pushing him into the Slough, and made off with the Booty; where he remained several Hours unable to get out, till a Waterman accidentally came by, and gave him Assistance.

The Proceedings of the Old Bailey contain many such incidents. These criminal cases are recorded as final fair copies of a question and answer process between the Justice of the Peace and the witness, and so cannot be taken as absolutely reliable accounts. The transcriptions expunge the stammerings of nervous witnesses and translate cant and dialect words into intelligible prose for the benefit of the reader. However, they are as close as we shall get to the voices of seamen and their women at this level of society and give a flavour of life in ports and dockside areas. A number of cases seem typical. On 27 June 1765 John Glass, seaman, was paid off from one of his Majesty's ships in Deptford yard. At about ten o'clock at night, 'a little in liquor', he made his way towards London Bridge. At Bright's Alley, by Nightingale-Lane, two women stopped him and asked him for something to drink. They took him to a room in a nearby house, where he offered one of them a shilling to stay with her all night. He had seven and a half guineas and six shillings in silver in a handkerchief tied round his neck. As he lay down, he put the handkerchief under his head. By this time, he was quite drunk. In the morning his money was gone. He went with a constable and searched likely public houses until he found the woman who had robbed him and her accomplice. The woman claimed that he had made a present of the money to live with her, and that she had slept with him before. She was found guilty of stealing and transported; her accomplice was sent to Newgate for keeping a disorderly house.

In another case, in April 1782, a seaman named Robert Cockrill claimed that Sarah Hatchett had stolen his money, his silver shoe buckles and silver knee buckles while he slept. Cockrill had picked Sarah Hatchett up at a public house and paid the owner of the house in which she had an apartment 1s to sleep with her. He had apparently been robbed when drunk. Next morning he fetched a constable and went in search of Hatchett and one of her accomplices, John Pinnick. Pinnick claimed that there had been 'singing & roaring' all night long so that he could not get any rest, and that when he got up at 5a.m. to go about his lawful work, he found the buckles at the bottom of the stairs. Both he and Hatchett were condemned to hard labour in the House of Correction.

Other cases reported in the press show that the conflicting testimonies of the accuser and the accused were not easily unscrambled. In 1794, Hannah Roper and Mary Burke were indicted for assaulting and robbing Christian Anderson, a seaman, of twenty-two guineas. He swore that as he was going home about ten at night one Saturday, Mary Burke ran out of a house in Gravel-Lane, snatched off his hat and ran into the house again. He followed her. At the time he had twenty-two guineas, kept in a handkerchief in his hand. The women knocked the money out of his hand on to the floor, and stole two guineas. Burke's defence was that the seaman had slept with her, and that in revenge for her not complying with some indecent liberties that he had proposed, he was bringing this charge against her. A witness was able to testify only that the seaman was spending his money in the lane with the girls. The court found Burke guilty of larceny but let Roper free.[36] Sometimes sailors would take matters into their own hands. They might return mob-handed to the bawdy house where they had been tricked and wreck it, ripping up mattresses and smashing furniture. Of course, if they were unlucky enough to be apprehended in the process, they could be charged with causing a riot.

Unmarried seamen might try to seek out the same women in port but this did not necessarily save them from becoming victims of crime. In 1785, a seaman called Henry Lane claimed his watch had been stolen while he slept. He began his evidence at the Old Bailey trial on 29 June with, 'I am a seaman, I have been several months at sea, and I went on shore to drink with my shipmates over night, that was on the 10th of June, I went home with a young woman as I knew very well, and slept with her'. His narrative illustrates how, once drunk, seamen were often at the mercy of those around them and easily robbed of money and valuables – though in this case he got his watch back. Watches were regarded as luxury items and in 1797 – 8 Pitt even attempted to put a tax on them to pay for the war. A well-made silver watch would cost around £3 to £5 and were certainly beyond the reach of the average artisan, though used silver watches might be valued at 40 shillings and metal ones at 20 shillings. An inquiry into the state of the police force in the metropolis in 1816 found that good patent silver watches fetched £2 and gold ones £5 or £6. Picking pockets and shoplifting were capital offences when the sums stolen were more than one shilling and five shillings respectively but since watches were a status symbol, there would have been a ready market for stolen ones; they found their way from pickpocket to receiver and many changed hands in London's underworld. Women accused of 'stealing from the person' were often prostitutes robbing their clients and it seems probable that many victims were reluctant to bring such women to justice out of embarrassment. Few men admitted to soliciting and preferred to present themselves in legal cases as having been 'tricked' by the woman. Women who kept bawdy houses often owned several properties in other parts of town so if robbery was committed in one, they simply moved off to another for a few weeks until affair had blown over and danger of arrest had passed. Nevertheless, judges in such cases often seem to have given the prosecutor a hard time, perhaps thinking they had brought their trouble upon themselves, and this applies even when the woman had a male accomplice. It is probable that such women did not perceive themselves as prostitutes at all, but rather thieves who used the methods of prostitutes to gain access to their victim's person. This would certainly apply to the case reported in *The Times* on 3 July 1816. Two women persuaded a sailor to take them out in a carriage for a day to Peckham. On the way back they stopped at a public house, and as he paid for the carriage they jostled and distracted him while a male accomplice ran out and stole the sailor's silver watch.

However much naval women longed for their partners to return from the sea, the man's arrival could sometimes cause domestic difficulty. For example, when sailors' women became pregnant within one relationship, the child's presence often threatened other long-standing relationships – not least because a seaman's long absences often made it impossible for the woman to pass off her latest child as her husband's 'legitimate' offspring (see Plate 29). *The Newgate Calendar*, in 1818, reported a sensational case: Margaret Dixon had re-married her husband in 1728, just a few days after being hanged for murdering her child.[37] Dixon's husband had been pressed into the navy and during his absence she became pregnant by another man. At this time Scottish law required that adulterous women be exposed publicly: they had to sit in church for three consecutive Sundays and be rebuked by the minister. Many women destroyed their illegitimate children rather than suffer such humiliation, and Dixon was found guilty of this offence and sentenced to be hanged. As her coffin was being taken for burial, the bearers stopped for a drink in a village and one of them saw the lid of the coffin move. He pushed it aside and Dixon immediately sat up. She was put to bed in the public house and soon recovered enough to be able to walk home. She could not be tried twice for the same crime and was therefore freed. The law held that her marriage had been dissolved upon her execution but she always maintained her innocence of murder, if not adultery, and her husband happily re-married her a few days after she was hanged. She was still living in Scotland in 1753.

The Times for 26 September 1789 carried the story of a Falmouth woman whose husband had been absent for several years and who had just murdered her bastard child. The body of the newborn infant was found in a small vault in her apartment used for hiding prohibited goods, implying that, like many sailors' women, she was involved in smuggling. The woman made no attempt to pretend that the child had been stillborn, as many in this situation did, and she was found guilty of murder and suffered the penalty. In yet another case, The London Chronicle for February – March 1790 reported that:

> A woman hung herself at Portsmouth last Tuesday, but was cut down time enough to save her life. The cause of this rash act is imagined to be her proving with child by a man she co-habited with in the absence of her husband, who was expected to arrive from the sea every hour.[38]

Some couples came to a happier accommodation. On 30 December 1816 The Times carried the story of a seaman from the East India Company who returned home after a long voyage to find his wife four months pregnant. The child was clearly not his, but as his wife had given him other children, he had no wish to turn her out of doors and break up his family. He took his wife to court and once her infidelity had been proved to the court's satisfaction, she was made to declare on oath the real father of the child with whom she had co-habited in her husband's absence. This other man was then required to pay three shillings a month towards the child's upkeep and the costs of the case.

The financial and emotional difficulties faced by the families of absent sailors are well illustrated in the letters of one seaman. James Whitworth, aged 34, was seized late in 1810 and served in the sloop Portia under Commander Henry Thomson in the North Sea. Both he and his wife, Charlotte, were literate and possibly aspired to the ranks of the middling sort. Whitworth came from Lincolnshire but the couple now lived with their two daughters in Back Lane (now Watergate Street), leading to the naval yard in Deptford, where they seem to have kept a shop. On 2 February 1812, Whitworth wrote home from North Yarmouth:

I shall not be able to write again before we sail as I expect it will be in a few days but hope you will write again by return as I shall be very anxious to hear from you, you must make the lodgers pay weekly else they will always use you the same, I am very well in my health but have got a bad pain in my back and have had for some time.[39]

At this period, shopkeepers often rented a whole house, kept their shop on the ground floor and lived with their family in the garret while renting out middle floors to subsidise their income. A freehold tenement in Back Lane Deptford in the early nineteenth century could be let for £10 a year, so the lodgers would not have brought in a large sum.

Whitworth did not shield his wife from his present dangers. On 4 February he wrote while in the North Sea, hoping to put into Hull or Leith soon so that the letter could be posted. The weather had been squally and he himself was 'very poorly of a bad cold and small pimples breaking out'. One man in the crew already had his head smashed on the bars of the capstan and his 'skull broke to pieces'. Yet Whitworth was still hopeful that if the ship returned to Yarmouth, he would get liberty to come to Deptford to see his family. He concluded by hoping he might at least earn some prize money:

My Dear you must not let gloomy thoughts be your companions and let us hope Providence has better days in store for you and me than we hitherto have had by one lucky price I may make a fortune who can tell.[40]

By 7 May he had learnt enough to help man a small boat and had been made a member of the cutter crew, but the *Portia* had met with terrible weather and taken no prizes at all:

You may depend on this I shall take the first chance I can to escape from this floating hell ... At present I am very well but have had a blow on one of my leggs [sic] which I am afraid will prove a laming stroke to me ... what an unhappy wretch I am and no prospect of relief or release.[41]

He explained that the surf was bad and he was not sure when a boat would be able to get to the ship to take the post off but he asked her to reply as soon as possible because he was desperate for news – 'Tell me how things go on as for peace or war, the price of bread etc'.

Later that month his ship put into Sheerness, but as he was 50 miles from London, he was doubtful that his wife would be able to travel to see him and he himself saw no prospect of getting leave to visit her. By this time, 29 May, he was seriously depressed, 'I fear but little happiness for us on this side the Grave. God grant our children may never taste the bitter cup we have had and at present are drinking.' He warned her to write as soon as possible as the ship would soon return to its station in the North Sea. He had been unable to write to her before since he had had to work from four in the morning to nine at night, nor could he answer her question about what his life is like on board, 'as for how I get on it is not in my power to make you understand for you can form no idea of this line of life'. She had also asked him why he continued to be lame and he replied that he thought the food was partly responsible. It was good but 'very salt'; the beef had probably lain in salt for 7 years. By this time, the dangers of salted provisions were well known. *The Craftsman; or Say's Weekly Journal* for 18 September 1773 had reported that in the American War of Independence, of the amazing number of seamen who had died of disease rather than wounds, 'half at least without exaggeration died of the scurvy, by living on salt provisions'. Such comments would have become common knowledge through the gossip networks and the newspaper had called on those in power to do more to preserve the lives of brave sailors.

Other aspects of Whitworth's life caused him distress: he had received six months' wages (£2 13s 6d) but he resented doing his own washing, since he was not used to it, and he hoped to lose his captain soon because he was a very 'divil'. By June, Whitworth had heard that all was well at home from another man's wife who had travelled from Woolwich, near Deptford, to visit her husband but he himself had received no reply to his recent letters. He complained to his wife that she might well be busy and have little time to spare but what time she had was her own, whereas he could steal few moments to write without the risk of being flogged. On 22 June he wrote in a more cheerful frame of mind to say that they had taken a prize off Norway and were returning to Yarmouth, but by 27 September he was imprisoned in irons for trying to desert – possibly seizing the chance, as he was one of the cutter crew. He wrote to his wife saying that he was 'sorry she should take it so much to heart for what am I but a piece of useless lumber a burden to myself and a plague to other people'. She had obviously suggested that she come to see him, but he asks her not to in his present situation, and not to tell the children. In fact, he wishes he had not told her what had happened since she can do nothing but worry.[42]

Yet Whitworth's wife would now be key to improving his situation. She was able to write to friends who pulled strings to ensure his case did not come to court martial. Obviously he also relied upon her to keep their home going. On

3 October he wrote from Sheerness, 'I hope my Dearest you are not ill as all and every thing depends upon you, with respect to my present unhappy situation.' He was beginning to feel more sanguine about his punishment: he thought that even if it came to a court martial, the worse that could happen would be that he would be turned over to another ship without leave. He also explained that his pay would go towards compensating for the damages caused in the attempted escape, so he would get no money for at least another six months. As the ship's pay book records that he spent £2 14s 1d on clothing supplied by the ship and 1s 6d on 'dead men's clothes', he would have been able to send very little money home. In November he was made a prisoner 'at large' and only confined to irons while the ship was in port. He had now been allowed to set up a little 'school' on board ship to teach others among the 86-strong crew to read and write. They could not pay him but did what they could to reward him. He hoped that his wife would soon be able to send him a specimen of his daughter Eliza's handwriting. Later that month he wrote cryptically that if she and an uncle were able to intercede with the captain for him, and he could get off the ship, he would try the new line of business she proposed for him. Presumably he could not be too explicit, and we do not know the outcome of her efforts, as the correspondence ends abruptly. The ship's muster book records that in November 1812 Whitworth was transferred to the *Solebay*. Yet it is clear that in September his only recourse had been desertion and that once this had failed his wife was key to his extrication. Earlier he had fantasized that were he ashore and able to come into their shop to buy a trifle she would not know him because of the alteration in his dress and person. Long separations clearly led to insecurities and in Whitworth's case the relation of his illnesses and pains may have been some attempt to regain an element of domestic support.[43]

At the end of a war, when seamen returned, there would be a glut on the labour market. Well-wishers suggested various solutions to the problem including, in 1763, settling them in the New Forest but such schemes proved impractical. At the end of the war against Napoleon, seamen were paid off in such numbers that they had little hope of finding work and became easy targets for radical groups agitating for social reform. In December 1816, a coordinated insurrection was planned to take place at Spa Fields in London and in manufacturing towns across the country where there was great distress. Ringleaders had deliberately targeted sailors, alongside other potentially disaffected groups, promising to pay them higher wages under the new government that they hoped to establish. The demonstrations failed, but one of the ringleaders, Cashman, who attained some notoriety at his trial and execution, was a seaman. Afterwards, measures were taken to relieve the immediate hardship of seamen and their families. Sermons were preached to distressed seamen in London workhouses, meetings were held in storeships docked in the capital aiming to set up subscription funds to relieve their wants, and the Marine Society pledged to clothe one hundred destitute seamen. Their families would never again have to endure such a prolonged period of severe want.

Yet at the end of our period, a telling anecdote appeared in the *Gentleman's Magazine* which indicates the deep impact that long periods of emotional stress and material want could have on poor seamen's wives. In 1820 at the town hall in Southwark, London, Hannah Baker, a miserable old woman, was charged with stealing an egg from a stall in the Borough market and an apple, orange, turnip, or potato, from other stallholders. When she was searched, there was found in a bundle of rags in her bosom notes amounting to £173, and in her pocket a substantial amount of silver, making in all £204 18s (about £8590 in today's money). She refused to give her address, but was traced to Garden Row in Shadwell where she lived with her son, who was poor but industrious and had no idea that his mother was worth so much. No one prosecuted the old woman, so she was set at liberty and the money given to her son. He had always believed that his father, who was a sailor, had died leaving some money but his mother had clearly felt so threatened and insecure that she obsessively hoarded the money where it would be safe and continued to live as a near scavenger.[44]

1. *GM* 36 (1766), 128.

2. Jessica Warner and Allyson Lunny, 'Marital Violence in a Martial Town: Husbands and Wives in Early Modern Portsmouth', *Journal of Family History*, 28, no. 2 (2003), 258 – 76.

3. See C. S Forester, ed., *The Adventures of John Wetherell* (London, 1954), p. 253.

4. Sim Comfort, *Forget Me Not: A Study of Naval and Maritime Engraved Coins and Plate (1745 – 1918)* (London, 2004), p. vii.

5. *The Times*, 24 October 1795, p. 3 col. c.

6. Thomas Wise, *The Newest Young Man's Companion* (Berwick, 1754), pp. 52, 54.

7. BL Add. MSS 75644. All subsequent extracts taken from these papers.

8. TNA, ADM 36 12168.

9. David Hannay, 'Odds and Ends of the Old Navy', *Mariner's Mirror*, 4 (1914), 181

10. *Morning Post and Fashionable World*, 25 Aug. 1794, p. 2 col 4.

11. 'Letter to the editor, 13 August 1809' in *Naval Chronicle*, 22 (1809), 102 – 04.

12. See Tony Henderson, *Disorderly Women in Eighteenth-Century London. Prostitution and Control in the Metropolis 1730-1830* (London, 1999).

13. George Pinckard, *Notes on the West Indies*, 3 vols (London, 1806), I, 38.

14. See Cindy McCreery, 'True Blue and *Black, Brown and Fair*: prints of British sailors and their women during the Revolutionary and Napoleonic Wars', *British Journal for Eighteenth-Century Studies* 23 (2000), 135 – 52; Geoff Quilley, *The Image of the Ordinary Seaman in the Eighteenth Century* (2004), www.nmm.ac.uk.mag accessed on 3 June 2005.

15. Jack Nastyface pseud. [i.e. William Robinson] *Nautical Economy; or, Forecastle Recollections of Events during the Last War* (London, 1836), p. 57.

16. Robert Wilson, 'Remarks on board his Majesty's Ship Unité of 40 guns' in *Five Naval Journals 1789 – 1817*, ed. by H. G. Thursfield, Navy Records Society, 41 (London, 1951), pp. 131 – 2.

17. Anon., *Statement respecting the Prevalence of Certain Immoral Practices in His Majesty's Navy: Addressed to the right honourable the Lords Commissioners of the Admiralty* (London, 1821), p.11. I owe this reference to Amy Miller.

18. Ivy Pinchbeck, *Women Workers and the Industrial Revolution 1750 – 1850* (London, 1930), p. 298.

19. TNA ADM6/385.

20. Ivy Pinchbeck, *Women Workers*, p. 3.

21. www.nmm.ac.uk/flinders accessed 18 Jan. 2007, 29 Nov. 1800, Flinders to Ann Chappelle.

22. 'Old-Bailey Intelligence', *The New Town and Country Magazine* (1787), 658. H. L. Cryer, 'Horatio Nelson and the Murderous Cooper', *Mariner's Mirror*, 60 (1974), 3 – 7.

23. *OBP*, www.oldbaileyonline.org accessed 28 Mar. 2005.

24. *The Bon Ton Magazine, Or, Microscope of Fashion and Folly*, 5 vols (1791 – 96), IV, 203

25. Anon. *The Lamentation of the Sailor's and Soldier's Wives for the loss of their Husbands* (London, *c.* 1800) www.crcstudio.arts.ualberta.ca/streetprint/Libraries/imagelibrary accessed 13 June 2005. Cf. the broadside *The Case of the Distressed Widows of the Commission and Warrant-Officers of the Royal Navy* (London, 1751).

26. TNA ADM 106/1118/80.

27. TNA ADM 106/1118/121.

28. TNA ADM 106/1118/294.

29. TNA ADM 106/1154/245 and 246.

30. TNA ADM 6/388.

31. TNA ADM 6/339.

32. All details of the case in TNA ADM 6/385.

33. TNA ADM 6/386, 25 Feb. 1813.

34. *GM*, 70 (1800) 299.

35. *The True Briton*, 2 Jan. 1798, p. 4, col. 3.

36. *The Morning Post and Fashionable World* (July to December 1794), p. 3.

37. William Jackson, *The New and Complete Newgate Calendar*, 6 vols (London, 1818), II, 153 – 6.

38. *The London Chronicle*, Sat. 2 Feb. – Tues 2 Mar. 1790, p. 208.

39. NMM WHW/1/1, 2 Feb. 1812, Whitworth to his wife Charlotte

40. NMM WHW/1/2, 4 Feb. 1812, Whitworth to his wife Charlotte.

41. NMM WHW/1/4, 7 May 1812, Whitworth to his wife Charlotte.

42. NMM WHW/1/5, 29 May 1812; WHW/1/6, 3 June 1812; WHW/1/9, 22 June 1812; WHW/1/10, 27 Sept. 1812, Whitworth to his wife Charlotte.

43. NMM WHW/1/11, 3 Oct 1812; WHW/1/3, 29 ? 1812, Whitworth to his wife Charlotte; ADM 35/3709; 51/2626; 37/3128; 37/4744.

44. *GM*, 90 (1820), II, 631.

Chapter Five
WARFARE AND WOMEN'S LIVES

Britain was almost continuously at war from 1750 to 1815 but the effect on society intensified particularly during the French Wars from 1793 since by the early 1800s, as we have seen, one in five adult males was engaged in some form of military activity. During these years the navy increased significantly in size, becoming the largest the country had ever maintained: when the war against Napoleon finally ended in 1815, the navy had 713 ships in commission and 140,000 men in service.

This work explores the impact this had on women at different social levels, an approach that requires some flexibility since individuals could move between different social ranks. Warfare had a marked effect on social ranking: during this period noble title, formerly the preserve of great landlords, increasingly became the reward for outstanding service to the state. Many of the peerages awarded during the French Wars went to naval heroes, although the practice began to attract criticism once successive governments found that they might have to support newly made peers financially to enable them to bear their titles with proper dignity. The navy was in any case a prime means of social mobility in wartime: individuals moved up the ranks more quickly as officers fell in battle and those who were fortunate enough to capture enemy prizes could find themselves with sufficient capital to purchase land, as demonstrated in Jane Austen's novel *Persuasion*, which she wrote in 1816.

During the French Wars, the social composition of the naval officer class narrowed somewhat since prolonged conflict highlighted the fact that a naval career offered fame and prize money, making the navy more attractive to men from good but impoverished families as well as younger members of the aristocracy. Yet arguably the aristocracy retained its powerful influence well into the nineteenth century because on the whole it readily assimilated the most talented from the middling sort, recruiting to its ranks key members of the military and new public service elite. This social mobility may help to explain why the middling sort did not challenge the elevated position of the aristocracy before the end of the century. Social advancement, however welcome, inevitably placed a strain on the wives of middle ranking naval officers. Captain Inglefield's social ambition, for example, seems to have exacerbated the tensions with his wife, who brought only a modest amount of money to the marriage and failed to shine in public. The letters exchanged between naval families also show how the responsibilities they shouldered and the constraints within which they operated helped to create a dynamic national culture and an evolving sense of 'Britishness'.

A study of the lived experience of naval wives in this period also adds to our understanding of the social expectations of gender relations and the proper role of women. The more capable and privileged naval women were to some extent able to traverse conventional boundaries, protecting their interests at home while supporting, with supplies and letters, their husbands at sea. On the other hand, there were certainly some wives, like Sarah Collingwood, who did not live up to expectations and who failed to run their homes or bring up children as their husbands would have wished. In 1809 Collingwood complained to his sister that one of his wife's relatives, the Rector of Bolden, County Durham, had died without leaving any money to his two daughters. He then reflected, 'perhaps he thought, what I by experience know, for every thousand pound he left them, two would have been spent on the credit of it.'[1] This was a bitter indictment of his family from a man who prided himself on succeeding in life through his own efforts and on never getting into debt. Mistresses could be similarly extravagant: Emma Hamilton amassed considerable debts as she renovated and furnished Nelson's home at Merton, exceeding by far his ability to settle them. At the extreme lower end of society, on the other hand, some wives were bereft of resources through no fault of their own, often left with young children and forced to depend on charity or resort to criminal activity.

Contemporary conduct books for women recommended strong religious faith as a means of coping with the vicissitudes of life that, it seemed to some commentators, would be sure to afflict them:

> Your whole life is often a life of suffering. You cannot plunge into
> business, or dissipate yourselves in pleasure and riot, as men too often
> do, when under the pressure of misfortunes. You must bear your
> sorrows in silence, unknown and unpitied. You must often put on a
> face of serenity and cheerfulness, when your hearts are torn with
> anguish, or sinking in despair. Then your only resource is in the
> consolations of religion [2]

When Anne Elliot, the heroine of Jane Austen's *Persuasion*, finally touches the heart of her former lover, Captain Wentworth, by explaining how women were constrained to suffer emotional distress in more searing ways than men, it would seem that Austen was simply re-pointing a sentiment that had become commonplace. In an intimate drawing room setting, where Wentworth is able to overhear the conversation, Anne tells Captain Harville:

> We certainly do not forget you as soon as you forget us. It is, perhaps, our fate rather than our merit. We cannot help ourselves. We live at home, quiet, confined, and our feelings prey upon us. You are forced on exertion. You have always a profession, pursuits, business of some sort or other, to take you back into the world immediately, and continual occupation and change soon weaken impressions.[3]

In the novel, Captain Harville strongly contests this argument, and surviving naval correspondence confirms that however distracted by the business of their ship, husbands were invariably anxious about their wives at home, particularly if they had children.

All the same, Anne's sentiments do help to emphasize a recurrent theme in the novel: that the happiest relationships are based on close partnership. Admiral Croft and his wife, though eccentric, are mutually supportive and face life's vicissitudes together. Rather unusually, Mrs Croft had accompanied her husband to sea for long periods. At Bath they were almost always in each other's company, though it was considered an unfashionable 'country habit' in an era when men rarely socialized with their wives. When doctors advised the Admiral to take walks to alleviate his gout, his wife accompanied him everywhere, walking just for his benefit. In this respect she offered a physical representation of all those naval wives who took special care of their husband's health, indirectly contributing to the war effort through their solicitude.

Austen's *Persuasion* also conveys the view that naval officers were mostly drawn to women possessing some strength of character, though the abortive relationship between Wentworth and Louisa Musgrove indicates that this strength should be 'steadiness of principle' rather than the 'obstinacy of self-will' that Louisa displayed. Anne is contrasted with her sister Mary who is always fancying herself ill and who spoils her children to such an extent that she is unable to control them. When Louisa falls during an outing to Lyme and concusses herself, Captain Wentworth is deeply impressed by Anne's presence of mind in this crisis and his feelings for her are re-kindled. Austen of course suggests that such robust, dependable qualities are desirable in any woman.

Fears of shipwreck

The general assumption during this period is that shipwreck and the possibility of their loved ones being lost at sea held the greatest terror for naval wives and women. During this 70-year period, 377 naval vessels were wrecked or lost at sea, on average, just over five a year. (A high proportion of these were smaller, more vulnerable ships rather than warships carrying hundreds of men; it was safer to be in a warship built to withstand all weathers with many hands to help in an emergency.)

Sailors' women rightly feared storms and shipwreck; few sailors could swim and no large warship carried sufficient boats if all the crew had to abandon ship.[4] Yet shipwreck was not a constant fear. Little evidence survives on which to judge emotional response but it appears that much depended on where their men were posted and on the time of year. Nelson, for example, reported to his wife from Minorca in May 1795 that he was enjoying the finest weather in the world and his health had never been better.[5] Captain Edward Codrington, writing from the Scheldt during the ill-fated Walcheren expedition of 1809, wrote teasingly to his wife: 'You probably are fancying me in danger both of shipwreck and disease, whilst I am in reality well moored in smooth water and as well as I ever was in my life.'[6] Yet in this age of sail, the dangers of the sea were often in the forefront of the mind of the population in general. Numbers of merchant and naval ships were wrecked or damaged each year through storm or accident. The UK shipwreck database shows that a staggering total of 8312 ships were wrecked off Britain's coasts between 1745 and 1815 – an average of 118 a year.[7] In 1763 it was estimated that during the Seven Years War alone around 4200 seamen, on naval and merchant ships, drowned annually.[8]

Given the uncertainty of communication, it is worth considering how the public would have found out about a shipwreck in the first place. Shipwreck was a fact of life but losses, naval shipwreck in particular, were well publicized. Under the heading 'Ship News', most newspapers listed arrivals and departures from London and other ports, and recorded ships lost at sea, thus helping to foster a 'maritime community' who shared the same interests and anxieties. They also reported seasonal storms around the coast when ships were lost or damaged and sailors killed. In this way merchants and ship owners tracked their investments, and families learnt the fate of loved ones.

We can gauge how such reports affected naval wives from Frances Boscawen's reaction when the *Lyme* foundered in the Atlantic in 1747. She wrote to her husband at sea, 'How shocking is the account of the *Lyme*'s fate, and that terrible storm the West India fleet met with. I could not read it without trembling.'[9] Newspapers and monthly magazines also published longer, first-hand accounts of disasters at sea from letters or official reports. These reports were often incorrect, deficient or liable to raise false hopes. For example, the *Gentleman's Magazine* for 1750 reported a destructive storm in the East Indies in some detail:

> His Majesty's ship *Pembroke*, of 60 guns, struck on Colderoon point, and over-set, having parted her cable the 13th, at 6 P.M. she made sail out of Fort St *David* road, but could not clear the point; twelve men only were saved, Capt. *Fineber* and about 330 men were drowned, and all the officers except a Capt. of *marines*.[10]

The very information the families needed, the names of the survivors, was not listed.

Even when shipwrecks were reported at length, readers would often be left in some suspense. In 1793 *The St. James's Chronicle or, British Evening-Post* printed the following dramatic extract from a letter sent from Plymouth on 16 December. It described the total loss of the cutter *Pigmy* near Plymouth:

> At six o'clock P.M. two anchors were let go, but the wind blew a hurricane, and they brought home; a few minutes after, she struck on the rocks, and continued there till ten o'clock, when the mast was cut away, on which, and in the boats, about 60 persons got on shore, but Lieut. PULLIBANK, her Commander, and five other officers, refused to quit the vessel, and unfortunately perished in her, as she went to pieces at eleven o'clock.

A woman who was on board, and who had the day before been delivered of a fine boy, was saved with her infant on the Cutter's mast.[11]

The Star for Wednesday 18 December reported the same event, noting that the Lieutenant 'with about eleven others, (the number not exactly ascertained) were unfortunately drowned'. It did explain, however, that the woman who was saved was married to one of the seamen. The wreck of the *Pigmy* does not seem to have been reported further but, after news of a significant disaster, a fuller list of those killed might be given in subsequent editions. When the frigate *Tribune* was wrecked at the entrance to Halifax harbour in 1798, the list of officers killed was printed in *The True Briton* on 6 February, and the list of women and children lost was printed the next day. Extended accounts generally emphasized dramatic details and elements of human interest that would appeal to readers. In the case of the *Tribune*, the newspaper noted that the Quartermaster, McGregor, had his wife on board and that, 'They were a respectable couple, and greatly attached to each other'. McGregor tried to get his wife to go ashore in one of the boats when ship lay on shoals but she refused to leave him. Both died.[12]

We know from the records of women claiming naval pensions from the Charity for the Relief of Officers' Widows that some who feared their husbands had been shipwrecked waited months in the hope of better news before reconciling themselves to widowhood. Contemporary entertainment may have encouraged wives to hope that loved ones would survive shipwreck. For example, a musical drama called *The Purse; Or, Benevolent Tar*, performed in Boston in 1797, features a sailor called Will Steady, who returns to his wife after shipwreck and eight years of captivity. Her ordeal is humorously glossed over in the dialogue. Will Steady hopes that he will not find that grief has 'shatter'd her hulk' or that she has 'founder'd in a hard squall of adversity'.[13] In *The Shipwreck*, a comic opera of 1797 played at the Theatre Royal, Drury Lane, the heroine's lover survives to marry her.[14] And it was sometimes right to hope against the odds. Some ships put to sea and were never heard of again but there were instances of vessels reported missing that later came safely into port. In 1793, the frigate *Aquilon* came home with news that the *Berwick*, which had been damaged in a gale off Toulon and given up for lost, had managed to limp back to Gibraltar. The ship's escape was subsequently reported in the press.

Consumer goods alluded to storms and shipwreck in sentimental terms and may have been intended to offer comfort. For example, a typical earthenware jug of the early nineteenth century commemorating Nelson is decorated with the popular lines, 'The sailor tost in stormy seas, | Though far his bark may roam, | Still hears a voice in every breeze, | That wakens thoughts of home, | He thinks upon his distant friends, | His wife, his humble cot, | And from his inmost heart ascends, | The prayer Forget me not'.[15] In contrast, contemporary poems alluding to shipwreck that were written by women strove for dramatic effect. A typical poem by Lady Manners called 'The Child of Sorrow', published in 1794, features a female narrator who from the coast sees her lover drowned. She describes the fury of the tempest, 'The floating wreck is driven towards the coast, | With seamen's lifeless bodies scatter'd round.'[16] This poem suggests that women were well aware of the particular conditions that sailors most feared.[17] Warships were built to ride out a storm at sea but faced real danger if driven towards a lee shore. Although captains tried to anchor in such conditions, the anchors rarely held.

The letters of naval wives suggest that some were able to calculate the risks their husbands faced though it is difficult to assess how far this understanding extended to the poorer classes since it is mostly the letters of the middling and aristocratic couples that survive. In April 1798, Nelson was anchored off Portsmouth with an unfavourable wind and unable to get to sea. His wife, Fanny, wrote:

> I can feel your disappointment in being contrary to your wishes detained at St Helens. I comfort myself in thinking you are safe and hope the ship runs no risk in losing any part of her masts etc. I see no daily paper and the Bath newspapers tell little Portsmouth ship news.[18]

In October 1747, Frances, Admiral Boscawen's wife, was actually anxious for her husband to put to sea because it was already late in the year. She writes:

> I wish you may sail so soon as this week. I want you safe out of the Channel before the November winds begin to blow. 'Tis a great distress to me here that I have no weathercock, but I believe the wind is fair just now. The black, cold air denotes it East.[19]

As it happened, Boscawen met with storms in the Bay of Biscay so severe that some of his squadron had to put into Lisbon to refit.

In due course, Frances wrote to Boscawen that news of this bad weather had caused her serious distress. The letters of sailors' wives to their husbands at sea required fine judgement. They had to show proper concern for the dangers their husband faced but it was best to avoid any suggestion of inconsolable grief: this would only make husbands feel guilty or irritated since they were quite powerless to do anything about their separation. Frances Boscawen was a consummate letter writer and always managed to hit a diplomatic note. In one of her letters she wrote:

> I might as well have gone to the Ridotto as lain awake all night disturbed, anxious, and miserable about you. The wind was excessive high. You had assured me you would sail in the morning, so that my fears suggested that you would not be able to recover the harbour with safety. Perhaps these fears appear so ridiculous to you that you cannot help laughing at them, but I assure you to me they were no laughing matter, and that I do not find myself at all the better for them this morning. I am going to see if the air of the Park, and the company of my children, will not recover me again. God bless and prosper you[20]

Here she demonstrates her affection and interest in naval matters, flatters a husband who can laugh off dangers, implies that she has reliable strategies to recover her spirits and reassures him that she is taking good care of their children. In contrast, Fanny Nelson told her husband in 1794 that she had been sick with worry, just as she had been the year before, and elicited this irritable response from Nelson, 'Why you should be so uneasy about me so as to make yourself ill I know not'.[21] Thereafter, all Fanny's references in her letters to her slow fevers, agues and hacking coughs must have seemed like a covert reproach to her husband.

But just how did husbands describe shipwrecks to their wives? Lieutenant Thomas Wells of the *Diomede* wrote to his wife from Madeira in 1805 to say that on the passage from Cork he and his squadron had met with a 'tight gale'. Three of his transports had been dismasted but he describes this as 'a trifling accident' and begs her to keep her spirits up as far as her circumstances will allow.[22] By 17 November, writing from the harbour of St Salvadores on the coast of Brazil, he described how the *Britannia*, a large East Indiaman full of troops, ladies, gentlemen and 300,000 worth of dollars (in all supposed to be worth at least half a million sterling), had struck a rock and been dashed to pieces (see Plate 30). The *King George* transport, a new ship also carrying many women and children, had shared the same fate so that his own ship, which had picked up survivors, was now crammed with extra passengers. His tone is extremely matter of fact, and for effect he seems to dwell more on the great wealth carried by the Indiaman, now at the bottom of the sea, than on the human loss. Wrecked East Indiamen always grabbed headlines due to the number of women and children carried on board and the great wealth of the cargo that went down with them. As Wells's wife had been very unhappy that he had given up a steady shore-based job on a prison ship to join the fleet at sea, he presumably wished to give her no cause to criticize his decision further. As we have seen, Codrington was similarly phlegmatic when he wrote to his wife about the shipwreck of the schooner *Sea Lark* off the Texel in 1809, when only one member of the crew survived.

In 1798 when Nelson was entrusted with a detached squadron and sent to assess French fleet movements in the Mediterranean, his ship *Vanguard* met a strong gale and was almost wrecked through poor seamanship. As he broke the news to his wife, he wrote as if this setback had been providential:

> MY DEAREST FANNY, - I ought not to call what has happened to the *Vanguard* by the cold name of accident, I believe firmly that it was the Almighty's goodness to check my consumate vanity. ... Figure to yourself this proud conceited man ... his ship dismasted his fleet dispersed and himself in such distress that the meanest frigate out of France would have been a very unwelcome guest. But it has pleased Almighty God to bring us into a safe port, where altho' we are refused

the rights of humanity, yet the *Vanguard* will in two days get to sea again as an Englishman of war.[23]

The *Vanguard* had lost its masts, a boat, and its best bower anchor; the quarters gallery had been washed away. Yet Nelson's letter was masterly in the way he both accepted and deflected blame. He asked Fanny to write a line to Lord Spencer, First Lord of the Admiralty, telling him that the *Vanguard* was now fitted tolerably for sea and that the accident would not hinder his operations. In fact, as Nelson may have hoped, she showed his letter to several friends, some of whom thought the sentiments in it so fine that they made copies. She also sent it to Lord Spencer so that he could read the original. In public she helped Nelson to put the best face she could on this setback. He had asked her to imagine not a terrible night of gales but an abstract morality lesson and in private she was not inclined to ask for further painful details. In her reply, she focused on her own trials at home rather than on his and wrote, 'It is impossible to say what I have suffered, I thank God you were saved. What a storm'.[24]

Matthew Flinders, writing to his wife Ann during his survey of the coast of Australia, also adopted a self-possessed, if more personal tone when explaining the loss of his ship's boat and the tragic death of John Thistle, the ship's master. He wrote from Port Jackson:

> It will grieve thee, as it has me, to understand, that poor Thistle was lost upon the south coast. Thou knowest how I valued him; he is however gone, as well as Mr Taylor and six seamen, who were all drowned in a boat. No remains of them were found; but the boat, which was stove all to pieces against the rocks, was picked up.[25]

Flinders then gave her an account of 'the politics of the ship', or how key members of the crew interacted with each other, intimating that the living should be a greater preoccupation than the dead.

In August 1803 Flinders himself was shipwrecked on his way home. He was travelling in the *Porpoise* with two other ships, *Bridgewater* and *Cato*, as his own ship *Investigator* had been condemned as unseaworthy. A Botany Bay paper dated 18 September 1803 brought news of the wreck to London, and the story was printed in *The Times* on 25 May 1804. No one would have known of Flinders' connection with the shipwreck until the following day, when *The Times* gave a full account. The three ships had been sailing from New South Wales to China when, on 17 August, both *Porpoise* and *Cato* struck a coral reef, 735 miles from Port Jackson. The *Bridgewater* managed to avoid the reef and just sailed on, though the account seems to attach no blame to this. *The Times* explained that when the weather moderated, Flinders and a lieutenant launched one of the *Porpoise*'s boats and rescued the crew of the *Cato*. Safe on a sandbank, the survivors managed to salvage enough provisions from the wrecked ships to last about three months. It was then agreed that Flinders and another captain should take the cutter that had been saved and steer for New South Wales to get help. They arrived on 28 August and the Governor there promptly ordered vessels to go in search of the crew so there was little doubt that the survivors would be saved. The Governor of New South Wales also gave Flinders a small schooner so that he could sail back to England but this vessel proved leaky and when one of the pumps gave out Flinders was forced to put into Ile de France. Unfortunately, the French Governor suspected him of being a spy and detained him.

Around the time that the news reached England of the shipwreck, Ann Flinders must have also have learnt of her husband's imprisonment. She wrote to Sir Joseph Banks who had sponsored the survey of the Australian coast. His reply, dated 4 June, was as helpful as it could be, though he could only guess at how Flinders had fallen into the hands of the French. He did have more details of the shipwreck and explained, 'the history of the Shipwreck is exactly as it is Stated except only that 8 of the Catos people were Lost & the whole of the Porpoises escaped safe & unhurt'.[26]

Ann did not get a letter from her husband until 16 December 1804. The first half had been written in Port Jackson, just after the *Investigator* had been condemned, the second part had been written at Ile de France. Flinders airily omitted to mention anything of his adventures on the coral reef:

> Various have been the turns of fortune, my dearest life, since the former part of this letter was addressed to thee; but since my brother will, I trust, have arrived before this can reach thee, my paper shall not be occupied by these.[27]

Flinders' brother Samuel had been wrecked with him but had sailed back to Britain with most of the crew in an East Indiamen, and there was every chance that he had arrived home by now. Flinders was to remain a prisoner at Isle de France for six years but in his surviving letters to his wife he never mentions the shipwreck, or his own part in it, though he could easily have represented his actions as heroic.

Men who were not sailors described tempests far less stoically. Edward Whitworth, an impressed seaman, wrote home to his wife in February 1812 that the fleet had experienced lengthy storms in the North Sea. Three lines of battle ships and one sloop had foundered with nearly all hands lost. On the *St. George*, only 4 out of 750 men had been saved and the officers and crew of his own ship had given two days' pay to their orphans and widows. He wrote, 'How soon it may be our lot God only knows, a storm at sea is a Dreadful sight. Indeed you can form no idea off it [*sic*].'[28] Whitworth, a reluctant seaman, had reason to feel victimized and unhappy. He does, though, suggest that sailors may simply have found it too difficult to describe the horror of storms and shipwreck to those who had no experience of such things.

Advances in navigational techniques, better instruments and improved training for officers, steadily reduced naval losses from shipwreck. Seafaring was still a dangerous profession and an estimated one in two seamen died unnaturally. But by 1810 it has been estimated – and recent research supports these findings – that only around 10 per cent of naval casualties were caused by shipwreck, fire or explosion while 50 per cent were caused by disease.[29] Of those officers commissioned between 1790 and 1794 who had brilliant promotion prospects at the outbreak of the French Wars, 39 per cent were dead by 1815. More than half of these died from disease, then (in descending order) from individual accident, shipwreck, and death in battle.[30] An insight into contemporary assessments of the risk of shipwreck is found in 1813 when an attempt was made to establish a private system of insurance for officers that would cover such expenses as uniforms lost in action or shipwreck. The scheme never got off the ground.[31]

As far as it is possible to judge, the prevailing code seems to have been for seamen to make light of storms and shipwreck. Women, on the other hand, were expected to be fearful and apprehensive, which cannot have been particularly welcome to married men who had chosen the sea as their profession. There were evidently some wives who could not bear separation and worry and who managed to deter their husbands from going to sea again. Commander William Foot wrote to Vice Admiral Sir John Duckworth in 1808:

> But my sister Richard has really suffered much during her Husband's absence & has never been able to reconcile herself for a moment to the situation afloat which he appears so fond of. I doubt much his obtaining permission to take another trip.[32]

However, some wives, like Frances Boscawen, were strong-minded enough to not burden their husbands with their fears. Such wives may have derived comfort from religion and the support of their families but they may also have had a more realistic appraisal of the risks involved.

The navy and material culture

Firm details are scant but just as today it is hard to avoid patriotic displays periodically associated with such international events as the football World Cup, so in this period it must have been impossible to avoid daily reminders of Britain's debt to the navy. Heroes and battles were represented in figurines and busts, on patch boxes, scent bottles, plaques, wallpaper, tiles, tooth-pick boxes, plates, punch bowls, mugs, jugs, teapots and other table wares (see Plate 31). When there was no specific battle or officer to celebrate, everyday items such as mugs and punch bowls were produced simply wishing commanders every success. The lower decks were also supported: earthenware bowls were decorated with images of ships and inscribed: 'Success to the British Tars'.[33] None of these goods would have been produced if there had not been a profitable market for them. Maritime decoration remained generally popular throughout the period; images of ships and shipping were used to decorate a range of ceramics, reminding people of Britain's dependency on the sea and on the navy. A growing print culture enabled commemorative goods to be advertised quickly and widely in newspapers, magazines, on trade cards and headed bills. Trade cards were particularly effective in reinforcing the link between fine taste and the goods offered. Attractively designed, and combining both advertisement and business card, they offered customers a token of good service and helped to win their loyalty. At the same time, women's magazines and almanacs promulgated the latest seasonal fashions for headdresses, ornaments, fans (see Plate 10) and gowns, which were also often adapted to commemorate victories and leading naval officers. Such advertisements and 'puffs' served to inform readers about new trends in portable objects intended for social display but also helped to shape taste and influence choice. Yet we cannot assume that all naval wives drew comfort from some of the goods on the market. For example, one Staffordshire earthenware mug of about 1800 is decorated with a version of a popular print by Collings depicting a press gang at work near the Tower of London. The mug is an ambiguous piece: humorous or subversive, depending on the context in which it was used.[34]

Some material possessions, such as tea sets commemorating naval victories, allowed people, particularly women, to exhibit their sense of national identity with the British as a maritime nation, particularly during invasion scares and other times of national crisis.[35] Successful naval officers from the middling sort who were rewarded with a noble title, and impoverished younger sons of the nobility who earned sufficient prize money to be able to live in a manner appropriate to their rank, often purchased impressive sets of tableware with armorial bearings from factories like Worcester and Wedgwood's Chelsea decorating studio which specialized in such goods. Sometimes, when porcelain tableware was commissioned to celebrate a victory at sea, less expensive versions might be produced in creamware or fine lead-glazed earthenware, presumably for popular consumption. Nelson's 'Baltic' set of Paris porcelain, which certainly belonged to Nelson himself, was reproduced in creamware in the months following the Battle of Copenhagen, 1801. Nelson also ordered a large service from the Worcester porcelain factory, which he visited with Sir William and Emma Hamilton on the way back from their excursion to Wales in 1802. Known as the 'Horatia' set, it was adapted from an existing Worcester pattern that was already flamboyant but was to be decorated further with parts of Nelson's personal insignia and coat of arms. Of the whole order only the breakfast set was made and none was ever paid for.

When naval families who might have grown up identifying with the service commissioned portraits, even of female members, they would often signal the family's patriotic connections with the nation's prime means of defence by including naval allusions in the symbolism of the painting and in the colours used. The frame might also be elaborately emblematic and include maritime symbols.[36] There were also occasions when women themselves helped to commemorate their husband's maritime achievements. Elizabeth Cook, whose husband, the explorer, was absent for so much of their marriage, embroidered a kerchief depicting the tracks of his three voyages superimposed on a world map. James Cook's navigational achievement was of immense national importance; his wife's embroidery asserts that achievement at the domestic level, showing how great national events could also be transferred to domestic settings. The time and personal care she invested in her work (now in the collection of the Australian National Maritime Museum), adds to its significance.

Ambitious oil paintings of naval victories were displayed in shows and galleries, attracting crowds who wished to view contemporary works of art but who also wished to be seen in fashionable civic spaces. Prints of naval heroes and significant battles were displayed in print shop windows, which functioned as galleries for the poor since the prints were on view to all passers-by regardless of their ability to purchase or hire them. We know that the wives of famous naval officers owned commemorative prints and often decorated their homes with these and other items celebrating their husband's achievements. They might themselves take their place in this visual domestic display: prints were produced of naval wives who became public figures, and when officers commissioned their own portrait, they often ordered one of their wife at the same time.[37]

Contemporary works of maritime art and maritime-related merchandise almost exclusively featured men but illustations and ceramic figures depicting the sailor's departure and the sailor's return, or the sailor and his lass, were significant exceptions (see Plate 32). These works generally represented naval women in a passive, dependent role unless sailors were depicted in alehouse scenes of drunken conviviality. Sailors' women were sometimes shown acting more assertively in theatrical performances, but for the most part women's participation in the visual landscape was restricted to the purchase and display of goods produced for the domestic market. Decorative items with a naval or maritime reference, increasingly associated with taste and 'politeness' would usually reflect the social standing of the owner, help cement social connections and allow owners to make a statement about personal wealth and style. At the same time, maritime ornament could be overdone. Emma Hamilton decorated Nelson's home, Merton Place, with so many images and souvenirs of the great hero that the diplomat Lord Minto, visiting in 1802, complained that the house was 'a mere looking-glass' in which Nelson could view himself all day and a ghastly tribute to bad taste.[38]

It is difficult to generalize about what commemoratives naval women would have sought to acquire but we know that, to some extent, purchases were influenced by gender. Both sexes collected china, but men were likely to be collectors of fine porcelain while women were much more closely associated with the purchase and use of everyday china, partly due to their central role in the ritual of tea drinking.[39] In wealthy households from the early eighteenth century, the library was the responsibility of the husband, while pictures and 'curious cabinet pieces' were 'under the custody' of the wife.[40] In the second half of the century, cheaper consumer goods increasingly became available to those lower down the social scale. Consequently at all social levels maritime-related objects helped to signify who their owners were and where their loyalties lay, building a sense of shared histories. A commemorative item might satisfy a desire to possess something that was currently fashionable but the object itself might also hold a personal resonance for any buyer who had a loved one at sea.

It is difficult to estimate the volume of naval commemorative ware that might have been in circulation. In the later eighteenth century, creamware became the standard product for everyday table use and it was also increasingly used for commemorative pieces. Creamware produced in Staffordshire might actually be decorated in Liverpool where firms such as Sadler and Green, active during the 1760s and early 1770s, specialized in transfer-printing. When this technique was used, we know that considerable numbers of each decorated item would have been produced in order to justify the expense of having a copper plate engraved for the printing of china. The copper plate would easily yield ten thousand prints, and it has been estimated that thousands more would be possible with careful handling and a few touch up repairs here and there.[41] Items produced to celebrate some topical event might have a fairly short shelf-life, which may explain why naval heroes (who may have been expected to stay famous for some time) were depicted far more than their particular victories, although at times manufacturers seem to have had scant regard for accuracy in portraiture as they hurriedly produced goods to celebrate a particular event. A creamware ale mug produced around 1800 was transfer-printed and hand-coloured with a portrait of an officer intended to represent Nelson, although exactly the same image had earlier been used to represent Rodney in 1782 (see Plate 33).[42] Another trick was to recycle prints of earlier battles and give them a new inscription to celebrate later events. Many of these products were of indifferent quality and clearly regarded as expendable, although items celebrating Nelson were an exception in that they remained popular over many years. From around the 1770s many of the larger potteries had agents supervising their warehouses in the metropolis, which meant that the latest prints could be sent by coach back to the factory so that in theory china could be produced more accurately to match the latest topical event. For example, after the Battle of the Nile in 1798, Liverpool's Herculaneum factory produced a creamware dinner service transfer-printed with Nelson's portrait.[43] This factory, founded in 1796, showed profits of £4786 6s 4½d in 1806 – 7 and nearly double that in 1813 – 14.[44] An account book also survives for Bow, the largest porcelain factory in mid-eighteenth-century Britain. The factory seems to have been exclusive producers of figures of a 'sailor and his lass' mid-century, although later there were Derby and other models (see Plate 34). The firm's account book shows a steady turnover despite the fact that by the late 1750s the pottery industry was in trouble, reviving only in the third quarter of the eighteenth century. From February 1752 to March 1753, for example, the value of the total sales was calculated to be £8403 7s 0½d or about £1,033,077 today.[45] Despite these figures, there are too few surviving business records to estimate accurately how much naval commemorative ware the potteries actually produced.

One reason why people would have been more exposed to commemorative goods is that throughout Britain during this period, good quality ceramics became more easily obtainable and more affordable as the growing canal system brought about a huge reduction in transport costs.[46] In London, shopping for semi-luxuries had become an elegant pastime and potteries situated in the north of England generally had their own warehouses in fashionable areas of London. There was Flight and Barr's warehouse for Worcester porcelain just off Piccadilly, and Fogg and Son's in New Bond Street. Wedgwood, recognizing that different ranges of stock attracted different customers, judiciously opened a showroom at the corner of Newport Street and St Martin's Lane that housed impressive displays of finely modelled figures and tableware.

While only a fraction of the pottery that was produced in this period survives today, there were clearly products to suit a variety of tastes and pockets. Probate inventories suggest that by mid-eighteenth century, prosperous artisans could afford to decorate their homes with china figures, and some potteries specialized in goods for the middle or lower ranks. These goods might be retailed in more down-market establishments in London, specializing in stone chinaware and earthenware. Coarser wares, flawed 'seconds' and other sub-standard pieces would be sold to the public more cheaply on city streets: hawkers who were too poor to establish a business went around crying their wares, which they carried in baskets on their heads or strapped to their bodies (see Plate 37). Pottery would also be sold at local markets and fairs, though there were tradesmen, known as chapmen, who hawked wares around the countryside. A decorative print might seem a luxury in poorer households but an earthenware mug celebrating a naval hero had the virtue of being a practical as well as a patriotic purchase. Since many such items were hardly well made and the transfer printing on them far from accurate, it seems that there was a ready market for cheap commemoratives at the lower end of the social scale. The quality of Staffordshire figures certainly deteriorated as the market for them grew, and the more topical they became, the more these coarser wares were reduced to the level of ephemera. Some Staffordshire busts of Nelson, produced at the time of his death, bore scant resemblance to him but as they stood on marbled plinths clearly stamped 'NELSON', there was little room for doubt.

If we knew the price charged for different items of commemorative ware, we would be able to form a more accurate estimation of how widely such goods penetrated different communities. The stamped, commemorative medals that men and women wore as smart accessories to mark victories at sea were produced in various metals to suit different pockets. But only a few price lists survive for any wares. Good quality Derby figures of a sailor and his lass sold at 2s 6d a pair in 1752 – 3.[47] A list for 1783 shows that the potter John Wood charged a wholesale price of 2s 6d per pair for figures of a sailor and his lass, a shilling for certain figures of reasonable quality and 6d or less for the cheaper ones – depending on size and painted finish. This price list relates solely to earthenware figures: porcelain would have been much more expensive. Interestingly, maritime subjects are rarely found in porcelain, which says something about the market for them. There is a record of the potters Enoch and Ralph Wood selling '12 sailors lasses' at 5d a pair to Wedgwood, which seems a rock-bottom price to which

Wedgwood would have added his own margin.[48] The evidence broadly suggests that an average price for a simple figure would have been 10d, increasing to 2s 6d for an enamel painted one.[49]

A price list for Liverpool's Herculaneum factory also survives for the year 1808. It sets down the net price of several common items from the factory, giving us some indication of what comparable naval commemoratives might have cost, for example, teapots might cost between 2s 2d and 2s 8d, according to quality. Unfortunately, it does not give the prices of the small busts of naval and military heroes that the factory produced in four different materials (buff stoneware, enamelled earthenware, enamelled porcelain and black basalt). Yet it does indicate the range of items available to those who wished to celebrate naval heroes. Herculaneum figures 22cm in height included Lord Duncan, the hero of the Battle of Camperdown (1797), and Nelson. Those 23cm in height included Admiral Earl St Vincent. At this period, Wellington's army had not overtaken the navy in popularity and such figures would have adorned many shelves, cabinets and mantelpieces. There are scant details of any individual purchase of commemorative goods or decorative items at any social level in domestic account books. However, the account books of the musician and writer William Ayrton, who married in 1803, show that in January 1804 they purchased Wedgwood tea and cream pots for 5s 9d. In 1805 they bought a jug for 2s 6d, a set of Wedgwood breakfast china that cost £1 17s, and also Wedgwood flower vases for 7s and a teapot for 3s 6d. They appear to have bought no more china until 1810 when Ayrton records that they purchased ornaments worth £1 8s 6d and two china pots and stands for 18s. These prices indicate that the Ayrtons bought good quality china. Other entries relating to decorative goods enable us to put these purchases into a context. For example, in 1806 he bought a panorama of the Bay of Naples in 1805 for 2s, and two framed coloured prints for £1 11s 6d. Ayrton was firmly of the middling sort: his income tax bill of £40 for the year 1808 indicates that his annual income was at least £400, and so his account books give an indication of the capacity people of this rank had to purchase semi-luxuries. Another indication is offered in the correspondence of Admiral Sir Charles Tyler, who in 1816 spent £2 6s 6d at Wedgwood's later sale room at York Street, St James's (see Plate 36). His purchases included a round teapot for 3s and a pint jug for 1s 2d but we know that Wedgwood generally priced his goods well above that of rival potteries to preserve the cachet of his brand.[50]

Yet if commemorative ware was produced at prices to suit most pockets, how likely was it that ordinary families could afford to buy such goods? Relatively few probate inventories now exist and anyway the cheaper commemoratives were not particularly durable. Wages could be as low as two or three pounds a year for a domestic servant, as they also received food, clothing and lodging. Female domestic servants earned less than men, their yearly wages ranging from £2 to £6 – £8 for a head housemaid, and up to £15 for a skilled housekeeper. In comparison, a footman could expect up to £8 per year and a coachman, more visible to the public, might earn anything between £12 and £26 per year. Independent workers who had to find their own food and lodging needed to earn much more than this. £15 – £20 per year was a low wage and close to £40 a year was needed to keep a family. The economist Adam Smith recorded in 1776 that common labourers in London earned nine or ten shillings a week and up to 40 or 45 shillings in a calendar month. Masons and bricklayers could earn between fifteen and eighteen shillings a week. Elsewhere in the country the weekly wages of common labourers fluctuated between four and six shillings.

In London most classes of workmen were paid about double those of the same classes in Edinburgh. Adam Smith wrote that £40 a year was considered very good pay for a curate but that there were journeymen shoemakers in London who could earn that amount. He reckoned that few industrious workmen of any kind in London failed to make more than £20 a year – though common labourers in many country parishes could often do the same. Women tended to be paid less than men, except in certain industries, including the potteries and in textile industries where selected skilled workers could earn more.[51] The increasing numbers of the middling sort helped to raise demand for new consumer goods and influenced consumer habits. By the later eighteenth century, the rural middling sort had an average income of £100 but those at the upper end lived more comfortably on incomes of between £150 and £700. In towns and cities, incomes tended to be higher and there was an even greater demand in urban areas for new, expressive goods. By 1803 when Colquhoun drew up his social tables, a high-ranking clergyman (not including bishops) might expect to earn £500 a year, many lawyers earned £350 a year and the average master manufacturer, £800.[52]

When considering the market for naval commemoratives, we also need to take into account the purchasing power of the pound, and the trend during this period did not favour poorer people. Between 1750 and the end of the eighteenth century prices roughly doubled while wages dropped in value, rising only by about 25 per cent. Bad harvests and wars caused steeper fluctuations in cost of staple items. For example, prices increased by 50 per cent during the period 1803 – 15, causing great hardship, with the least skilled suffering most because their wages were very low. In normal times a loaf of bread could be purchased for a penny, while a basic meal of meat, broth and beer would set you back three pence. Half a pint of gin cost two pence but a quart of beer might be had for a penny and a cup of coffee for the same price. In London, two pence a night would get you a shared bed in a cheap lodging house while a basic, unfurnished room could set you back 1s 4d a week. A modest house, suitable for better-off artisans, might cost £10 a year to rent but a suite of rooms in a more fashionable area could cost £40 a year. Only the upper tier of the middling sort could afford to buy a £700 house in London. If some of these prices now seem low, proportionate to income, certain items were much more expensive than their modern equivalents: in 1805, for instance, a toothbrush retailed at 1s. In an age when most things were made by hand, clothes accounted for a much higher proportion of an individual's spending than they do now. A man's suit might cost £8, and if clothes were made at home the materials alone were still a significant cost: in 1801 cottons for common gowns sold at 1s 8d a yard.

Other contemporary naval celebrations

Other forms of popular culture served to keep the navy in the public eye and would have helped to give naval women a sense of belonging to a distinct group. During the wars against Revolutionary and Napoleonic France, naval battles were regularly re-enacted on the popular stage so that the theatre became an important means patriotic experience. Verses in honour of specific commanders found willing publishers. For example, in January 1806 *The Times* advertised an ode on Nelson's victory and death at Trafalgar 'by a Lady' to coincide with his funeral, embellished with an elegant engraving offering a true likeness of him. Alternatively, readers could purchase a sermon preached on the day of thanksgiving for the victory for half the price at 1s, or two historical prints of the hero, one showing him with and the other without his right arm. Songbooks contained the latest patriotic songs about the navy, which theatres helped to promote (and were often the source in the first place), and panoramic displays also took their cue from wartime events. The nobility organized public breakfasts and suppers in honour of successful naval officers. The birthdays of popular heroes such as Admiral Edward Vernon (1684 – 1757), who captured Porto Bello in 1739, were celebrated annually as popular anniversaries. Great numbers of medals were cast to mark particular naval events, and fans were also made which may have seen repeated use on such anniversaries.[53] Public interest in naval officers was increased by the fact that many were also Members of Parliament and therefore implicated in the politics of the day. Throughout the period, charitable giving to various naval funds and charities became a public testimony to an individual's commitment to the war effort since personal contributions were often openly listed. Not until Waterloo did the army attract such widespread support and adulation.

The material and popular culture surrounding naval warfare at this period cannot be said to have reached a mass market in the modern sense of the term but it permeated all social levels, particularly the diverse middling ranks. Since the vast majority of commemorative pieces featured notable naval figures from the middling and higher ranks, the acquisition of such pieces might signify the purchaser's social aspirations as well as an uncomplicated patriotism. A few items were overtly designed for female consumers, for example a fine enamel and copper patch box was decorated with the female figure of Fame who is depicted on the shoreline celebrating the naval heroes of the French Revolutionary War. Alongside her is a young woman representing Peace and bearing a laurel wreath. There is a cornucopia below, and above the figures an inscription reads, 'Fame Proclaiming her Heroes Peace with Plenty' (see Plate 38).[54]

One thing is clear – in such an arena, populated by so many commemorative items, it was impossible for ambitious officers not to see the opportunities for self-promotion. They were concerned that visual representations of battles should be accurate, and wished at least to ensure that their own position in the fighting had been adequately represented. Wives who were ambitious on their husbands' behalf tried to ensure that their husbands' professional actions and decisions were presented in the best possible light, even if their part in this process, as wives, extended only to the commissioning of household goods commemorating their victories, helping to circulate their portraits or sharing their more informative letters.

All popular culture tends to be transient and any new fad can be followed by a backlash. In the case of naval commemoratives, the process may have been hastened by the fact that some pieces show little taste. For example, an earthenware mug mourning Nelson's death has this glib verse inscribed below a transfer-printed portrait of the hero: 'Shew me my Country's Foes, the Hero Cry'd. | He saw – He fought, He conquer'd and he di'd'. The re-working of Julius Caesar's famous boast: *veni, vidi, vici* (I came, I saw, I conquered), produces unintentional bathos. A pair of singular earthenware jardinières, produced to commemorate the hero, boasted gilded lugs on each side in the shape of dolphin heads. Though designed to cater for those with a genteel interest in gardening, the gilt dolphin heads are strangely sinister and repellent. A contemporary, painted ivory locket, encased in a gilt setting, depicts a marine lifting his hat and bears the hearty inscription, 'NELSON FOR EVER HUZZA' permitting the wearer to send an uncomplicated patriotic signal to all who came close enough to read it. Some lockets and brooches, mourning or celebrating Nelson, have compartments for human hair. Since few purchasers would have had access to Nelson's hair, wearers presumably felt no incongruity in placing a lock of their loved one's hair behind the image of the national hero.

The navy helped to provide a market for a variety of goods that fostered a sense of national belonging, and encouraged naval women to keep up morale while their men were at sea, but commemorative fashions were susceptible to criticism. Commentators of the time poked fun both at the extreme styles inspired by Nelson's victory at the Battle of the Nile and at the manufacturers who capitalized on the event in order to make money.[55] Women exhibited their patriotism in this way may simply have laid themselves open to ridicule, either for their taste or their politics.

High-ranking women, who celebrated naval victories in order to burnish their own social reputation or who exploited naval officers by inviting them to social gatherings in order to add cachet to the proceedings, were certainly criticized. The epistolary romance, *A Sailor's Friendship, and a Soldier's Love*, published in pastel pink and blue binding in 1805, features a Captain Byron who complains bitterly of such treatment. A lady of quality gives a public breakfast to honour his bravery but succeeds only in causing him embarrassment. He explains:

> Just as I was seated at the banquet, and preparing to console myself for all my miseries, down comes (to the tune of Rule Britannia) a huge crown of gilt laurel, from the ceiling, or the Lord knows where, and anchors upon my hair. ... I brandished my knife, with as much fury as if it had been a sword ten yards long, tore off the crown, started from the table, stammered out something about not bearing it any longer, and fairly made my way through beaux and belles, without either ceremony or remorse. ... If there had really been but one atom of enthusiasm for my poor services in all this mumming, I would not have been brutish enough to have wounded it; but when I know that these folks only want something to worship out of mere idleness ... I confess I have no patience with their absurdity.[56]

But if this work criticizes empty-headed, high-ranking women, it also allows the author to criticize the war while neatly avoiding censure by adopting the voice of a naval officer. Captain Byron imagines peace has been announced and meditates on the blood uselessly shed, 'It seemed to me then, as if we had fought only to make widows and orphans. Such a peace rendered the war criminal'.[57]

In *Persuasion* Jane Austen similarly criticizes Anne's snobbish sister Elizabeth for inviting Captain Wentworth to her house party for entirely superficial reasons. Bath was a place where the sick and elderly went to try the waters and where many naval officers repaired to restore their health. Consequently there was often a dearth of fit young men at social gatherings in an age when married couples infrequently socialized together. Anne's sister invited Wentworth not for his own sake but because, with his military air and bearing, she saw that he would greatly ornament her drawing room. As in all lifestyle issues and matters of taste, discrimination was essential. Particular criticizm seems to have been reserved for the *nouveau riche* and for the gentry or middling sort who were tempted to ape the aristocracy rather than fill their own responsible role in life conscientiously and with dignity.

A range of experiences

This study offers an insight into the various support networks that helped naval women to carry out heavy responsibilities in their husband's absence or, in some cases, simply to survive. It appears from surviving letters that women from the upper ranks felt it their duty to help seamen's women from the middling and lower ranks, if they appeared deserving. They helped to smooth communications by passing on news and letters, and might exert their influence to secure the husbands of their acquaintance better ships or promotion. Such women would also help financially, by forwarding money that was owed or by paying money in advance that could be reclaimed later. Where families with a connection to the navy lived in close proximity, they seem to have formed a community with a distinct identity. This certainly seems to have been the case in Pembrokeshire, where the Tylers, Foleys and Grants lived, and the fact that such communities existed at home seems to have given reassurance to husbands at sea. However, this support and generosity of spirit did not extend to poor women of dubious respectability who might be intent on deceiving them for money: Codrington, for example, specifically warned his wife not to believe the stories of poor women hanging around dockyards. Additionally, women who tried to cheat the authorities out of grants and pensions often found that neighbours proved willing spies and informants.

As has often been remarked, there was more than one eighteenth-century Britain. High ranking naval wives might not have enjoyed their domestic situation while their husbands were on active service but they seem on the whole to have come to terms with separation and with the help of servants and advisors to have coped rather well with the additional responsibilities. Wives from the nobility and gentry often exceeded their perceived roles during their husband's absence; they took on additional household tasks and derived satisfaction from the competence with which they administered the management of estates and finances. Their correspondence reveals the ways in which such women were able to support and promote their husband's careers, working especially through networking and patronage. When such scrutiny is applied more widely to women from lower ranks, it is possible to appreciate the degree to which, in successive conflicts, the war effort and indeed victory depended on women as well as men, and also to see how imperial endeavour and the demands of national security, which depended so heavily on the navy, often entailed the sacrifice of women's happiness. This investigation of naval women and the contribution they made in supporting their partners and maintaining home life offers an opportunity to re-consider the apparently masculine nature of the British imperial enterprise and adds to our understanding of power and social relations at home.

Manliness and femininity, then as now, were not fixed categories but were continually being tested and re-worked in all areas of daily life, and relations between the sexes were affected by local, practical circumstances as well as by ideological and cultural precepts. In this period, the activities of naval wives informed this process to a high degree and, in the case of middling sort and above, women seemed to have attained a greater sense of partnership in the married state than perhaps they did in the period that followed. Jane Austen reflects this in her conclusion to *Persuasion* when writing that only the dread of a future war could dim Anne's happiness after her marriage to Captain Wentworth, 'She gloried in being a sailor's wife, but she must pay the tax of quick alarm for belonging to that profession which is, if possible, more distinguished in its domestic virtues than in its national importance.'[58] The 'domestic virtues' exemplified by naval officers in her book seem to be those which support a marriage founded on trust and mutual support. The 'tax' of nagging anxiety that came with Anne's marriage to Wentworth alludes to the burden which Austen recognized all naval women carried during wartime, and which has been largely neglected in favour of studies of strategies, heroes and victories at sea. This work helps to redress the balance and adds nuances to an evolving sense of national distinctiveness of culture and identity.

1. Edward Hughes, ed., *The Private Correspondence of Admiral Lord Collingwood*, Navy Records Society, 98 (London and Colchester, 1957), p. 293, 20 Sept. 1809, Collingwood to his sister.

2. John Gregory, *A Father's Legacy to His Daughters* (Dublin, 1774), p. 7.

3. Jane Austen, *Persuasion* (1818), ed. D.W. Harding (Harmondsworth, 1965), p. 236.

4. N. A. M. Rodger, *The Wooden World: An Anatomy of the Georgian Navy* (London, 1986), p. 53; The *London Chronicle*, 3– 5 April, p. 7 c. 3.

5. George P.B. Naish, ed., *Nelson's Letters to His Wife and Other Documents 1785 – 1831*, Navy Records Society, 100 (London, 1958), p. 209, 22 May 1795, Nelson to Fanny.

6. NMM COD 21/1a, 24 Sept 1809, Codrington to his wife.

7. Richard and Bridget Larn and Alan Jones, *Shipwrecks UK* www.shipwrecks.uk.com accessed 25 January 2006.

8. John Wilkinson, *Tutamen Nauticum; or, the Seamen's Preservation from Shipwreck, Diseases, and other Calamities incident to Mariners* (London, 1763), p. i.

9. Cecil Aspinall-Oglander, ed., *Admiral's Wife. Being the Life and Letters of the Hon. Mrs Edward Boscawen from 1719 to 1761* (London, 1940), p. 55.

10. *GM*, 20 (1750), 46.

11. *The St. James's Chronicle or, British Evening-Post*, Tues. 17 to Thurs. 19 Dec 1793 p. 4. c. 3. Burney Collection, vol. 845 II.

12. *The True Briton*, 7 Feb 1798, p. 3. c.4 and p. 4 c. 1, Burney Collection, vol. 925 II.

13. J.C. Cross, *The Purse; Or, Benevolent Tar* (Boston, 1797), p. 9.

14. Samuel J. Arnold, *The Shipwreck, a Comic Opera, in Two Acts* (London, 1797).

15. NMM AAA5162.

16. Catharine Rebecca Manners, 'The Child of Sorrow' in *Poems* (London, 1794), p. 70.

17. N. A. M. Rodger, *Wooden World*, pp. 46 – 7.

18. Naish, p. 424, 7 April 1798, Fanny to Nelson.

19. Cecil Aspinall-Oglander, p. 54.

20. Cecil Aspinall-Oglander, p. 34. A ridotto was a public ball, typically a masquerade, and popular in the eighteenth century.

21. Naish, p. 186, 31 Oct. 1794, Nelson to Fanny. Cf. pp. 252 – 3, 30 September 1794, Fanny to Nelson.

22. NMM MSS/86/051, 1 Oct. 1805, Captain Thomas Wells to his wife.

23. Naish, pp. 396 – 7, 24 May 1798, Nelson to Fanny.

24. Naish, p. 448, 11 Sept. 1798, Fanny to Nelson.

25. www/nmm.ac.uk/flinders accessed 5 Dec 2006, 25 November 1802, Matthew Flinders to Ann Flinders.

26. www/nmm.ac.uk/flinders accessed 5 Dec 2006, 4 June 1804, Sir Joseph Banks to Ann Flinders.

27. www/nmm.ac.uk/flinders accessed 5 Dec 2006, 25 June 1803, Matthew Flinders to Ann Flinders.

28. NMM X2002.047.1, 2 Feb. 1812. Edward Whitworth to Charlotte Whitworth.

29. B. Lavery, *Nelson's Navy: the Ships, Men and Organisation 1793 – 1815* (London, 1989), p. 212.

30. Charles Consolvo, 'The Prospects and Promotion of British Naval Officers 1793 – 1815' in *Mariner's Mirror* (May 2005), 137 – 159, p. 155.

31. N. Tracey, ed., *The Naval Chronicle*, 5 vols (London, 1998), II, 366.

32. NMM MS66/026, 1 August 1808, William Foot to Vice Admiral Sir J. T. Duckworth KB.

33. Double-faced mask cup of Rodney, c.1782, NMM AAA4374 . For 'tars' see a bowl of c. 1800, NMM AAA4438. Cf. NMM AAA4439 and NMM AAA4771.

34. NMM AAA4892, NMM AAA6026, NMM AAA5030, NMM JEW0202, NMM AAA6329.

35. Tim Edonsor, *National Identity, Popular Culture and Everyday Life* (Oxford and New York, 2002), pp. 17, 21.

36. Marcia Pointon, *Hanging the Head: Portraiture and Social Formation in Eighteenth-Century England* (New Haven and London, 1993), pp. 35 – 7.

37. See *Captain Justinian Nutt and his wife*, NMM BHC2915 and NMM BHC2916; *Captain Ferguson and his wife*, NMM BHC2688 and NMM BHC2689.

38. Quoted by C. Oman, *Nelson* (London, 1947), p. 498.

39. E. Kowaleski-Wallace, *Consuming Subjects: Women, Shopping, and Business in the Eighteenth Century* (New York, 1996), pp. 52ff.

40. See Marcia Pointon, *Strategies for Showing: Women, Possession, and Representation in English Visual Culture 1665 – 1800* (Oxford, 1997), p. 44.

41. T.A. Lockett and P.A., Halfpenny eds, *Creamware & Pearlware*, (Stoke-on-Trent, 1986), p. 22.

42. NMM AAA4783. Cf. AAA4370. A similar image is captioned 'Right Honble LORD HOWE' see NMM PAD0120.

43. NMM AAA4761. AAA4766.1.

44. Peter Hyland, *The Herculaneum Pottery. Liverpool's Forgotten Glory* (Liverpool, 2005), p. 101.

45. BL Add. MSS 45905, Accompt-book of the Bow porcelain factory. Calculation made using the 'How Much is That? tool on the Economic History Services website.

46. Robin Hildyard, *English Pottery 1620 – 1840* (London, 2005), p. 189.

47. William Duesbury's London Account Book 1751 – 1753 (London, 1931), p. 19.

48. Pat Halfpenny, *English Earthenware Figures 1740 – 1840* (Woodbridge, 1991), pp. 314 and 322. I am indebted to Robin Emmerson for this reference.

49. Robin Hildyard, p. 163.

50. NMM TYL/1 part 2, receipt from Josiah Wedgwood, 29 April 1816. Cf. David Drakard and Paul Holdway, *Spode Printed Ware* (London, 1983), p. 3.

51. Adam Smith, *An Inquiry into the Nature and Causes of the Wealth of Nations*, ed. William Playfair, 3 vols (London, 1995), I, 155 – 229; Maxine Berg, *The Age of Manufactures 1700 – 1820: Industry, Innovation and Work in Britain*, 2nd edn. (London and New York, 1994), p. 143.

52. P. J. Corfield, *Power and the Professions in England 1700 – 1850* (London, 1995), p. 234.

53. E.g. an ivory and paper fan made in 1740 to celebrate Porto Bello, NMM OBJ0421.

54. NMM OBJ0057.

55. See *Dresses a la Nile, respectfully dedicated to the Fashion Mongers of the Day*, published by W. Holland, 24 Oct. 1794, NMM PAF3864.

56. Anna Maria Porter, *A Sailor's Friendship, and a Soldier's Love*, 2 vols (London, 1805), I, 99 – 100.

57. Ibid., I, 143.

58. Jane Austen, *Persuasion*, p. 254.

BIBLIOGRAPHY

Manuscripts

British Library
Additional Manuscripts
Accompt-book of the Bow Porcelain Factory, Jan. 1751 – Dec. 1755: Add. 45905
Althorp Papers: 75643 – 45
Ayrton Papers: 52344, 60360 – 60366
Charles Babbage Papers: 37200 f. 90
Bridport Papers: 35198 ff. 84, 91
Robert Brown Papers: 32439 f. 266
Davison Papers: 79200 ff. 65, 66
Harwicke Papers: 35376, ff. 132 – 5
W. Locker Notebook, last manager of the old china factory, Derby, *c.*1810 – 1851: Add. 54574
Sir C. J. Napier Papers: 54534 f. 86

Nelson Papers
Nelson family correspondence: 34988
Nelson to Emma Hamilton: 34989

Sidney Smith Papers: 37778 f. 60

Young Papers: 46712

National Archives: Public Record Office
To Principal Officers & Commissioners of his Majesty's Navy
ADM 106/1154
ADM 106/1118

Papers submitted by widows asking for pensions from the Charity for the Relief of Officers' Widows
ADM 6/335

Papers submitted by widows asking for pensions from the Charity for the Relief of Officers' Widows – doubtful cases
ADM 6 385 – 402

Minute books of the Commissioners of the Charity for the Relief of Officers' Widows, 1732 – 1819
ADM6 332 – 334

First admission papers for various widows for 1802
ADM 6 339

Log books
Portia 1811 – 16: ADM 51/2626

Muster books and ships' pay books
Culloden 1794   : ADM 36 12168
Portia 1811 – 12   : ADM 37/3128, 4744
                    : ADM 35/3709

Staffordshire Record Office
D615/P(S)/1/3/G: Lady Anson to Mr Thomas Anson, 1749 – 50

National Maritime Museum
Personal Collections
Admiral Lord Bridport: BRP/
Philip Carteret: CAR/8A
Samuel Carteret: CAR/8B
Admiral Codrington: COD/
Admiral Lord Collingwood: COL/
Admiral Sir William Cornwallis: COR/
William Foote: MS66/026
Jean Tyler Grant: GRT/23
Admiral Lord Hood: MKH/
Samuel Hood (1762 – 1814) MKH/244
Admiral Lord Howe: HOW/1, HOW/4
Susannah Maria Middleton: MDT
Admiral Sir Charles Pole: WYN/104
Admiral Purvis: PRV/
Captain Riou: RUSI/R/1
Admiral Rodney: AGC/
Troubridge Papers MS 84/070
Admiral Tyler: TYL/
Rear-Admiral Webley-Parry: WEB/3
Captain Wells: MSS/86/051
James Whitworth: WHW/
William Wilkinson: WIL/

Artificial Collections
Francis Collier letterbook: LBK/
Nelson-Ward: NWD/
Phillipps-Croker: (Letters to and by Nelson purchased by John Wilson Croker, later owned by Sir Thomas Phillips): CRK/Sutcliffe-Smith: SUT/1 – 2

Individual items
MSS/86/080 0: Accounts kept by Lady Mary Duncan (1731 – 1804) MSS/87/053.3: Emma Hamilton to John Scott

Newspapers and Periodicals

The Annual Register, 1798
The Bon Ton Magazine, Or, Microscope of Fashion and Folly, 5 vols, 1791 – 96
Cobbett's Weekly Political Register, 1804
Gentleman's Magazine, 1747 – 1825
Lloyd's Evening Post, 1763
The London Chronicle 1790, 1798, 1800
London Magazine, 1756
'Old-Bailey Intelligence', *The New Town and Country Magazine*, 1787, 658.
Read's Weekly Journal, or British Gazetteer, 1751
Schofield's Middlewich Journal or General Advertiser, 1756
The Craftsman; or Say's Weekly Journal, 1773
The Evening Advertiser, 1756
The General Advertiser, 1784 – 90
The General Evening-Post, 1795
The Ladies Magazine; or, Polite Companion for the Fair Sex, 1750
The Lady's Magazine, 1760
The Morning Chronicle, 1793, 1801 – 02
The Morning Herald, and Daily Advertiser, 1785
The Morning Post and Fashionable World, 1794
The Morning Post, 1794, 1803 – 04
The Naval Chronicle, 1810, 1815
The New Town and Country Magazine, 1787
The Penny London Post; or, Morning Advertiser, 1750 – 1
The Police Gazette, 1797 – 1810
The Portsmouth Gazette, and Weekly Advertiser, 1795
The Public Advertiser, 1760

The St. James's Chronicle; or the British Evening-Post, 1763, 1793, 1795

The Star, 1793

The Times, 1787 – 1820

The True Briton, 1798

Books, Pamphlets and Articles

(*Place of publication is London, unless otherwise stated*)

A Civilian, *Free Thoughts on Seduction, Adultery, and Divorce* (1775)

A Civilian of Doctors' Commons, *A New Collection of Trials for Adultery* (1799)

Ackermann, R. *The Repository of Arts, Literature, Commerce, Manufactures, Fashions and Politics* (1809)

Adams, Max, *Admiral Collingwood: Nelson's Own Hero* (2005)

Aiken, John, *Evenings at Home; or, the Juvenile Budget Opened*, 2nd edn, 6 vols (1794 – 98)

Anon., *Harris's List of Covent-Garden Ladies: or, Man of pleasure's kalender, for the year 1788* (1789)

Anon., *Statement respecting the Prevalence of Certain Immoral Practices in His Majesty's Navy* etc. (1821)
———. *The Cuckold's Chronicle; being select trials for adultery, imbecility, incest, ravishment etc.*
2 vols (1793)

———. *The Arguments of Counsel in the Ecclesiastical Court in the Cause of Inglefield ... on the twenty-second of July, 1786, at giving judgment* (1786)

Arnold, Samuel J., *The Shipwreck, a Comic Opera, in Two Acts* (London, 1797)

Aspinall-Oglander, Cecil, *Admiral's Wife. Being the life and letters of The Hon. Mrs. Edward Boscawen from 1719 to 1761* (1940)

Austen, Jane. *Persuasion* (1818), ed. by D.W. Harding (Harmondsworth, 1965)

Barker, H. and E. Chalus, eds, *Gender in eighteenth-century England: roles, representations and responsibilities* (London and New York, 1997)

Barker, Theo and Dorian Gerhold, *The Rise of Road Transport, 1700 – 1990* (1993)

Barry, Jonathan and Christopher Brooks. *The Middling Sort of People: Culture, Society and Politics in England 1550 – 1800* (Basingstoke, 1994)

Baudino, I, J. Carré and C. Révauger, eds, *The Invisible Woman: Aspects of Women's Work in Eighteenth-Century Britain* (Aldershot, 2005)

Beattie, J. M., 'The Criminality of Women in Eighteenth-Century England', *Journal of Social History* 8 (1975), 80 – 116

Beckett, J. V. and Michael Turner. 'Taxation and Economic Growth in Eighteenth-Century England', *The English Historical Review* 43 no. 3 (1990), 377 – 403

Bell, Susan Groag, 'Women Create Gardens in Male Landscapes: A Revisionist Approach to Eighteenth-Century Garden History', *Feminist Studies* 16 No. 3 (1990), 471–91

Bemrose, William, *Bow, Chelsea and Derby Porcelain* (1989)

Berg, Maxine, *Luxury and Pleasure in Eighteenth-Century Britain* (Oxford, 2005)

———. *The Age of Maunfactures 1700–1820*, 2nd edn (London & New York, 1994)

———.and Hellen Clifford, 'Commerce and the Commodity: Graphic Display and Selling New Consumer Goods in Eighteenth-Century England', in *Art Markets in Europe, 1400 – 1800*, ed. by Michael North and David Ormrod (Aldershot, 1998), pp. 187–200.

Bermingham Ann, and John Brewer, eds, *The Consumption of Culture 1600 – 1800: Image, Object, Text* (London & New York, 1995)

Bland, E. and Cross M., eds, *Gender and Politics in the Age of Letter Writing, 1750 – 2000* (Aldershot, 2004)

Bodleian, Library, *The John Johnson Collections, Catalogue of an Exhibition* (Oxford, 1971)

Boulton, Jeremy, 'Clandestine Marriages in London: an examination of a neglected urban variable', *Urban History* 20, pt. 2 (1993), 191 – 200

Brewer, J., Mckendrick, N. and Plumb, J. H., eds, *The Birth of a Consumer Society: The Commercialisation of Eighteenth-Century England* (1982)

Brewer, J., and Porter, R., eds, *Consumption and the World of Goods* (1993)

Brewer, J., *The Pleasures of the Imagination: English Culture in the Eighteenth Century* (1997)

———. 'English Radicalism in the Age of George III', in *Three British Revolutions*, ed. by J. G. A. Pocock. (Princeton, N.J., 1980).

Campbell, R., *The London Tradesman* (1747)

Cannon, John, *Aristocratic Century: The Peerage of Eighteenth-Century England* (Cambridge, 1984)

Carter, Philip, *Men and the Emergence of Polite Society 1660 – 1800* (2001)

Chalus, E., 'Elite Women, Social Politics and the Political World of Late Eighteenth-Century Britain', *Historical Journal* 43 (2000), 669 – 97

Chapman, R.W., ed., *Jane Austen's Letters to her Sister Cassandra and Others*, 2nd edn (Oxford, 1952),

Cocks, Anna Somers, 'The Nonfunctional Use of Ceramics in the English Country House during the Eighteenth Century', *Studies in the History of Art* 25 (1989), 195 – 215

Colley, Linda, 'The Apotheosis of George III: Loyalty, Royalty and the British Nation 1760 – 1820, *Past and Present*, 102 (1984), 94 – 129

———. *Britons: Forging the Nation 1707 – 1837* (New Haven and London, 1992)

———. 'The Multiple Elites of Eighteenth-Century Britain. A Review Article', *Comparative Studies in Society and History* 29, no. 2 (1987), 408 – 13

———. 'The Politics of Eighteenth-Century British History', *The Journal of British Studies* 25 no. 4 (1986), 359 – 79

Collingwood, C. L. Newnham, ed., *A Selection from the Public and Private Correspondence of Vice-Admiral Lord Collingwood*, 2nd edn (London, 1828)

Comfort, Sim, *Forget Me Not: A Study of Naval and Maritime Engraved Coins and Plate (1745 – 1918)* (London, 2004)

Cordingly, David, *Women Sailors and Sailors' Women: An Untold Maritime History* (Waterville, Maine, 2001)

Corfield, P. J., *Power and the Professions in England 1700 – 1850* (1995)

Cross, J. C., *The Purse; Or, Benevolent Tar* (Boston, 1797)

Cryer, H. L., 'Horatio Nelson and the Murderous Cooper', *Mariner's Mirror*, 60 (1974), 3 – 7

Daunton Martin, and Matthew Hilton, eds, *The Politics of Consumption* (Oxford, 2001)

David Syrett, ed., *The Rodney Papers. Selections from the Correspondence of Admiral Lord Rodney, Volume 1, 1742 – 1763*, Navy Records Society, 148 (Aldershot, Hants, 2005)

Davidoff, Leonore, and Catherine Hall, *Family Fortunes: Men and Women of the English Middle Classes, 1780 – 1850* (1987)

Davis, Sally, *John Palmer and the Mailcoach Era* (Bath, 1984)

Davis, J., *Letters from a Mother to her son: written upon his return from his first voyage at sea* (Stockport, 1801)

Deutsch, Phyllis, 'Moral Trespass in Georgian London: Gaming, Gender, and Electoral Politics in the Age of George III', *The Historical Journal*, 39, no. 3 (1996), 637 – 56

Drakard, David, *Printed English Pottery: History and Humour in the Reign of George III, 1760 – 1820* (1992)

Earle, Peter, *The Making of the English Middle Class* (1989)

Earle, Rebecca, ed., *Epistolary Selves: letters and letter writers, 1600 – 1945* (Aldershot, 1999)

Eatwell, Ann and Alex Werner, 'A London Staffordshire Warehouse, 1794 – 1825', *Journal of the Northern Ceramics Society*, 8 (1991), 91 – 224

Edensor, Tim, *National Identity, Popular Culture and Everyday Life* (Oxford and New York, 2002)

Ellis, Joyce, '"On the Town": Women in Augustan England', *History Today*, (Dec., 1995), 20 – 27

English Ceramic Circle, *William Duesbury's London Account Book, 1751 – 1753* (1931)

Erskine, David, ed., *Augustus Hervey's Journal: The Adventures Afloat and Ashore of a Naval Casanova* (Rochester, Kent, 2002)

Finn, Margot, 'Women, Consumption and Coverture in England', *The Historical Journal*, 39, no. 3 (1996), 703 – 22

Forester, C. S., ed., *The Adventures of John Wetherell* (1954)

Freemantle, Anne, ed., *The Wynne Diaries*, 3 vols (1935 – 40)

———. *The Wynne Diaries: The Adventures of Two Sisters in Napoleonic Europe* (Oxford, 1982)

French, H. R., 'The Search for the "Middle Sort of People" in England, 1600 – 1800', *The Historical Journal*, 43, no. 1 (2000), 277 – 93

Goldsmith, Elizabeth C., ed., *Writing the Female Voice* (1989)

Gregory, John, *A Father's Legacy to his Daughters* (Dublin, 1774)

Guest, Harriet, ed., *Small Change: Women, Learning, Patriotism, 1750 – 1810* (Chicago and London, 2000)

Halfpenny, Pat, *English Earthenware Figures 1740 – 1840* (Woodbridge, 1991)

Hannay, David, 'Odds and Ends of the Old Navy', *Mariner's Mirror*, 4 (1914), 179 – 182

Hay, Douglas, 'War, Dearth and Theft in the Eighteenth Century: The Record of the English Courts', *Past and Present*, 95 (1982), 117 – 60

Hay, M. D., ed., *Landsman Hay: the Memoirs of Robert Hay 1789 – 1847* (1958)

Heal, Sir Ambrose, *London Tradesmen's Cards of the XVIII Century, an account of their Origin and Use* (1925)

Henderson, Tony, *Disorderly Women in Eighteenth-Century London. Prostitution and Control in the Metropolis 1730 – 1830* (1999)

Hildyard, Robin, *English Pottery 1620 – 1840* (2005)

Hillier, Bevis, *Pottery and Porcelain 1700 – 1914* (1968)

Honan, Park, *Jane Austen: Her Life* (1987)

Hufton, O., 'Women Without Men: Widows and Spinsters in Britain and France in the Eighteenth Century', *Journal of Family History*, 9:4 (1984), 355 – 76

Hughes, Edward, ed., *The Private Correspondence of Admiral Lord Collingwood*, Navy Records Society, 98 (1957)

Hunt, Margaret, *The Middling Sort: Commerce, Gender and the Family in England 1680 – 1780* (Berkeley, 1986)

———. 'Wife Beating, Domesticity and Women's Independence in Eighteenth-Century London', *Gender and History*, 4, no. 1 (1992), 10 – 33

———. 'Women and the Fiscal-Imperial State in the Late Seventeenth and Early Eighteenth Centuries' in *A New Imperial History: Culture, Identity and Modernity in Britain and the Empire, 1660 – 1840*, ed. by Kathleen Wilson (Cambridge, 2004)

Hyland, Peter, *The Herculaneum Pottery: Liverpool's Forgotten Glory* (Liverpool, 2005)

Inglefield, Ann, *Mrs. Inglefield's Justification, containing the proceedings in the Ecclesiastical Court …
on July 11 and 17, 1785* (1787)

Inglefield, J., *Captain Inglefield's Vindication of his conduct: or, a reply to a pamphlet intitled Mrs.
Inglefield's Justification* (1787)

Jackson, William, *The New and Complete Newgate Calendar*, 6 vols (1818)

Jenks, Timothy, *Naval Engagements: Patriotism, Cultural Politics and the Royal Navy, 1793 – 1815*
(Oxford, 2006)

Kay, George, *Royal Mail* (1951)

Kidd, Alan and David Nicholls, eds, *The Making of the British Middle Class? Studies of Regional
and Cultural Diversity since the Eighteenth Century* (Stroud, Glos, 1998)

Kirkham, Linda M. and Anne Loft, 'The Lady and the Accounts: Missing from Accounting
History?' *The Accounting Historians Journal* (2001), 1 – 6

Knight, Roger, *The Pursuit of Victory: The Life and Achievement of Horatio Nelson* (2005)

Kowaleski-Wallace, Elizabeth, *Consuming Subjects: Women, Shopping, and Business in the
Eighteenth Century* (New York, 1996)

Land, Isaac, 'The Many-Tongued Hydra: Sea Talk, Maritime Culture, and Atlantic Identities
1750–1850', *The Journal of American Culture* 25 (2002), 412 – 17

Lane, Penelope, Neil Raven and K. D. M. Snell, eds, *Women, Work and Wages in England
1600 – 1850* (Woodbridge, Suffolk, 2004)

Langford, Paul, *Englishness Identified: Manners and Character 1650 – 1850* (Oxford, 2000)

———. *A Polite and commercial People: England 1727 – 1783* (Oxford, 1989)

Lavery, Brian, *Nelson's Navy: The Ships, Men and Organisation 1793 – 1815* (1989)

———. ed., *Shipboard Life and Organization 1731 – 1815*, Navy Records Society (Aldershot, 1998)

Le Fevre, Peter and Richard Harding, eds, *The Precursors of Nelson* (2000)

Lemmings, David, 'Marriage and the Law in the Eighteenth Century', *The Historical Journal*, 39,
pt. 2 (1996), 339 – 60

Lewis, Judith, '"'Tis a misfortune to Be a Great Ladie": maternal Mortality in the British
Aristocracy, 1558–1959', *The Journal of British Studies* 37, no. 1 (1998), 26 – 53

Lewis, Randle, *Reflections on the Causes of Unhappy Marriages* (1805)

Lincoln, Margarette, *Representing the Royal Navy: British Sea Power, 1750 – 1815* (Aldershot, 2002)

Lockett, T. A. and P. A. Halfpenny, eds, *Creamware & Pearlware* (Stoke-on-Trent, 1986)

McCahill, Michael W, 'Peerage Creations and the Changing Character of the British Nobility',
The English Historical Review, 96, no. 379 (1981), 259 – 84

McCreery, Cindy, 'True Blue and *Black, Brown and Fair*: prints of British sailors and their women during the Revolutionary and Napoleonic Wars', *British Journal for Eighteenth-Century Studies*, 23 (2000), 135 – 52

McGuffie, T. H., 'The Walcheren Expedition and the Walcheren Fever', *The English Historical Review* 62, no. 243 (1947), 191 – 202

McIntosh, Carey, *The Evolution of English Prose, 1700 – 1800: Style, Politeness and Print Culture* (Cambridge, 1998)

Manners, Catharine Rebecca, *Poems* (London, 1794)

Morris, Lydia, *The Workings of the Household: A US – UK Comparison* (Oxford, 1990)

Morris, Marilyn, 'Marital Litigation and English Tabloid Journalism', *British Journal for Eighteenth-Century Studies*, 28, no. 1 (2005), 33 – 54

Morrison, Alfred, *The Collection of Autograph Letters and Historical Documents Formed by Alfred Morrison: The Hamilton and Nelson Papers*, 2 vols (privately printed, 1893 – 4)

Mui, H. Mui and L., *Shops and Shopkeeping in Eighteenth-Century England* (1989)

Naish, George G. P. B., ed., *Nelson's Letters to his Wife and Other Documents 1785 –1831*, Navy Records Society, 100 (London and Colchester, 1958)

Nash, S., 'Prostitution and Charity: The Magdalen Hospital, a Case Study', *Journal of Social History* 17 (1984), 617 – 28

Nastyface, Jack, pseud. [i.e. William Robinson], *Nautical Economy; or, Forecastle Recollections of Events during the Last War* (1836)

Nelson, James, *An Essay on the Government of Children, Under Three Heads: viz, Health, Manners and Education,* 2nd edn (1756)

Nenadic, Stana, 'Middle-Rank Consumers and Domestic Culture in Edinburgh and Glasgow 1720 – 1840', *Past and Present*, 145 (1994), 122 – 57

O'Donoghue, Louise and Jim Goulding, 'Consumer Price Inflation Since 1750', *Economic Trends*, 604 (2004), 38 – 46

Ogborn, Miles, and Charles W. J. Withers, eds, *Georgian Geographies: Essays on Space, Place and Landscape in the Eighteenth Century* (Manchester and New York, 2004)

Oman, C., *Nelson* (1947)

Pawson, Eric, *Transport and Economy: The Turnpike Roads of Eighteenth Century Britain* (1977)

Pettigrew, Jane, *A Social History of Tea* (2001)

Pinchbeck, Ivy, *Women Workers and the Industrial Revolution 1750 – 1850* (1969)

Pinckard, George, *Notes on the West Indies*, 3 vols (1806)

Pocock, J. G. A., *three British Revolutions* (Princeton, N.J., 1980)

Pointon, Marcia, *Strategies for Showing: Women, Possession and Representation in English Visual Culture 1665 – 1800* (Oxford, 1997)

———. *Hanging the Head: Portraiture and Social Formation in Eighteenth-Century England* (New Haven and London, 1993)

Porter, Anna Maria, *A Sailor's Friendship and a Soldier's Love*, 2 vols (1805)

Prentice, Rina, *A Celebration of the Sea* (1994)

Quilley, Geoff, 'Duty and Mutiny: the Aesthetics of Loyalty and the Repreentation of the British Sailor *c.*1789 – 1800' in *Romantic Wars*, ed. by Philip Shaw (Aldershot, 2002)

———. *The Image of the Ordinary Seaman in the Eighteenth Century* (2004) <www.nmm.ac.uk/mag>

Richards, Sarah, *Eighteenth-Century Ceramics: Products for a Civilised Society* (Manchester, 1999)

Rodger, N. A. M., *The Command of the Ocean. A Naval History of Britain, 1649–1815* (2004)

———. *Naval Records for Genealogists* (1984)

———. *The Wooden World: An Anatomy of the Georgian Navy* (1986)

Rolt, Richard, *A new dictionary of trade and commerce, compiled from the information of the most eminent merchants, and from the works of the best writers on commercial subjects in all languages* (1756)

Royal Naval Club, *Historical Memoirs of the Royal Naval Club of 1765 and the Royal Navy Club of 1785 to the time of their Amalgamation as the Royal Navy Club of 1765 and 1785 United 1889* (1925)

Rubinstein, W. D., 'New Men of Wealth and the Purchase of Land in Nineteenth-Century Britain', *Past and Present*, 92 (1981), 125 – 47

Schaw, Janet, *Journal of a Lady of Quality: being the narrative of a journey from Scotland to the West Indies, North Carolina and Portugal in the years 1774 – 1776*, ed by E. W. Andrews (New Haven, 1934)

Scott, A. F., *Everyone a Witness. The Georgian Age* (1970)

Sheldon, Ann, *Authentic and Interesting Memoirs of Ann Sheldon*, 4 vols (1790)

Shesgreen, Sean, *The Criers and Hawkers of London. Engravings and Drawings by Marcellus Laroon* (Aldershot, 1990)

Skipp, Jenny, 'Masculinity and Social Stratification: Eighteenth-Century Erotic Literature, 1700 – 1821', *British Journal for Eighteenth-Century Studies*, 29 (2006), 253 – 269

Smith, Adam, *An Inquiry into the Nature and Causes of the Wealth of Nations, ed. by William Playfair*, vol. 3 (1995)

Southam, Brian, *Jane Austen and the Navy*, 2nd edn (2005)

Spavens, W., *The Narrative of William Spavens, a Chatham Pensioner Written by Himself*, ed. by N. A. M. Rodger (2000), first published 1796

Spinney, David, *Rodney* (1969)

Stark, Suzanne J., *Female Tars: Women Aboard Ship in the Age of Sail* (Annapolis, Maryland, 1996)

Steele, Ian K., *The English Atlantic 1675 – 1740. An Exploration of Communication and Community* (Oxford, 1986)

Stone, Lawrence, *Broken Lives: Separation and Divorce in England 1669 – 1857* (Oxford, 1993)

Stone, Lawrence, *The Road to Divorce: England 1530 – 1987* (Oxford, 1990)

Sweet, Rosemary and Penelope Lane, eds, *Women and Urban Life in Eighteenth-Century England : "On the Town"* (Aldershot, 2003)

Tague, Ingrid H., 'Love, honor, and Obedience: Fashionable Women and the Discourse of Marriage in the Early Eighteenth Century', *The Journal of British Studies* 40, no. 1 (2001), 76 – 106

Thompson, E. P., 'Eighteenth-century English Society: class struggle without class?' *Social History*, 3.2 (1978), 133 – 65

Toppin, Aubrey, 'The China Trade and Some London Chinamen', *English Ceramics Circle Transactions* 3 (1935), 37 – 57

Trumbach, Randolph, *The Rise of the Egalitarian Family: Aristocratic Kinship and Domestic Relations in Eighteenth-Century England* (New York, 1978)

Vickery, Amanda, *The Gentleman's Daughter: Women's Lives in Georgian England* (New Haven and London, 1998)

Vincent, J., ed., *Disraeli, Derby and the Conservative Party: Journals and Memoirs of Edward Henry, Lord Stanley 1849 – 1869* (Hassocks, 1978),

Wahrman, Dror, *Imagining the Middle Class* (Cambridge, 1995)

Wall, Richard, 'Women Alone in English Society', *Annales de Demographie Historique* (1981), 303 – 17

Ward, Valentine, *A Short Essay on the Duties of Husbands and Wives* (Liverpool, 1809)

Warner, J. and A. Lunny, 'Marital Violence in a Martial Town: Husbands and Wives in Early Modern Portsmouth', *Journal of Family History*, 28, no. 2 (2003), 258 – 76

Warner, Oliver, *The Life and Letters of Vice-Admiral Lord Collingwood* (1968)

Walters, S., *Samuel Walters, Lieutenant RN: his Memoirs*, ed. by C. Northcote Parkinson (Liverpool, 1949)

Weatherill, Lorna, *Consumer Behaviour & Materials Culture in Britain 1660 – 1760* (1988)

———. 'The Business of Middlemen in the English Pottery Trade before 1780', in *Business in the Age of Reason*, ed. by R. P. D. Davenport-Hines and J. Liebenau (1987), 51 – 76

———. *The Pottery Trade and North Staffordshire 1660–1760* (Manchester, 1971)

West, Jane, *Letters to a Young Lady*, 3 vols (1806)

Wheeler, David, 'The British Postal Service, Privacy, and Jane Austen's "Emma"', *South Atlantic*

Review, 63, no. 4 (1998), 34 – 47

Williams, Samantha, 'Poor Relief, Labourers' Households and Living Standards in Rural England *c.*1770 – 1834: a Bedfordshire Case Study', *Economic History Review* LVIII, 3 (2005), 485 – 519

Wilkinson, John, *Tutamen Nauticum; or, the Seamen's Preservation from Shipwreck, Diseases, and other Calamities incident to Mariners* (London, 1763)

Williams, Kate, *England's Mistress: the Infamous Life of Emma Hamilton* (2006)

Williams-Wood, C., *English Transfer-Printed Pottery & Porcelain* (1981)

Wilson, Kathleen, ed., *A new Imperial History: Culture, Identity and Modernity in Britain and the Empire, 1660 – 1840* (Cambridge, 2004)

Wilson, Robert, 'Remarks on board His Majesty's Ship Unité of 40 guns', in *Five Naval Journals 1789 – 1817*, ed. by H. G. Thursfield. (1951)

Wise, Thomas, *The Newest Young Man's Companion* (Berwick, 1754)

Young, Hilary, *English Porcelain, 1745 – 94* (1999)

INDEX